JOYCE CARY
A CRITICAL STUDY

A. NIRMALA

ATLANTIC

ATLANTIC PUBLISHERS AND DISTRIBUTORS

Published by
ATLANTIC PUBLISHERS AND DISTRIBUTORS
B-2, Vishal Enclave, Opp. Rajouri Garden, New Delhi-27
Phones : 5413460, 5429987
e-mail : info@atlantibooks.com

Sales Office
4215/1, Ansari Road, Darya Ganj, New Delhi-110 002
Phones : 3273880, 3285873, 3280451
Fax : 91-11-3285873
web : www.atlanticbooks.com

ISBN 81-7156-993-5

Typeset at
APD Computer Graphics, Delhi
Printed in India at
Mehra Offset Press, Delhi

FOREWORD

The notion of canon in literature is an important concept governing the act of recognition of classic works. Canons change but the notion of canon remains. In the history of modern English novel, the canonical writers were authors like Henry James, E.M. Forster, D.H. Lawrence and so on. However, readings of such writers varied with the emergence of new schools of thought and methods of approach. With the rise of post-colonial theory, there has been a significant shift in the focus towards major Victorians and modern writers, leading to a revaluation and a rethinking on their ideological positions. Even such time-tested classics like Joseph Conrad's *Heart of Darkness* and E.M. Forster's *Passage to India* have been deconstructed and their greatness reconstituted. It is in this context that we must place the relevance of the much neglected Anglo-Irish novelist like Joyce Cary on whom Dr. A. Nirmala has chosen to write her book.

Although there has been the tradition of 'Political Novel,' Joyce Cary has given a different depth and dimension of the genre, moving away from the trend set by writers like Benjamin Disraeli, C.P. Snow and George Orwell because of his involvement in a colonial situation as an officer of the British Empire in Nigeria. He is justly famous for his three significant African novels : *An American Visitor, The African Witch* and *Mister Johnson.* Although they have provoked controversies, none can deny their profound implication for understanding post-colonial politics. Cary may be said to have cast the political novel in the dialogic mode deviating from the existing practices. This is one of the central arguments in A. Nirmala's book. She places her study of Cary's African novels within the framework provided by Frantz Fanon's work on the national liberation ideology and within that provided by Cary himself in his political treatises, *Power in Men, The Case for African Freedom* and *Britain and West Africa.*

A. Nirmala studies Cary's critique of colonialism within the white national context in his novel on Irish politics, *Castle Corner.* She argues that there is asymmetry in any colonial situation, be it white or black, between the colonizer and the colonized. We may say that A. Nirmala's study of Joyce Cary attempts a rehistoricizing of the power struggle that marked the colonial situations. She argues that Cary may be considered a pioneer of post-colonial writing although he was writing about colonialism.

I also wish to mention the refreshing light A. Nirmala throws on Cary's trilogy on British politics. Although in these novels his preoccupation is not colonialism, he makes an incisive study of the operation of power in politics proper. A. Nirmala offers a very useful contextual location of these novels within liberal humanism, its rise and fall. She also brings into relief the parallel between micro and macro politics in studying the role and structure of family in that trilogy.

I am sure the academic readers as well as researchers will find Dr. A. Nirmala's book thought-provoking.

DR. C.T. INDRA
Reader
Department of English
University of Madras
Chennai

PREFACE

Despite the ordeals I faced in my efforts to collect materials, I managed to secure practically all the primary works of Cary, except *The Process of Real Freedom* and a few miscellaneous works. A few significant secondary sources like A.G. Bishop's *A Gentleman Rider*, G.D. Killam's *Africa in English Fiction* 1874-1939, and Abdul R. J. Jan Mohamed's *Manichean Aesthetics : The Politics of Literature* were beyond my reach.

In the book, the word 'liberalism' is spelt with capital 'L' to refer to the system of philosophy and to the political party. In other places it is spelt with small 'l'. 'Nonconformist' is spelt with capital 'N' to refer to the specific sect of Protestants. In general context it is spelt with small 'n'.

A. NIRMALA

ACKNOWLEDGEMENTS

This book would not have become a reality if I had not received the timely advice and valuable guidance from Dr. C.T. Indra. For enabling me to exploit my potential as researcher to the utmost, I owe her my first sincere expression of gratitude. Late Prof. V.S. Seturaman who helped me in understanding the seminal perception of Joyce Cary as a political novelist still remains a pervasive influence.

I profoundly thank Prof. Molly Mahood for sparing her time for me during her brief visit to Madras in 1991 and for guiding me to other leading Cary scholars who were deeply interested in the subject, besides lending to me her own copy of the most valuable book by Cary, *The Case for African Freedom and other Writings on Africa*. I sincerely thank Prof. Barbara Fisher for sending me her book, *The House as a Symbol* : *Joyce Cary and The Turkish House* and Prof. Tim Hansen for offering more insight into Cary's indebtedness to William Blake.

What I owe to my father Mr. N. Aiyaswamy is beyond words. It would have been a difficult task for me to complete this book but for his labour of love. I also like to record my sincere thanks to Dr. Nandini Iyengar, Dr. R. Azhagarasan, Mrs. Geetha Mohan and Mrs. Kanthi Shenbagaraman for readily sharing their views and knowledge on this subject.

I duly admit the affectionate patronage of my husband Dr. A. Ganesan and my children Ms. G. Lara and Mr. G. Arun Mozni Varman for their help in all possible ways in the preparation of this book.

A. NIRMALA

LIST OF ABBREVIATIONS

AR	Art and Reality
AV	An American Visitor
AW	The African Witch
CAF	The Case for African Freedom and Other Writings on Africa
CC	Castle Corner
EL	Except the Lord
MJ	Mister Johnson
NHM	Not Honour More
PG	Prisoner of Grace
PM	Power in Men
SE	Joyce Cary : Selected Essays
TP	To be a Pilgrim

CONTENTS

1
The Case for Cary

Joyce Cary (1888-1957), the Anglo-Irish novelist, has been a rather misunderstood writer of the twentieth century. He has been widely regarded either as a minor novelist with rich potential, or as a naive celebrant of Life Force. However, the misconception about this writer which was invariably due to the prejudices of the times in which he lived have indeed slowly lost their ground and his credibility as a profound writer has come to be better appreciated in the recent past.

As one who breathed zestful optimism with a staunch faith in the sustaining force of humanity at a time when there was hardly any sign of hope around him, Cary has often been treated as an anachronism. But a proper understanding of the age in which he lived and the system of thought which moulded him, will enable us to see him in relevant perspective, not excluding the prospect of discerning him as a political writer.

Cary was born in a declining Anglo-Irish family of landed gentry which witnessed its complete ruin along with the other landlords when the Irish Land Act was passed in 1882: And at a young age, he had the misfortune of experiencing the impact of the prevalent politics on everyday life due to the friction between the settlers and the native in Ireland. The sufferings of the resident landlords which in his opinion was not justified, exposed him to the horrors of a blind fate. As a sickly child, who was ill-fated to lose both his beloved mother and later his equally loving step-mother, he saw again the darker side of life. These two factors consequently acted as a chief source of his deep conviction about "the fundamental injustice" (SE, 64) of life. Nevertheless, "family affection" which he experienced "as the one trustworthy thing among so many treacheries" (*Ibid.*) could sustain his faith in humanity and thanks to it, he could remain a thinker who would not allow his sense of frustration to affect his balance. He became a crusader for the ultimate truth of existence.

Cary's deep interest in politics as one of the shaping forces of man's day-to-day life was further enhanced when he underwent the traumatic experience of being a British Assistant District Officer in Northern Nigeria (1913-1920). He became acutely conscious of the differences in cultures and races and experienced the inevitable crisis of a lack of compatibility and understanding between two races. It led him to focus on the 'war of cultures,' as one of his main themes. It further accentuated his obsession with the question of the efficacy of the British policies towards the colonized [here Africans]. Particularly it raised his interest in the dialectics of British Imperialism and the philosophy of Liberalism.

The politics of the times was generally practised in the name of Liberalism. However, Cary's liberal conviction went far beyond the historical and politicized versions of Liberalism. It is true that his liberalism took its origin in the historical context of English Imperialism and German/European metaphysics. Yet he could keep a balance between the political pressure and the ideological pressure. Cary so assimilated the thought and spirit of Liberalism that he could perceive 'liberalism' as a habit of mind as well as the creed of a single party. His earnest attempt, for instance, to annihilate himself provisionally as a member of the ruling class and to view the Africans, also as human beings with an innate urge for freedom raises him to the level of a Liberal Humanist, notwithstanding the instinctive imperialistic pull in him.

In the British context too, he revealed an equal measure of maturity and discretion and refused to be a mere spokesman of Liberalism, for he could identify the pros and cons of the complex Liberal system of thought. Cary's significance indeed lies in his reluctance to confine himself to the narrow bounds of a dogmatic admirer of a particular political system. He emerged as a complex writer who could translate the liberal dilemma into the novel form cast in a dialogic manner.

Cary, after equipping himself well with a thorough background of European social and political thought, stepped into English literary scene, only during his forties. His rich and wide range of first-hand political experience enabled him to contribute sixteen novels (one unfinished), four political treatises and a few brilliant short stories, essays, articles and miscellaneous works — all within a relatively short time of twenty-five years. The following eight novels, which are saturated with rich political content, have been taken up for our study : *An American Visitor* (1933); *The African Witch* (1936); *Castle Corner* (1938); *Mister Johnson* (1939); *To Be A Pilgrim* (1942); *Prisoner of Grace* (1952); *Except the Lord* (1953) and *Not Honour More* (1955). The three political treatises *Power in men* (1939), *The Case for African Freedom* (1941) and *Britain and West Africa* (1946) have been extensively used as choric, sometimes dialogic, commentaries on the concerns of Cary's fiction.

The Clark Lectures delivered by Cary, which were later published as a book, *Art and Reality* (1956) and A.G. Bishop's edition of Cary's essays and interviews in *Joyce Cary : Selected Essays* (1976), threw light on Cary's views about life, art and politics. By contributing to the understanding of the metaphysical and political basis of Cary's ideology, these two works also help us to clarify Cary's stand as a political writer who can render the feel of politics in every walk of life.

The study attempts to make an assessment of him as a writer who has explored the theme of politics with all its ramifications unlike the conventional political novelists like George Orwell, C.P. Snow and Aldous Huxley.

Politics has been one of the vital elements in literature at all times. Many writers have their own ideologies. In the case of any political novelist, the expression of his ideology may be related to his grasp of politics as a discipline. Hence in this study there is an attempt to place Cary's political convictions in their historical perspective.

In England, the political novel, the very form with its aspect and feeling, indeed goes back to the eighteenth century. Politics was generally assumed to be the science or art of government and so the term 'political novel' originally referred to a work of fiction which dealt with a particular issue or a theory of public conduct. But now the term 'politics' means much more than that for it has slowly started accommodating the various kinds of power relations in its arena. The range of a political novel has also consequently widened. The various definitions of the political novel offered by some leading critics, indeed, bring out the modifications which have marked the genre.

Morris Edmund Speare (1924) offered a very narrow range of approach to the genre when he declared that a political novel "is a work of prose fiction which leans rather to 'ideas' than 'emotions'; which deals rather with the machinery of law making or with a theory about public conduct than with the merits of any given piece of legislation; ...."[1] He asserted that "... the political novelist, if he is to be true to his craft, must be dominated, more often than not, by *ideas* rather than *emotions.*"[2] Joseph L. Blotner (1955) too was inclined to emphasize the dominance of political ideas in any political novel. But he viewed it as an artistic representation of the complexities of any society as well : "As an art form and an analytical instrument, the political novel, now as ever before, offers the reader a means for understanding important aspects of the complex society in which he lives, as well as a record of how it evolved."[3]

But this idea has assumed a different dimension in the hands of a critic who has done significant work on the genre, Irving Howe (1957). He looked at the political novel as an extension of the social novel, thereby bringing under its banner a variety of books which might not have been viewed from that angle in the past. In his opinion, a political novel is "... a novel in which we take to be dominant political ideas or the political milieu, a novel which permits this assumption without thereby suffering any radical distortion and, it follows, with the possibility of some analytical profit."[4]

The significance Howe attaches to the subjectivity of the readers in identifying the political element in a novel both discredits the inordinate importance attached to 'labels' in general and also widens the latitude of the novel. Joyce Cary reiterates this idea in his article "A Novel is a Novel is a Novel."[5]

Critics have now become even more conscious of the widening range of politics, and in turn, the political novel. The recognition of the power struggle in its most intensified form, not only at the national stage but also in the arena of complex human relationships, has helped to expand the horizon of the political novel. Politics is now regarded as implying an attitude of the mind more than the realities of a particular form of Government. Morroe Berger (1977) while discussing the works of Ignazio Silone and T.S. Stribling, declares that "politics in its broadest sense refers to the relations among power, moral ideas, and social institutions."[6] Thomas Mann's thought-provoking remark that the destiny of man nowadays assumes its meaning in political terms may be recalled here. Michael Wilding (1980) demands more from the political novelists than remaining within the narrow bounds of politics in its exclusive sense : "Fiction dealing with politics successfully is responsive to the forces of society; these forces manifest themselves in the cultural area, have their aesthetic expression. In political fictions we would expect to find not only the political conflicts of social choices but also the aesthetic conflicts of fictional choices."[7] In the Preface to *The American Political Novel : Critical Essays* (1984), the Indian critic Harish Trivedi expresses a similar view. He points out how politics refers to "the idea of dominance and power equation in almost every sphere of human activity, and has thus become an all — pervasive concept". In his view the fascination of a political novel lies in "its creative balancing of ideas with art."[8]

The brief survey of the definitions of politics and the political novel offered by a variety of critics reveals how politics per se and the political impulse in man are interlinked. According to Joyce Cary, "politics is the art of human relations, an aspect of all life."[9] As a writer who perceives life itself as a political act, he deals with politics at several levels. Besides being an objective analyst of certain aspects of the prevailing politics of his time, he also studies everyday life as political activity. And hence, he translates his conception of politics into the form of the novel, evoking family life itself as a paradigm of a political situation.

The perception of Cary as a political writer is not a new one. George Orwell, the renowned political writer, in his Foreword to the 1941 edition of *The Case for African Freedom*, praised Cary as "a man who has thought deeply over the problems of our time, and has been above current political movements and their characteristic jargon." Walter Allen in his article "Joyce Cary" (1954) regarded Cary's deep interest in English democratic history as the correlative of the Protestant Nonconformist trend, thereby bringing out in his novels the religious appeal of politics and the political appeal of religion. Yet Cary seems to have impressed him rather as a social historian. Molly Mahood (1964), an intensive analyst of Cary's African novels, both extolled him as a skilful and imaginative political writer and acknowledged some of the weaknesses of his work. And she is just in her estimate of Cary. Cornelia Cook (1981) has also made a sincere attempt to establish Cary as a liberal writer. However, Cary's African novels which reflect the liberal's dilemma in a deeply disturbing manner, have not been included in Cook's study.

Several other critics have focused attention on Cary's deep interest in the concept of free man : for example, Andrew Wright (1959), Charles Hoffman (1964), R.W. Noble (1973), Michael Echeuro (1973,1979), Hazard Adams (1983) and Kinley E. Robey (1984). Cary made an earnest effort to examine what he called 'the fundamental question' which is the 'root of all politics, all arts,' "what do men live by? What makes them tick and keeps them ticking;...."[10] The critics mentioned above have noted this point, but only in passing, although they have acknowledged the intrinsic political thrust of the Second Trilogy [*Prisoner of Grace, Except the Lord* and *Not Honour More*]. The special issue of *Adam International Review* of 1950 and the special number of *Modern Fiction Studies* which came out in 1963, have come a long way in enlightening the readers about the various dimensions of Cary's works. Malcolm Foster's detailed picturization of Cary's life in *Joyce Cary : A Biography* (1968).[11] and Barbara Fisher's exhaustive studies of Cary[12] have also indisputably aided to clear many misconceptions of Cary's standing and reputation as they facilitate a better understanding of Cary's work on its own intrinsic merit. Cary is no more looked upon as "a minor novelist with the gifts of a major one", as Frederick Karl puts it.[13] The growing popularity of Joyce Cary in the United States especially among the feminists who discern in Cary a writer of woman-oriented subjects has enhanced his position to a large extent. He has indeed been considered, though not fully acknowledged, as one of the major writers of the 1940's. In the view of A.C. Ward, "Joyce Cary...was the most original and versatile novelist of his generation, and, alone among his contemporaries, in the main stream of English fiction."[14] G.S. Fraser also in a similar vein admits that "young writers see a leading novelist in Cary" but not without reservation : "one respects Cary, but one does not feel that he was a master."[15] A few famous critics in the then colonies[16] and even the reputed African novelist Chinua Achebe have discussed Cary extensively, though often as a target of attack. A comparison between Chinua Achebe and Joyce Cary has also become the fashion of the day. For instance, Robert Wren and Morroe Berger compare Joyce Cary's famous novel *Mister Johnson* with Achebe's *Arrow of God* and *No Longer at Ease*, respectively.

Notwithstanding the significant works on Cary, the political direction in Joyce Cary's novels has been somewhat obscured by the other interests in his fiction. The fact that Cary's works have not been cited in any major critical works exclusively on political fiction, save a few like Joseph Blotner's *The Political Novel*, needs to be mentioned here. Critics, in general, have evinced more interest in paying tribute to Cary and rate him highly for the vitality and gusto of his writings. Andrew Wright who wrote a pioneering study of Cary in 1952, remarked in 1963 that although Cary had been viewed as "the happy Browning--hearty, superficial, and myopic;...."[17] "Time, however, is once again on Cary's side.... The slump is over. Already good work is being done on Cary."[18] The developing image of Cary, however, seems to persist in foregrounding his vitality as a 'joyful trout' as an anonymous writer in *Time* once called him.[19]

Contrary to the established notion of Cary, this book highlights Cary's complex view of history and ideology which makes him all the more relevant in the era of decolonization.

The main reason behind the cold reception meted out to Cary may be traced to the intricacies involved in the discussion of political novels in general. The political bias in a literary work and the subsequent exposition of a particular creed has very often tilted the balance either in favour of or against the writer despite the merits and demerits of the literary work. In other words, critics have a tendency to err while perceiving the significance of a political writer owing to their own political bias. In his book *Political Fictions* Michael Wilding regrets the fact that as a result of the political prejudice of critics some thought-provoking literary works of writers like D.H. Lawrence and Mark Twain have been dismissed somewhat unjustly as lacking in any political seriousness. He laments "the attempts to depoliticize" and "deradicalize"[20] Lawrence's works by hostile critics; these men have done him this injustice mainly because they could not accept a writer who wrote in a manner which did not suit their convenience and taste. The proletarian novels which were the craze of the 1930s have been over-praised by those critics who were fascinated merely by the idea of the poor man on the street and the wicked capitalist, and the same kind of eulogy was later paid to the anti-fascist and anti-communist novels. The intrusion of the critic's prejudice, thus, plays a major role in determining whether a novel is worth being looked at from a political angle or not. When a writer gives an impression that his ideas and the temperament of the people of his age do not coincide, he is cast aside as an insignificant writer and his message is completely obscured. This has not been an uncommon occurrence.

Such victims of prejudice have been sometimes fortunate enough to be better understood and appreciated in later times. In Cary's case, justice has been done to some extent in recent years by occasional references to him as one of the major novelists of this century. But there has not been any path-breaking work which can offset the hostile reception received by Cary in the hands of a few pungent critics like Robert Bloom and Dennis Hall.

While examining the treatment of the works of Cary one finds that the African novels with which he began his career as a novelist have prevented a balanced appraisal of him. His writings seemed to go against the spirit of Imperialism nurtured and kept alive by writers like Rudyard Kipling who in a patronizing spirit accepted the natives in the colonies as 'white man's burden.' Cary's stand was also the opposite of that of Joseph Conrad's who very often viewed Africa through the white man's eyes. Max Cosman feels :

> As a representative of the ruling class he [Cary] would have been prejudiced but he does nothing of the kind. In his African novels as well as in scattered bits elsewhere,... at times in the consorting of people, one cannot tell who is ruling whom and that in the final analysis, since a master-slave set up is untenable, one might act in favour of getting the subject race ready for self-government.[21]

Cary's books which seemed less like eulogies to and more like scathing attacks on colonialism, proved to be anathema to his age. The possibility that he might have seemed a renegade cannot be ruled out. His ambivalent attitude towards the contemporary British political situation, neither partaking of the spirit of the Leftist extremists nor that of the fanatical Rightist further strengthens the misconception of the thrust of his writings. Malcolm Foster aptly remarks :

> Since he did not bemoan the fate of Western society or point a damning finger at capitalism (or socialism) or screech that the individual was being crushed in a world of machines and faceless bureaucracy, he was not treated as a 'serious' writer by those circles in which 'serious' is equated with moans, groans, and continual damnation. On the other hand, since he did not say that everything was sunshine and roses, he was not apt to be a popular writer.[22]

The juxtaposition of dualities which distinguishes this liberal writer is the major obstacle in the way of the appreciation of his work. Joyce Cary never takes a 'monological' stand on any issue but tries to strike a balance between the two extremes, especially if it is politics. Cary well knows that "There are no easy answers in politics, especially nowadays" (CAF, 224). So what he intends to do in his novels is to give the readers "the real feel of politics" (TP, 427) (to echo the wish of Edward Wilcher in *To be a Pilgrim*). He must show "what a muddle and confusion it is ..." (TP, 428). Cary, in fact, baffled the readers and critics alike, by refusing to share unquestioningly either the prevailing mood of euphoria of the Imperialists or the blind faith of the Liberals who dreamt of saving the world by their 'individualism' and 'freedom.'

Joyce Cary has been recognized as a writer whose main theme is freedom. Throughout his career he was obsessed with the idea of exhibiting a wider canvas of life but always emphasizing the intrinsic greatness of the creative imagination of free men. His keen interest in the individual which indeed is the essence of Liberalism, combined with his Blakean worship of the artistic imagination (Vide Chapter II), no doubt, makes him an impressive portrayer of private worlds. He is also 'protean' enough to enter into the thoughts of his characters. The 'chameleon' (V.S. Pritchett's label for Cary) among the contemporary writers has emerged so successfully as an artist that the political content of his novels has been relegated to a lesser position. Cary is no doubt a great artist but he has also remained a conscious political thinker.

Cary's predicament, however, is not uncommon. Long ago, G.D.H. Cole, while discussing political literature in England, remarked that "In a people so given to politics, and with so great a literary tradition, the two streams have often flowed inevitably together."[23] A later critic, J.A. Morris also feels that

> .... English writers must have felt an innate refusal to allow ideology to disturb more than the surface of British political life and this refusal can be extended to literature. Many writers in Britain, as abroad have been rebels of a political or quasi-political nature but almost without exception, they have remained ultimately loyal not so much to the continued political life of the country as to the literary and linguistic tradition to which they belong.[24]

Cary justifies this stand though other self-conscious political novelists like Benjamin Disraeli and George Orwell have remained a singular exception to the rule. Cary has used the novel as a medium to express his political views by transforming them into an emotional experience. In an interview with John Burrow and Alex Hamilton, Cary remarked that "a novel should be an experience and convey an emotional truth rather than arguments"[25] and for him "the best way to be a bore is to write a novel of ideas" (SE, 145). Obviously Cary regarded the novel as a spectrum of human experiences and not a treatise.

The changing trend in recent times to view the political novel as a work encompassing all human relationships which are inherently political, thereby widening the latitude of the genre, enables us to see his relevance in the post-modern context. Bakhtinian emphasis on the plurality of voices substantiates the increasing recognition that a political novel need not be univocal in its exposition of even a single dominant ideology or issue. As pointed out by Robert Boyers, "There are always, in the political novel, several points of view in which the novelist wants us to be interested, even when he deplores most of them."[26]

Though the acknowledgement of the co-existence of several points of view is not uncommon in modern times, several critics have alleged Cary for the absence of a stable center in his fiction which almost baffled them arousing their empathy. The myth of 'indeterminacy' built up strongly by a number of critics starting with Robert Bloom (1962) and including Dennis Hall (1983) has contributed immensely to the adverse criticism on Cary. Being a liberal in his outlook, Cary has aptly chosen a method of narration where different points of view are presented so equally effectively that it becomes a challenge to the reader to identify the author's point of view.

In the orthodox studies of Cary, it has been noted that Cary's attitude to the political problems within his country and in the colonies was marked by an uneasiness. However, in Cary's case, this particular tendency assumes a fascinating dimension because of the dichotomy between Cary the Essentialist who believes in a transhistorical core of human nature and Cary the product of a particular culture of a particular time such as Edwardian Liberalism. It may be noted here that his affinity for the goals and values of the Liberal Humanist tradition (which was severely threatened between the two World Wars) provided him a sense of poise, a hope for humanity and a way to reconcile the contradictions between humane politics and the pragmatics of government (within Britain and in the colonies).

The recognition of the rich and complex legacy of Liberalism in the last two decades enhanced by the reappraisal of the Liberal ideology in Ian Bradley's, *The Strange Rebirth of Liberal Britain* (1985) gives a new perspective to Cary's works, especially his

British novels, by aiding the re-examination of his affiliations with Liberalism. Mention may be made here of D.J. Manning's *Liberalism* (1976) and E.K. Bramsted and K.J. Melhuish's *Western Liberalism* (1978) for they have enabled us to comprehend the whole ideology in a much needed historical perspective. Cary's complex perception of politics as embedded in history and history as determined by power relation, no doubt, will establish him as an enduring force in English literature. That Cary recognizes in politics, especially in a colonial situation, a variety of competing centres of cultural powers is of equal interest to readers and critics. This reiterates the necessity to rehistoricize Cary's political position and resituate him in the context of post-colonial awareness, assuming the text to be a site for an engagement in polemics.

With the trend of decolonization strengthening the literary and cultural voices of the erstwhile colonies, we are now in an advantageous position to revalue Cary's ideological stand to find out how far his fiction represents the complexity in cultural politics.

Frantz Fanon's deep exploration of the psychological complexity involved in the issue of acculturation might have completely changed the nature of assessing power-relations in a post-colonial set-up during the sixties. But long before the theorists and critics are confronted with the problems of colonialism, Cary had the foresight of post-coloniality. This enabled him to comprehend the contradictions in the colonial ideology at all levels — individual, social, cultural and political — in its totality.

This study attempts here to discuss a few queries raised about Cary. Is he contradicting himself? If so, is it deliberate or unconscious? Or is his indeterminacy to be accounted for by the times when colonization had a benign imperial goal to accomplish, *i.e.*, civilizing a primitive people like the African, Irish, Indian? Above all, how should one see his relevance in the context of post-colonial political writings? The work also aims to focus on the 'polyphonous' texture of Cary's political fiction which accommodates all these issues raised above placing his heterogeneous concerns with politics in Bakhtinian terms because they help to project the subtleties and dialectics of Cary's ideology of life.

2

The Philosophical and Political Basis of Cary's Ideology

David Daiches in the essay, "Religion, Poetry and the Dilemma of the Modern Writer" observes how "the old question of theodicy of the Justice of God, or, if we prefer, of the way in which the universe is organized so far as it affects man, has long been a central theme in literature." And in his view, "The answer is generally given in terms of attitude rather than of logic."[1] Joyce Cary may be placed in the literary tradition referred to above, and the philosophical basis of his Liberal ideology substantiates this. Cary's significance, however, lies in his earnest attempt not to sketch a mere literary answer but inculcate in the reader a pragmatic political attitude. The focus of this chapter, therefore will be mainly on how Cary's political ideology has been repeatedly formed and undermined by the heterogeneous political and cultural complexes which affected his career as a writer and as an administrator of the Imperial regime. Further there is a touch of metaphysical preoccupation in Cary's thinking which also invites attention.

There has always been a conflict in the European Christian thought between the despair that man has been condemned once and for all by his Original Sin and the optimism that man has been at the same time endowed with adequate resourcefulness to secure freedom out of this very condemnation. He can achieve glory if not the eternal innocence or bliss, which was lost by his Fall. Basil Willey explains the human predicament, highlighting how the belief in Natural Law with all its ramifications through different ages has been the source of hope :

> ... the existing system was sanctioned by God and Nature for the preservation of order, and departures from it would be unnatural. Yet still the idea of the first and pure Natural Law hovered in the background, and man, though severely damaged by the Fall, could feel that he had not yet lost all his original brightness. Liberty, equality, and fraternity were still the perquisites of his ideal if not of his actual nature, and even in the Middle Ages the established order could be criticized from this stand point.[2]

At this juncture, it is interesting to note that few writers have gone to the extreme point of dismissing civilization as a curse and advocated 'primitivism' as a prop to the buckling happiness of mankind. Rousseau's worship of instinct and feeling swept the whole of Europe in no time when the cult of Reason of the Age of Enlightenment appeared to lose its hold on the European thinking. As early as the seventeenth century we have writers, starting with Milton, who were champions of the massive energy of man resisting civil order and if needed, moral law too. Some of them were even attracted to the glamour of the imaginative rebels, however roguish the rebels may be. For, such writers identified their own passion for freedom with them. The rebels seemed to give them a chance to unleash their boundless energy, transcending all barriers. The epic grandeur which surrounds Milton's archangel Satan has attracted the attention of many critics. One can readily concur with the view of Thomas R. Edward that some readers at least

> can see in Satan's introspective moral consciousness, without embracing it, a significant image of intensity of will modulating into a painful assertion of will after it has infact faltered, an idea of freedom being sustained even as one almost sees through it to discern one's passivity and helplessness.[3]

Even the writers who cherish intellectual freedom have not managed to cut themselves off from involvement with the two contradictory theories of anarchism and progressive nonconformism. Joyce Cary, with his watchword 'freedom', is no exception. In spite of his logical analysis of the absurdity of the cult of primitivism, he does not seem to want to disentangle himself completely from its hold over him and his African novels bear this out. The fascination that primitivism and the cult of innocence hold for Cary cuts into his Christian conditioning. However, being a nonconformist, he can imaginatively grant the credibility of the devil's claim to freedom. Indeed the "charm of the devil" (EL, 94) who took upon himself all guilt and defied the very lightning of Heaven, "carried an irresistible appeal" (EL, 94) not only to Joyce Cary's Chester Nimmo, the protagonist in the Second Trilogy, but to the author himself. The force of evil defeating that of virtue is one of the chief concerns of Cary as projected in most of his novels, especially in both the trilogies. Looking back at the history of his own family Cary once remarked : "To us, from earliest childhood, in England or Ireland, the fundamental injustice and instability of things, the cruelty of blind fate, was as natural as the air we breathed, and, as I think now, probably as important to our health" (SE 64).

He made an early tryst with scepticism, in the days when he was still at school. In Clifton, his teacher Mr. Rintoul could not help him when he "found geology incompatible with Genesis."[4] Cary raised doubts about "the Trinity, the Incarnation, the problem of evil, miracles and so on" (*Ibid*, 34). He confesses :

> ... my faith began to wither like a plant whose root has been cut, and when I went to Oxford I was calling myself an agnostic and, in fact, existing in a cheerful muddle. I accepted the world as science described it, a complex kind of machine; I also admired poets, painters, as great creative minds; and deeply respected goodness, courage, wherever I saw it. (SE, 69).

But the fire of enquiry about the problem of nature kindled in him by A.E. Prichard, the Philosophy tutor at Trinity College, inevitably led to a long, laborious mental exercise. It resulted in the discovery of some power beyond reason with the help of which the realities of the world can be comprehended more extensively. The study of writers like Immanuel Kant, William Blake, Thomas Hardy and Joseph Conrad greatly influenced Cary, enlarging his vision.

It was Kant who helped Cary to consider the free mind as the basis of man's freedom. Kant emphatically says that objects do not exist apart from the receptivity of our senses.

> ... space and time, as the necessary conditions of all our external and internal experience, are merely subjective conditions of all our intuitions, in relation to which all objects are therefore mere phenomena, and not things in themselves, presented to us in this particular manner. And for this reason, in respect to the form of the phenomena, much may be said *a priori*, whilst of the thing in itself, which may lie at the foundation of these phenomena, it is impossible to say anything.[5]

Kant's philosophy, no doubt, instilled a new life into the young Cary who had been desperately looking for someone to bring order to his confused thoughts. In arriving at his idea of the private world and the impossibility of knowing the 'thing-in-itself,' Cary explicity acknowledges his indebtedness to Kant : "Everyone but a lunatic has reason for what he does. Yes, in that sense I am a determinist. But I believe with Kant, that the mind is self-determined. That is, I believe intensely in the creative freedom of the mind."[6]

Cary further argues that man "requires to be free, he requires his independence and solitude of mind, he requires his freedom of mind and imagination. Free will is another matter--.... It is the mind, the reason, the imagination that steers."[7] Though Cary is equally bewildered by the possibility of the counter-argument that even ideas are determined entirely, his firm belief in the free mind remains with him till the end. Kant's view of object helped him to arrive at the notion of reality and freedom of mind and its importance in our view of the world, *i.e.*, human society.

William Blake, the poet, an apostle of the Imagination, guided Joyce Cary in shaping his theory of the creative imagination. Cary's adherence to Blake assumes many forms. His worship of Blake seems to occupy all his thoughts as a young man. In an unpublished letter Cary acknowledges that "I have been a devotee of Blake since my nonage." He adds :

> No one conveys more sharply the unique quality of

> the particular thing or event, no one is more consistently aware of the world character in which all particulars have universal significance and all events relate to final causes. No one more completely despised on one hand the worm's eye view of the materialist, and on the other, more successfully escaped the dazzled myopia of the idealist philosopher or transcendental poet confounding the limitless novelty of concrete living experience in some empty abstraction called spirit or the absolute, destitute of form or significant action. For him the thinghood of reality was as immediate as its energetic soul, its person; he knew them both in their eternal and pungent quality.[8]

Cary, who had been impressed by the idea of the individual in isolation, found the means to make it more aesthetic and fruitful in Blake's theory of Imagination. Cary's creed of creative imagination seems to have derived its nourishment mainly from Blake's dictum, "Exuberance is Beauty"[9] leading to the affirmation of Cary's belief in nonconformism as the basis of Protestant religion and later the liberal creed. Blake's unconventional idea of Beauty allows the unleashing of its strange patterns which can even be "fearful and twisted." Cary echoes Blake in claiming that the success of art lies in inspiration and enthusiasm. That is why all his novels are dotted with inspired artists in different walks of life : Elizabeth, Johnson, Gulley Jimson, Chester Nimmo, Coker and Porfit, characters who are all vested with the 'power' of a special kind. They involve themselves whole-heartedly in the creation of their world, which itself is an artifact, unhinging themselves from any kind of convention. One may recall Blake's words :

> Men are admitted into Heaven not because they have curbed & govern'd their Passions or have No Passions, but because they have Cultivated their Understandings. The Treasures of Heaven are not Negations of Passion, but Realities of Intellect, from which all the Passions Emanate Uncurbed in their Eternal Glory.[10]

Blake's idea of art as "an imaginative ordering of sense experience"[11] immensely appealed to the young Cary who was determined not to yield to the nihilistic tendency. Creative imagination, thus became his beacon light. In other words, Cary longed to see a world of fulfilment and boundless energy and freedom through the imaginative pattern one imposes upon the existing crude reality, instead of accepting the mundane world in its chaotic form merely through memory or sight. In Blake's view, the supernatural Imagination coheres with our own and so the 'Without' is 'Within' : "In your Imagination, of which this World of Mortality is but a Shadow."[12] In the words of K.D. Sethna, it is left to man to exercise the Divine Arts of Imagination "through his mental ability to create and commingle, to be artist and lover, to enter sympathetically into modes of life outside us and to aspire to an ideal."[13] The faculty of Reason restricts the spectrum of the senses. Blake holds, "... the Reasoning Spectre/Stands between the Vegetative Man & his Immortal Imagination."[14] The creative activity of imagination and transformation of experience through it are possible only through the release and exercise of awful powers. Exuberant energy is allowed. But it becomes evil only when it is distorted. In other words, evil is misdirected energy. Blake's sincere identification of Imagination with God and his firm faith that the more creative a man, the more God-like he is, naturally enabled Cary to remain nonconformist and at the same time believe in the existence of Divine order. Cary might be groping towards evil, but thanks to Blake, he never became an atheist.

To say that Blake was influential in shaping Cary's growing ideology of freedom does not mean that Cary's conception of creative imagination is identical with that of Blake's. A whole host of Blake scholars have pointed out that there is no Blakean aesthetics without a transcendental metaphysics. The line of interaction between Blake and Cary is the exaltation of the freedom of the being to know and be itself.

However intense Cary's admiration for Blake may be, he juxtaposes Blake's idea with that of Spinoza whose intellectual energy has been diverted altogether in another direction. In spite of Blake's bold comment that "This world of Imagination is Infinite & Eternal whereas the world of Generation, or Vegetation, is Finite

& Temporal,"[15] day-to-day life smeared with evil and good of all kinds is too complex to be condensed into a small capsule. As an antithesis to Blake, the thought of Spinoza is introduced in *The Horse's Mouth* although the novel is a tribute to the artistic genius of Blake. Michael Echeruo rightly points out that "Spinoza is the novel's alternative to Blake."[16] and adds that the

> two ways of looking at the ugly world — as a subject for transcendent creativeness or as an object for transcendent contemplation — are really two alternative means to the inner freedom of man. The free man may either transcend the fact of evil by seeking to create a world of beauty out of the facts of evil or, by postulating an indifferent and unsympathetic Providence, he can take heart at the beauty and the magnificence of the universe of which he is only a puny part.[17]

Spinoza relies on knowledge as power and freedom and its pursuit as the only source of permanent happiness. He brushes aside free will as an impossibility, reducing human action to a mathematical study : "... an idea of each individual composing the body must necessarily exist in God; therefore the idea of the human body is composed of these several ideas of the component parts. The idea which constitutes the formal Being of the human mind is not simple, but is composed of a number of ideas."[18] This indeed seems to extend the scope of the attitude embodied in a character like Gulley Jimson. Spinoza's belief that passion is an inadequate idea, free will an abstraction and thought "necessarily one of the infinite attributes of God,"[19] may not seem to have any correlation with Cary's views, if surveyed superficially. But it may be borne in mind that Cary has never dismissed reason as a state of passivity. He makes it clear in *Power in Men* :

> Man with reason is born ignorant. He is therefore adaptable to circumstances. He learns the world anew, and if it is a changed world, he has a changed knowledge and can change his action. But since he is born ignorant, he can learn wrongly; and since by reason he can study a situation and do right in it, he can also do wrong.

> For man, therefore, progress depends on the use of his reason. He realizes for himself his instinctive desires, what we call his nature, by the use of independent judgement. That is his means and his only means of self-development (PM, 266).

However, Cary disagrees with Spinoza's conception of God. To Spinoza :

> Since,..., the reason or cause which could negate the divine existence cannot be outside the divine nature, it will necessarily, supposing that the divine nature does not exist, be in His nature itself, which would therefore involve a contradiction. But to affirm this of the Being absolutely infinite and consummately perfect is absurd. Therefore, neither in God nor outside God is there any cause or reason which can negate His existence, and, therefore, God necessarily exists....[20]

On the other hand, Joyce Cary's God is imperfect because love is imperfect and He is definitely not omnipotent. If He is so, there cannot be any freedom for Man. Cary is certain that there is a God who exists as a person : ".... love and beauty are emotions and emotions do not exist except in personality .... The goodness, the love we find in the world is personal. That's why we know God as a person, and only a person."[21]

The manner in which Cary rates reason and imagination which vary according to the time and situation, naturally baffles his readers. The realization that there is hardly any character in his novels who exercises his reason unless it is goaded by his instinct, further adds to the discomfort. However, the contradiction can be interpreted as a sign of the growth of the writer who tries his best to strike a balance between the two, listening to the voice of the longing in his heart to see a beautiful world and to the voice of reason which exposes him to the stark realities of life. The significance of this disparity indeed lies in the fact that he is neither an escapist nor an idealist philosopher. Cary's modification of the faith of the anarchist in "love working as absolute ruler" into "Love working in liberty by reason" (PM, 156) opens a new vista of thought.

However, the overall credit of shaping Cary's philosophy of life goes to Blake. Blake's analysis of Man's Fall as the beginning of his journey towards the destination of freedom is the starting point of Cary's political theory. Though man found happiness in Eden, it was undoubtedly the challenging world, with its various pitfalls, which actually gave him the chance to choose, thereby giving some meaning to his life. Hazard Adams feels that "we can see that Blake's apocalyptic transcendence of the fallen world could have provided him [Cary] with the detachment that sees the comic in the tragic rather than the tragic in the comic."[22]

Cary is an artist not only by profession but also by nature and hence his interest in affirming aesthetic freedom is understandable. He is half-Irish by birth and so his zest for politics is also as natural to him as the air he breathes. His capacity to capture the beauty of the natural landscape and the spontaneous outburst of man's passion in any form, in a lucid, poetic, and evocative manner, has indeed resulted sometimes in the arbitrary handling of his material and looseness of organization. Even his serious political novels abound in descriptive scenes making it difficult for the conservative critics to accept him as a political writer. But since the forties, it has been agreed that political issues are involved in any kind of literature either overtly or by implication. It is interesting to watch the way in which this artist starts from the point of view of an individual and stretches his horizon towards a slightly bigger circle called family where all kinds of political attitudes originate, affecting its members, either enhancing or distorting their outlook. This in turn leads to the question of the bigger society where somehow the individuals have to preserve their freedom and procure their rights to the maximum extent. This preoccupation makes Cary a serious writer with a political direction, though not an obsessed political novelist like George Orwell. In the Prefatory Essay in *An American Visitor* he puts forth his view that "The situation in family life as in politics is always unique; it has to be dealt with by the imagination, by a creative effort of the mind" (AV, 11). It is this fresh dimension which he gives to the term 'politics' which makes his treatment of the political themes entirely different from that of others. Cary explains his view in another essay too :

> ... all human relationships have what I can call a political aspect, they have to be managed. Every lover, every parent, knows that, and if you listen to children in a nursery you will hear them entering into political relations with each other all day long. One says to the other, 'If you leave my horse alone, I won't knock down your fort.' Here you have an elementary social contract and we all know how much questions of justice and its opposite, special consideration, both crop up every day in handling children (SE, 114).

There have been several hostile critics who have questioned the validity of Cary's political stand. Nevertheless most of them have found it difficult to ignore the fact that Cary has conscientiously attempted to give a proper political slant to the attitudes of the individuals as displayed in everyday life. Even so the pervasive mood among Cary critics in regard to his politics is one of apathy.

Cary's soul seeking freedom and enlightenment finds a means in the creed of Liberalism as a political way of life as well as a habit of mind. Although he was by upbringing pious, religion and orthodox Church could not soothe his heart, and the clergymen who were concerned more with the rituals than with the essence of faith, had no power to invigorate his spirit. Cary is sensitive to this lacuna in the institution of religion and almost draws back from faith. The vein of agnosticism in him aided by his obsession with the individual as a primary factor in life, has led some to mistake him to be an existentialist in Sartre's sense. Of course, he strongly refutes such a reading in an interview with John Burrow and Alex Hamilton.

> The French seem to take me for an Existentialist in Sartre's sense of the word. But I'm not, I am influenced by the solitude of men's minds, but equally by the unity of their fundamental character and feelings, their sympathies which bring them together. I believe that there is such a thing as unselfish love and beauty. I am obliged to believe in God as a person.... Of course, if you say I am an Existentialist in the school of Kierkegaard, that is more reasonable. But Existentialism without a God

> is nonsense, — it atomises a world which is plainly a unity.[23]

Generally speaking, religion and politics are inseparable in Cary's novels and his other works as well. His affirmation that "Religion is full of aesthetic feeling and political action; politics uses aesthetic and religious appeal; ..." (SE 121) reveals how interlaced they are. It is mainly on account of this fact that British liberalism which has absorbed into its fold the Protestant spirit of religion, has made such a strong appeal to Cary's imagination and has enabled him to arrive at a political theory of his own.

In Cary's view, the world is a place where love is bound up with selfishness and good is mixed with evil. The investigation into how to make the best out of one's life leads him to start with the potential of the individuals to cope with the various situations very often forced upon them. The question of morality from the point of view of the so called earthly standard becomes secondary to him as against the presence of the coveted freedom of man. Like any other conscientious writer, Cary starts his 'pilgrimage' with the aim of establishing a norm by which the quality of one's life can be judged, and concludes that liberty is the end point. In this context he avers that

> Bentham's norm [happiness] does not apply. But there is a norm which would, in the past, have applied to all three conflicts — for votes, for education, for economic power — a norm of liberty : the greatest liberty; that is, the greatest power of mind and body to the greatest number (PM, 76).

Cary asserts that the same norm should hold good for the individual too. He proceeds to judge the worth of an individual by the yardstick of how far he has exercised his native power, in other words, his liberty, in making his life enjoyable, if not a fulfilled one. The state is likewise rated by its provision of a conducive atmosphere for the play of the power of the individual.

In spite of the utilitarian touch about Cary's theory, what makes it different from regular Benthamite Utilitarianism is the religious touch in it. In Cary's opinion, it is the religious fervour with which a person's native power is exercised that determines the quality of his action. Malcolm Foster points out that "... to Joyce religion, politics and love were fused together in the philosophy at which he had begun to arrive."[24] It should not be forgotten that Cary's ideology, like that of many progressive liberals, has been derived mainly from the Nonconformist Protestantism.

The starting point of Cary's political theory is his nonconformist assertion of the free mind. When the protesting ministers could not be coerced to accept the doctrines of the Common Prayer Book, nonconformity raised its head in defiance of the Act of Uniformity of the Church of England in 1662. It did not take long for this trend to become the essence of the British stream of thought which in course of time came to shape Liberalism which held up nonconformism as its creed. The strong moral fervour with which one holds on to one's belief regardless of the tyranny of the majority, gives one's act a religious colour and it is this sacred form of nonconformity which is highlighted by the liberals in general. L.T. Hobhouse rightly observes :

> The heart of Liberalism is the understanding that progress is not a matter of mechanical contrivance, but of liberation of living spiritual energy. Good mechanism is that which provides the channels wherein such energy can flow unimpeded, unobstructed by its own exuberance of output, vivifying the social structure, expanding and ennobling the life of mind.[25]

The Nonconformists belonging to the various churches like the Baptists, Quakers, Methodists and Unitarians, remained an unpopular minority with their emphasis on "the freedom of conscience as 'a natural and inalienable right.'"[26] The novel *To be a Pilgrim* where various sects are referred to, is charged with this religio-political spirit. For Cary, this kind of worship of the nonconformists in every walk of life turns out to be a powerful force in shaping his characters.

In some ways, Cary is closer to John Stuart Mill who upheld the value of spontaneity and man's capacity for choice. "Though the customs be both good as customs, and suitable to him," Mill argued, "yet to conform to custom, merely as custom, does not educate or develop in him any of the qualities which are the distinctive endowments of a human being."[27] The division of Cary's characters into two sets of people, creators and preservers, may be based on the model provided by the philosophy of J.S. Mill. Cary also shares Mill's admiration for the people who are capable of making their own choices. Mill holds, "Strong impulses are but another name for energy. Energy may be turned to bad uses; but more good may always be made of an energetic nature than of an indolent and impassive one."[28] These words remind us of Cary's *To be a Pilgrim*, especially of the way he has peppered the novel with passages idolizing strong and impulsive characters. In such passages, the author seems to give himself away. His Sara was "as persistent as a natural force" (TP, 479) and "... Lucy carried a nervous force which charged the air about her so that when I [Tom Wilcher] waked to find her in my room, I was suddenly carried out of its narrow domestic comfort and security into that mysterious universe of passion and faith in which she lived" (TP, 250-51).

Nonconformity as an aspect of liberalism with its religiosity leads to different kinds of private worlds built on a sturdy foundation, none of which can be fully understood by others. For they are the creations of individual experiences. Cary's interest in such private worlds has very often landed him in trouble. The 'pluralism of value system' in society which is one of the chief contributions of John Stuart Mill, has been effectively translated by Cary into the novel form, but unfortunately at the expense of his reputation as a writer with a firm view of life.

The range of Cary's creative art does not, however, stop with the portrayal of the private worlds. The reason is, as Foster puts it, "He always enjoyed being on the inside of a situation, seeing how it worked and politics was one of his greatest interests."[29] His scrutiny of the individual as a social being, and the function of the state, compels him to decide whether Man or the State is superior and his answer is naturally in favour of the former. That is why he holds that "The power in the man is real, but the power of a nation is derived. It is the creation of men" (PM, 1). These words instantly remind us of the radicals like John Wilkies who decided "to go back to the roots, to the 'original fountain of power.'"[30]

As the champion of new liberalism, Cary is close to the Radicals of the nineteenth century who found the old notion of freedom as 'absence of restraint' inadequate and stressed on State action as a necessary evil. Cary is convinced that freedom is not a commodity which can be simply granted to the people without creating the circumstance where the individual has the capacity to use his liberty. If his African novels, especially, he analyzes this problem in fictional terms with deep sight, *The Case for African Freedom* is a powerful theoretical exposition of this idea. Elsewhere, Cary points out in "Britain's Liberal Influence" that "the liberals .... made one capital error, which still haunts their thought, when they defined freedom as 'absence of restraint'" and further adds that "Freedom is power, the power to do what you like" (SE, 216).

During the period preceding the First World War, the basic tenets of Liberalism had begun to be attacked for various reasons. But long before that Edmund Burke in the eighteenth century and Bentham in the nineteenth century had already expressed their reservations about the doctrine of natural rights and the notion of man existing independently of the state. The aftermath of industrialization which brought to the fore the limitation of the laissez-faire policy, the degeneration that had set in the national life, and the general social unrest in England, exploded the myth of 'classic liberalism' as the epitome of unrestrained economic competition and 'atomistic individualism.' The rather naive faith of the Victorians in automatic progress was suavely mocked by Matthew Arnold in his *Culture and Anarchy* (1869). Even E.M. Forster, a widely acknowledged liberal humanist of our century, could not remain blind to the unwillingness on the part of the early liberals to recognize the magnitude of the danger which may be caused by the demonic growth of science, and became critical of the classic liberal tradition from within. Joyce Cary went a step further and not only welcomed but advocated a shift from 'classic liberalism' to 'new liberalism' which substituted the theory of minimal state intervention and developed into a more collectively oriented ideology. However, he could not concur with the group of thinkers represented by T.H. Green who glorified the state as a custodian of the individual's liberty and happiness. Cary points out that "Green's thought is really Platonic. He imagines his ideal state as existing solely for the realization of goodwill in its members and this goodwill is conceived in moral terms" (PM, 68). The reason for such an assessment is that Cary strongly feels that "moral judgement is not opinion; it is tied to the facts" (PM, 69). He observes,

> This was the flaw in Kant's notion of a man bound to tell the truth, even to a murderer who asks where his victim is hiding. To tell the truth in such a case would be a crime. A man has no right to conceive of himself as the machine tool of a principle; he cannot get rid of the responsibility of moral freedom. He must study the facts and use his invention to devise the right means of obtaining from them the highest possible good (PM, 69).

When the radical leaders proposed many kinds of State Acts in the name of justice and liberty, like the Pension Act, the Insurance Act and the Factory Act, they were, no doubt, unconsciously treading the foot-path of the Socialists but nevertheless, they were democratic in their approach. The dialectic of Liberalism, which is the outcome of the unavoidable shift from the individual to the state, resulted in a great deal of confusion and confrontation among the liberals. But Cary has no second thoughts about the power of the liberal creed to survive in any situation though it may assume different forms and is sure to suffer set-backs in the temporal order of history. This is made clear when he makes a prophetic remark that "The liberal revolution of the last two centuries in Europe is not a phase that will pass." (SE, 218). Cary explains the plight of the liberals of his day in particular as follows :

> They had to attempt a demarcation of private interest and state interest; and everyday the lines shifted, but always in the same direction.
>
> They did not see that the Asquith government had not diminished real liberty but enormously increased it and that it could still be increased. The liberty of the subject is not coming to an end — it is beginning; and the state is as necessary to it as subjects are necessary to the state. But it must be a state organized for the distribution as well as the increase of power,

> and not for centralization; that is, it must be a democratic state (PM, 31).

In the novel *Castle Corner* while Felix discusses certain "big fundamental discoveries" (CC, 85), he makes a comment on some radical changes which finally prove that after all "'politics is only the expression of moralities'" (CC, 85) : "Watch a new moral truth smashing its way into politics and economics and upsetting everything and everybody. Look at the idea of employer's responsibility — the Factory Acts and so on" (CC, 85-86). And he adds :

> When I was young, even thirty years ago, people still said that it was wrong to educate the poor. They got very angry with the Government for forcing parents to send their children to school. But now it's obvious to everybody that deliberately to leave children uneducated, even on the highest economic grounds is a moral crime (CC, 86).

In Cary's analysis of the ways by which the liberty of an individual can be enhanced, education has been given top priority, for he upholds John Stuart Mill's view that education is the 'key of liberty.' The stigma attached to education as the destroyer of the innate power and spontaneity in man and the exploitation of the education system by the dictators and the opportunists, however, make Cary cautious in his treatment of the subject. His choice of education as a source of liberty is therefore not made without reservation. The fear that state education may crush the distinct original free will in man had gripped even the early liberals like John Stuart Mill and Von Humboldt, though they believed that it may help society to achieve a degree of equilibrium. Von Humboldt expresses his uneasiness thus : "such an artificial equilibrium ... leads to sterility or lack of energy; while on the other hand, the pursuit of particular objects, which is characteristic of private education, produces an equilibrium more surely without sacrifice of energy, through a variety of relationships."[31]

Besides this, the way in which the dictators and scientists have distorted the nature of education makes Cary all the more wary. The dictator's argument goes thus : "Liberty is to do what a man likes. Therefore, if we teach him to do what we like, he will still have liberty. He will feel no restraint. He will be the most valuable slave who delights in his blind obedience" (PM 18). And the scientists pose a threat to the humanistic goals of education with their "conditioned reflexes" (PM, 19). Wilcher in *To be a Pilgrim*, for instance, makes a cynical remark about Ann that "'she doesn't even know she's a woman — that's something these chromium-plated schools don't put into their test-tubes'" (TP, 206). Cary expresses the fear that compulsory education may destroy individuality :

> Where it succeeds in obtaining uniformity or any high degree of uniformity, it produces stagnation and political weakness. It destroys all initiative, all progress even in the arts, and makes great races the easy prey of foreign conquerors. A pattern authoritarian education almost ruined even so great a civilization as the Chinese (PM, 22).

He further remarks that "mass education, even when it is limited to forming a standard political or religious mind, can succeed only among illiterate peasantry. It produces then stagnation" (PM, 23-24). Cary extensively explores in *The Case for African Freedom* the problem of education in a backward country. And the helplessness of the educated Africans like Aladai in *The African Witch* can be easily apprehended and justified given their background. But it is rather surprising to note that even the British characters like Ann, Amanda, John, Richard etc., in the various novels of Cary are women and men who have not been enriched but crippled by education, for they display less of moral courage and heroism than the uneducated. The reason underlying their dullness and lack of creative power may be that they are the recipients of education in its negative aspect. Cary's reluctance to show at least a single model of a respectable, admirable, educated gentleman, creates a suspicion that he is torn between his desire to see a full-fledged educated man on the one hand and his fear that a man's original charm might be marred by education. Yet, it cannot be denied that as a conscious thinker, he does not question the validity of education as a liberating force : "Since education has this power to help or cripple, it is the most important function of society" (PM, 25).

Another problem which confronted the liberals who were already in a bewildered state, was the question of Britain's participation in war. Interference with the affairs of any nation, though it goes against the liberal conviction in its original form, is at times highlighted as a necessary evil for safeguarding the interests of the weaker nations. It is also considered as a part of the modified liberal creed as it concerns the liberty of the individual. Cary is neither for nor against war but he is certain that the state's decision should be determined by the nature of the prevailing situation.

The anti-war propaganda by Cobden and Bright during the Crimean War provided a pacifistic tinge to the contemporary radicalism. 'Peace, Retrenchment and Reform' became the slogan not only of Gladstone but of thousands of his admirers. But Cary reacts to it adversely and questions the credibility of a world of eternal peace and this finds its full expression in *To be a Pilgrim*. He is certain that "Love truly overcomes evil. This is probably the most important truth of religion. But it does not overcome all evil, as religion itself insists.... Injustice, disease, inequality of powers belong to the nature of reality and the perpetual conflict of good and evil within that nature" (PM, 155-56). This realization forbids him from being an uncompromising pacifist. Moreover, Cary is unwilling to consider war as a danger peculiar to democracy. Even in a democracy war-mongers are not the majority; sometimes the pacifists themselves acknowledge the need for war as an inevitable exercise of liberty. If absolutism, by denying liberty, can guarantee peace, Cary is not the one to embrace it. For life cannot go on for long without evil raising its head in some form or the other and the denial of the reality of evil is itself a folly. "For evil is real. A cancer which kills the young mother of a family is a real evil. A brute who cripples a child for life does real and irreparable evil" (PM, 155). This is why Cary's creative men are not flawless. They are at least unconsciously attracted by this evil and hence his novels are a study of evil as a corollary of the liberty of mind. Such insights are plentiful in *To be a Pilgrim*. For instance, Tom Wilcher playfully makes the following remark : "I remembered Edward's old advice, founded on history, that, with the white arm, the thrust has always defeated the cut. So in this little battle, the force of evil, better instructed, utterly defeated that of virtue, which was left breathless on the ground" (TP, 466).

The duality of good and evil finds a more complex expression in other places where he deals with morality in public life. He feels that "The double standard of morality, allowing a statesman more latitude than the ordinary private man, is so widely accepted that it is made an excuse for the greatest crimes" (SE, 229). He has no doubt that "Lies are always lies, evil is always evil; public and private morals are governed by precisely the same law" (*Ibid.*). As a political theorist he does not contradict himself, for the essence of liberalism has never been a faith in a fixed standard but in fixed motive. Liberals judge any action not by its nature but by the purpose behind it and the sense of conviction with which it is carried out. The latitude thus allowed to the pubic man is not a matter of compromise with one's own conscience but of practical necessity. He makes his stand lucid when he says in *Power in Men* that moral judgement is 'tied to facts', as mentioned earlier. "A man who is convinced that war is evil may volunteer to fight against a bigger evil, such as the domination of injustice, cruelty, and violence in the world" (PM, 69). It is not therefore surprising that Cary had been very tolerant towards the changing attitude of the contemporary political leaders (as elucidated in the fifth chapter) during the time when each move of Lloyd George's and that of his successors were questioned by their rivals. The fascination a character like Chester Nimmo holds for Cary which finds a subtle expression in the Second Trilogy, is explicated in his letters and interviews. No doubt it goes against his theory to some extent. For the demarcation between the opportunist and the moralist in Chester Nimmo is rather narrow. The apparent discrepancy between Cary's idealism and pragmatism may perhaps be better understood if Blake's influence on Cary is recalled. Cary's conviction that "... the creative liberty of man .... realizes the good, as well as the evil, in an infinity of new forms" (PM, 70) seems to have an upper hold over him when he is so full of the character, Chester Nimmo. Yet, what distinguishes Cary is the fact that as a true liberal, he does not allow himself to be beaten by the pervasive evil around him and he even scoffs at men like Aldous Huxley as pessimists because they lament that the world had gone awry and there is no redemption. Cary says :

> ... what I mean by faith, a living faith, see any child enjoying itself on any muck heap. All that faith, in spite of defeatists like Huxley (who is really not very strong in the head) is perfectly sound and real. It exists as certainly, as really, as the muck heap, and has a good deal more effect in the world. The silly pessimist is just as deluded as the silly optimist — the Huxleys, I suspect, are escapists who dodge the troublesome job of moral and political decision by going up a rabbit hole and saying 'All is darkness.' The optimist blinds himself by gazing at the sun and says all is light, for just the same reason, to dodge the conscription of life.[32]

Such a pungent attack is possible only from a person of Cary's intellectual calibre. Like James Joyce, he makes a strong assault on the Christian dogma of suffering. He can very well visualize the yearning of the heart to yield to this soothing temptation as the character Tom Wilcher confesses : "The dark wave was rising over me, and I had longed to drown in it; to get rid of self; to find what? A cause. Excitement. The experience of suffering, of humiliation, so attractive to my sense. Above all, an answer to everything" (TP, 234). But Cary is not a writer who is interested in such people who are "defeated by it [muddle] or grew resigned to it, or escaped from it into some bolt-hole of juju" for he says that "... muddle doesn't interest me except as a necessary accident of life, like the weather" (SE, 117). He further adds :

> ... a character like Rose in my novel *The Moonlight* fascinated me, because she tried with all her soul to make order in the world .... And her success and failure were both due to the nature of the world, of a reality shot through and through with creative freedom, with imagination (SE, 117-18).

Cary's cognizance of evil as well as human resourcefulness compels him to take a stand different from that of absolutists like Plato and Hobbes who believed more in the power of the state, and that of the anarchists who found an unalloyed goodness in the natural man. Cary looks at anarchy rather as a temptation which victimises the liberals : "Anarchy is the natural temptation of every liberal; he believes in the perfectibility of mankind. His instinct is against all government, and even Marx prophesied the end of government. He too believed in the automatic progress" (SE, 243).

Cary is an apostle of individuality. Yet unlike Rousseau he has been tempered by the realization that however important an individual may be, he can never claim to be an entity who can stand alone, independent of the state.

Rousseau believed "that nature made men happy and good but that society depraves him and makes him miserable."[33] He also boldly proclaimed, "I venture to declare that a state of reflection is contrary to nature; and that a thinking man" [an "intellectual", as we would now say] "is a depraved animal."[34] Cary's innate urge to believe in a natural simple life and his simultaneous cognizance of its inadequacies is yet another source of the dialectical tension discernible in his works. Cary's experience of life in Africa convinced him that "it was life in a vacuum, life more as an automaton or an animal than as a man."[35] If in totalitarian state there is no scope for the flourishing of the individual, in a tribal society man has no opportunity to exploit his imagination and creativity though he has the freedom to do it. The predicament of man in both the societies is the same.

Even Tolstoy whose ideas have made a tremendous impression on Cary's writings has not escaped Cary's criticism with regard to the political ideas underlying his works.

> Tolstoy's anarchism carried such weight because it was the simplest of all. Tolstoy said in effect, do nothing, leave it all to God, who is found in our own human nature. This fiction carried a unique emotional appeal. It offered a golden age of peace and love and happiness, which was to be attained at once, much sooner than the Marxian. Tolstoy did not promise merely that the state would wither when evil had vanished from the world and all men were always good; he said that if the state were at once

> abolished, all men would be good, and universal happiness would begin, (AR, 23).

The two famous anarchists mentioned above, as well as the systematic anarchists of the nineteenth century like Proudhon, Bakunin and Kroptokin appear to be rather idealistic in their approach. Although Cary confers honour upon them, he is reluctant to agree with them. The vehement anti-capitalist of France, Proudhon talked about a society based on the theory of mutuality : "Through the energy of its principle ... it will make both capital and the State subordinate to labour. Through the genuine nature of exchange it will create true solidarity between peoples."[35] Bakunin praised a government which is "that of a man by himself agreeing freely to obey natural laws," to use the words of Cary (PM, 55). And Kroptokin over-emphasised the instinct of mutual help. Along with Tolstoy the above three philosophers have provoked Cary to contend that

> Anarchists, nevertheless, deny liberty. The power they set above individual man, whether they call it serial dialectic, natural law, or God, is absolute. Moreover, in practice each of them — Proudhon, Bakunin, Kroptokin, Tolstoy — like Hegel, reads the will of this power in his own will (PM, 57).

The fact that some strains of anarchism which proposed single acts of symbolic, pointless violence gave rise to the bomb throwing anarchist in the popular imagination of the 1890's has also not escaped the attention of Cary. In *Except the Lord*, Chester is shown in direct contact with such an experience, which puts him off completely in the end. Through Marie in *An American Visitor* Cary effectively elucidates his view on anarchism , affirming its negativity. Though Cary shares to some extent Marie's sentiment regarding primitivism and tends to adore anything in its natural state as picturesque and gorgeous, he manages to overcome his instinctive romantic inclination by conscious speculation. And therein lies Cary's significance as a man who knows how to mould instinct by experience.

As a staunch believer in progressive liberalism, Cary not only disapproves of the moderate measures of the British Government but also its colonial policy, as expatiated in the third chapter. When he first went to Africa, Cary was somewhat paternalistic in his attitude to the Africans. He firmly believed that the native people had not attained the maturity and responsibility required to accept, understand and execute the democratic form of government.

> Finch's rule, of course, was paternalism, now so much decried. But paternal rule where it is still possible, that is, among primitive tribesmen, has two great advantages. It is flexible and its reasons can be explained. The police state with its cruelty, its indifference to the individual, and bureaucratic democracy with its complications and its bylaws, defeat and discourage simple people till they rebel or simply lose the wish to live. What they want is an actual ruler to whom they can state their special case (SE, 93).

But in course of time Cary was impressed by the enthusiasm of a few progressive natives who wanted to have at least a glimpse at civilization. They were searching for a talisman to free them from their boredom and moral stagnation. As Malcolm Foster puts it, Cary realized that "Being (order) must give way to becoming (freedom), the static to the creative, or else man, society, and civilization will sicken and die."[37] Cary's experience in Africa enlightened him on the nature of politics which enabled him to arrive at the idea of democracy as the inevitable destination of humanity. He was fully aware of the paradox of the situation as may be seen in "Policy for Aid" :

> The democratic machinery — votes, elections, parliaments — except in a developed industrial state with literate workers and a responsible middle class, are merely forms. They not only increase confusion and turmoil, they are dangerous to the unity and continued progress of the state. Nevertheless, these dangers must be accepted. The catastrophe of the Russian Czardom lay primarily in its refusal to accept turmoil and change as the price of representative government (SE, 104).

Cary's African novels are in fact the platform from which he delivered the above message in fictional terms.

Above all, the African experience enabled Cary to witness rapid changes taking place on their own in spite of various human forces trying either to resist them or to mould them to suit their taste. This corroborates his faith in the continuity of history and his idea of the world of everlasting conflict. Change may result in insecurity, disorder, in the ruin of the favourite old customs and those who still cling to them, but it cannot be curbed by any external force. He explains it thus :

> Roughly, for me, the principal fact of life is the free mind. For good and evil, man is a free creative spirit. This produces the very queer world we live in, a world in continuous creation and therefore continuous change and insecurity. A perpetually new and lively world, but a dangerous one, full of tragedy and injustice. A world in everlasting conflict between the new idea and the old allegiances, new arts and new inventions against the old establishment.[38]

Cary's African novels treat this theme, illustrating the chaos and confusion generated by the cultural revolution which in turn was ushered in by the political changes. *The Horse's Mouth*, in particular, deals with the tragedy of an artist who becomes outmoded once his heyday is over. None of Cary's novels, in general, fails to point out the inevitability of change. It is born out of his conviction that no revolution can put an end to this conflict which is the basis of human life. Cary seems to be influenced by Henry Bergson's idea of evolution. Bergson holds that an original impetus, "... an internal push that has carried life, by more and more complex forms, to higher and higher destinies"[39] need not always result in order. He adds :

> Evolution is not only a movement forward, in many cases we observe a marking time, and still more often a deviation or turning back. It must be so, as we shall show further on, and the same causes that divide the evolution movement often cause life to be diverted from itself, hypnotised by the form it has

> just brought forth. Thence results an increasing disorder.[40]

It is this Bergsonian perception which helps Cary later in his speculation about the changing political condition, especially in Europe, as well as the plight of the individual in a world which is in a flux. That is why, though as an imperialist he believed in England as a liberating force, he could realize that all the colonies will undoubtedly become free one day, whether for better or for worse, thereby prophesying the nadir of Imperialism.

Cary comes to anchor at the port of democracy after his 'pilgrimage' in pursuit of the best that different forms of Government can offer. His political theory commences with the acknowledgment of the "fundamental political condition of the individual soul; dynamic energy of imagination, ambition, curiosity, more or less restrained by private interest, private ideals and the policy" (SE, 216). This factor has been generally viewed at from two extreme points of view, in the name of either autocracy or anarchy. The former emphasizes the need of the government to condition the exercise of the free will whereas the latter encourages it, sometimes even at the expense of the general social welfare. Cary no doubt, understands the spirit underlying these forms but according to him, neither extreme form of freedom nor that of authority can be a proper solution to the present problem. The modern democratic state "has developed by something like a natural course of events, and it does pursue, however erratically, the good life for its people; ...." (AV, 10) and hence democracy alone can be the most appropriate remedy among the available remedies.

It does not mean that Cary is blind to the seamy side of democracy. The devastating art of rabble-rousing has indeed been one of the targets of attack since the time of Plato.

> Mob rule is a rough sea for the ship of state to ride; every wind of oratory stirs up the waters and deflects the course. The upshot of such a democracy is tyranny or autocracy; the crowd so loves flattery, it is so 'hungry for honey' that at last the wiliest and most unscrupulous flatterer, calling himself the 'protector of the people' rises to supreme power.[41]

Cary too admits that "The demagogue is the disease of democracy, as the brute is the disease of autocracy, whatever its name" (SE, 231). But he is not prepared to accept demagoguery as the evil peculiar to democracy. He argues that "It is a delusion that democracies are more corrupt than autocratic states. The corruptions are only of a different order. The tricks of a demagogue cannot be hidden; the blackmail of a police state is secret. It is also much more dangerous." He further argues that what such spellbinders indulge in is not the "art of lies;" their's "is a selected, an arranged, truth" (SE, 231). The Second Trilogy focuses on this particular problem and the Cary reader immediately recalls Nina's words justifying Chester Nimmo's approach to politics : "What he meant by truth was the *practical truth*, something that worked" (PG, 219).

Another problem which confronts democracy is bureaucracy which Cary knows, is necessary "to maintain national defense and guard standards of life while keeping the essential freedom to use organization for the increase of freedom."[42] Cary also knows what a tricky affair this is but feels that somehow it has to be sorted out. Cary is no idealist to promise heaven on earth. He concludes that

> All one can do is to salvage the victims, and nothing can give a cripple two sound legs again or restore the dead to life. The aim of democracy should be to give everyone his chance, to see that it is a fair chance and that even, if he fails with it, he suffers as little deprivation as the state can contrive.[43]

Whether Cary also feels like E.M. Forster that democracy deserves only two cheers is discussed in the last chapter.

As an exponent of democracy with emphasis on Liberalism as a political creed Cary demands our attention, but what makes him persist that it is a living force is the idealization of liberalism as a habit of mind. According to Ian Bradley :

> Liberalism is much more than a party creed. There are liberals in every walk of life and in every political party. What characterizes them is not their particular political beliefs but their general tendency to exhibit those qualities of generosity, open-mindedness, receptivity to new ideas and also that robust and

> cheerful optimism which are the distinguishing features of the liberal spirit.[44]

The relevance of this definition to Cary's ideology has been taken up for discussion in the fifth chapter. Suffice it to note here that Cary has not ignored the two main offshoots of the liberal creed, nationalism and the changing role of women. Dictated by his general tendency to accept the world as a heterogeneous consortium of people with their varying immutable instincts and cravings, his attitude towards nationalism is ambivalent. In his letter to his wife, dated 16th November 1918, Cary states that

> ...nationalism is the most dangerous of spirits, and it is strong everywhere. It rests on the best as well as the worst, and strongest of human nature — the love of home, the suspicion and therefore hatred of the stranger. On one hand admirable virtue, on the other, the evil ignorance & prejudice which attack an innocent person merely because he is foreign.
>
> The theory is that all races should have their own land. But there is scarcely a land in Europe not of mixed race. It will have to go by majorities; and the boundaries will cause as much heart burning jealousy and bickering as any arbitrary division. Each country will have its Ireland.[45]

Cary's dual feelings towards the nationalists whose psychological problem is beyond any simple solution, are reflected in the African novels and in *Castle Corner* as well. Yet, he rests his hopes on international organizations like the League of Nations to tackle the problem at the political level and believes that the inherent sustaining force in humanity will preserve some sort of order :

> Of course, that world, as I see it, is not merely a flux of senseless change. Underneath all the turmoil there are certain fixed and permanent things too. In daily life there is always affection, family love and responsibility, ambition, the things people really live for;.... (SE, 115)

This belief in family affection seems to run counter to the contemporary idea of the emancipation of women. His novels abound in distorted versions of progressive women like Ann and Amanda (in *To be a Pilgrim* and *Moonlight*). This feature contradicts his avowed conception of women as stated in his prose :

> Women are great adventurers in their own lives. A young woman, carefully brought up in some strict school and affectionate, guarded home, having got her man, will cheerfully set out to the other end of the world in order to do her job, which is not by any means in subordination. It is constructive, creative. She builds a society, a relationship, a spiritual world (SE, 126).

His visualization of woman as a destroyer of man, bringing him salvation in Blakean terms, is generally what we find in his novels. There are exceptions like Aunt Mary in *Castle Corner* who display the same attitude as Cary's own Aunt Moll who is "a giant in strength and grasp" and "understood life itself" (SE, 65). As a theorist he is against those who decry the emancipation of women. He welcomes the fact that

> Women nowadays emphasise their sex as never before. The modern mother is even too nervously concerned for her children. Human nature, the character of the sex, has proved much too strong for politics .... no modern girl could endure the old life again; it is not happiness that matters to her, but power, freedom to act, richness of life. And that new richness is all our richness (SE, 241).

But the impression one gets out of his novels is the reverse. Cary's treatment of women, above all, seems to strengthen the idea that though he is a liberal by outlook, at heart he is a conservative just like his Tom Wilcher. Such conflict in him may be the origin of his dualities but it is at the same time the source of his deep sense of enquiry too.

To conclude, it is necessary to see whether Cary has succeeded in forging a suitable form which can fulfill his ambition as a writer with a purpose Cary admits in his letter to Professor Mark Schorer, dated 13-10-51, that it is Blake who has paved the way for the formation of his artistic theory :

> My novels are all about one world--as much so as Blake's poetry is about his world, and I want, like him, to make people *feel* that world which might be described as that of freedom.
>
> ...but of course my theme is far wider than any religious construction. It includes aesthetic and political freedom, the whole problem of the created symbol.
>
> ...unlike Blake who invented his own mythology.... I use a quite different method of approach ...I detest allegory — my people are real people in a real world or they are nothing.[46]

Tolstoy's theory of artistic creation has also evoked mixed responses from Cary. He dismisses the slogan 'art for art's sake' as Tolstoy does and strongly asserts that the function of a writer is to provide the greatest experience of truth as perceived by the artist. Like Tolstoy, Cary also does not approve of the expressionist school of Croce. But he differs from Tolstoy in one important point. He explains his stand as follows :

> I have to admit that for all Croce's brilliant argument, I think his theory fails to meet the facts. I suspect also that it has been disastrous to artists who have attempted to believe that all intuition is expression, all expression art. For if intuition is expression, how does the artist know anything but his expression? He is cut off from reality by his own act. He can't ask himself, like Tolstoy, 'Does this expression fairly represent this intuition?' because for him intuition does not exist objectively. It is to him like Kant's thing-in-itself. He knows it only by his own expression. He is compelled, that is, to accept the word for the thing. He is isolated in his own ego. And in practice he falls back upon expression for the sake of expression. This, I think, is what Tolstoy meant by 'art for art's sake.' But of course he was wrong in condemning what he called exclusive art. Almost all great art has begun as exclusive art, and every great artist has been received with suspicion

> and called obscure, immoral or eccentric. The first duty of the artist is to find the right form for his intuition (SE, 135-36).

As in the case of Blake, for Cary also "Meaning is form, and form is meaning" (SE, 145). Like Blake, he thinks that a great writer is "one whose world of organised experience harmonises into one coherent impression in the largest area of actual confusion" (SE, 151) and is interested in breaking the crust and communicating his 'intuition.' In doing so, words become symbols and they are built into 'a total symbol' called the novel which is a living history. Cary's novels are treasure-houses of symbols and many critics, especially Barbara Fisher have evinced keen interest in his symbols, though it has not been incorporated in the domain of our study.

Cary knows well that "... men live so entirely by feeling that reason has extremely small power over even our most intelligent, our geniuses like Marx and Tolstoy" (AR, 23-24). A novel then should be an experience : "a novel, like all art, is aimed at the feelings. It has to be an experience. So far as it deals directly in ideas, they must be ideas that convey feeling" (SE, 145). Above all, it is the fulfilment of one's duty as a novelist which heightens his achievement. Cary poses the question to himself and answers thus : "What can the author, the artist, the novelist reply to the question, are you doing any good in the world, and what good. He can say that education is the principal force for good in the world and that artists are the chief educators, perhaps the only true educators."[47]

To the question whether the artist being an educator should provide any ready-made answers, Cary's reply is a definite 'no.' And on this issue we may give Cary the last word :

> An artist does not start with literature, but life, and the deeper he can go into life, the better. He would also be well advised to suspect any ready-made answers, whether political, religious, or psychological. Where are the Freudians of yesteryear? Where are the Marxists, the behaviourists? All of them have a little bit of truth wrapped up in a mass of nonsense. What you want to do is to dig out the truth, or as much of it as you can pry loose (SE, 128).

3

White Imperialism and the 'Noble Savage'

Writers evincing interest in a setting alien to their culture and milieu is not a strange phenomenon in the history of any literature. Only it is more common among the British writers as many of them had the opportunity of obtaining a rich colonial experience derived either from first-hand knowledge or from received information, strengthened by the built-up image of the concerned land. In the case of West Africa, it has been ironically the non-West African writers (white) who have written about the land earlier than the native writers, unfortunately to the disappointment and disapproval of the natives. The non-African writings on Africa go back to the records of the Arab geographer- explorers and Portuguese historians and were strengthened by the memoirs of the European explorers between the fifteenth and the eighteenth centuries. Defoe, in his novel *Captain Singleton* introduced Africa for the first time as an exotic setting, focusing on the enchanting, romantic side of Africa with its invincible superstitions and deplorable irrationality. He provided a distinct image of Africa which the later writers seemed to perpetuate. The writers of the nineteenth and the early twentieth centuries who had imbibed the spirit of Imperialism in its heyday, used Africa more as an interesting and impressive setting to appeal to the light-hearted readers and less as an intrinsically relevant subject. Hence, their representations of Africa were amusing, tickling the vanity of the white as benevolent and condescending rulers. However, from the 1930s a change in the trend of writing became obvious, as pointed out by Emmanuel Obiechina :

> From the 1930s onward this kind of fantasy —

> spinning gave way to an attempt at realistic exploration of African themes. In West Africa, this took the form of exploring the problem of Westernization and its impact on Africans and the African traditional culture. Some of the novelists concerned also began to explore the personal and psychological factors of colonization, especially in the European colonial officials carrying the 'white man's burden.'[1]

The assessment of Cary at this juncture to perceive how far his experience as a colonial officer had enriched his political sense and to see to what extent he could remain unbiased may prove to be an interesting endeavour.

The political stand taken by Joyce Cary on the matter of colonization cannot be easily comprehended for various reasons. A mere exhaustive analysis of the early novels which have Africa as their setting will not carry us far in the task of arriving at the essence of his thought if it is not based on a thorough knowledge of the contemporary situation. A proper study of the various political forces which operated in Britain under the banner of Imperialism will help us greatly in achieving a near-correct perspective of Cary's novels. Our attempt in this study is not only to extract the political essence of his novels but also to see how far this "reluctant sage" (to use the phrase of Robert Bloom), was a prophetic voice, especially when we go through a variety of post-colonial writings. This results in problematizing accepted colonial texts.

Generally speaking, Cary's African novels deal with the 'war' of incompatible ideas, the intensity of which was felt more with the passing of time, as suggested by him in one of his manuscripts :

> This war of cultures... is now being intensified every year by the rapid organisation of the nations. Up to now only Germany, America, Russia, the English Public School, the Jesuits etc. have deliberately set about this work of construction which has been carelessly and inefficiently performed by every parent and educator since before the self-invention of man.

> But soon the inefficient and with them the *laissez-faire* school of the pseudo-Freudians, Russel [l] etc., will not be tolerated any longer ....[2]

This passage reflects Cary's urge to tackle the problem of cultural clash, taking it beyond the narrow boundaries of a particular continent or nation. No doubt, his opportunity to study the Africans as the products of a particular political situation resulting from colonialism enabled him to focus his attention on a particular problem, namely a collision of ideas, caused by the forcible interaction among various races. Yet this has to be considered only as a microcosm of world politics, for the issues which captivated his attention have universal significance.

Cary's African novels, in general, analyze the problems connected with the colonization of Africa, a subject which gripped the attention of the people in Britain during the Victorian and Edwardian periods. The cleavage in the Liberal Party, the consequence of the divided opinion among its members in their approach to the colonies, resulted in a split in the mind of every rational English man. The collision between the followers of Gladstone and the rising new imperialist groups with their motto 'maximum exploitation with minimum violence,' caused a lot of inconvenience to the party men. The problem of how to reconcile oneself to any situation which arose due to the complexity caused by the reaction "from those who believe that the African is not fit for civilization, and from those who are convinced that civilization is not fit for him" (CAF, 33) could not be easily solved. The image of the British abroad became the preoccupation of some of the Liberals and non-intervention appeared to them as the panacea. Bramsted and Melhuish observe :

> While English travellers abroad were generally found 'to be upright, high-minded, brave, liberal and true,' he [Gladstone] remarked, they had too high an opinion of themselves and 'too little disposition to regard the feelings, the habits and the ideas of others.' Gladstone argued that Palmerston's determined interventionist policy contributed to this deplorable stereotype. The remedy was clear. Britain should in future 'refrain from all gratuitous and arbitrary meddling in

> the internal concerns of other States,' just as the British would resent the same sort of interference practised by others to themselves.[3]

The dialectic of liberal doctrine as propagated by famous Liberal philosophers like John Stuart Mill who started revising their works, added another dimension to the political texture of the day. A humanistic approach marked their writings. Mill in his *Considerations on Representative Government* emphatically asserts that he would assess the goodness of a government by "the degree in which it is adapted to take advantage of the amount of good qualities which may at any time exist, and make them instrumental to the right purposes."[4] Whereas, Rousseau's theory of the 'Golden Savage' captured the imagination of the Americans, the prevalent mood in England was one of cynicism. Molly Mahood elaborates on this point in her work *Joyce Cary's Africa*. After the publication of the Dual Mandate in 1922, many writers and former administrators began to question the validity of leaving the primitive men in status quo (65). Cary who had assimilated into his system of thinking the spirit of liberalism in its totality starting from the earliest nonconformist, 'Protestant strain' coloured by its rational humanistic approach which later formed the basis of the British political policy, is undoubtedly an enigmatic but unique writer.

The question of what kind of policy was to be adopted towards the colonies became more than a political problem to be studied with detachment when Joyce Cary at the age of 25 entered the strange land of Africa towards the close of 1913. The English explorers and traders who entered the Dark Continent with a solely commercial purpose, had to take, in course of time, some measures to safeguard themselves against the natives and the foreign forces. Their gradual interference with the internal affairs of the natives became inevitable when they began to feel that the abolition of slavery and witchcraft was their task. They started exercising their power, imposing themselves upon the strong and defending the weak, though not always devoid of lust for material gains. Sir C.P. Lucas in his book *A Historical Geography of the British Colonies*, Volume III, quotes several instances which justify the British stand. But to decide the extent to which their authority had to be exercised at the expense of certain powers of the Native

Administration was not an easy task. This immediate problem disturbed the minds of not only the rulers in Britain but also their representatives who had been sent as District Officers to the various colonies. The dialectical tension which marked the temperament of the age is reflected in Cary's novels. Cary himself while serving as a political officer in Nigeria, had to face this conflict very often. In the Prefatory Essay in his novel *An American Visitor* he voices this tension : "The everlasting conflict between authority and freedom was not an academic subject in Nigeria, it cropped up every day in a country where the traditional frame was in collapse and law had to be built while the queue waited" (AV, 9). His African novels, especially *An American Visitor* and *The African Witch*, are the results of the recollection of his experiences. They are tinged with conscious reflection, guided by his authentic knowledge of Africa. His arduous attempt to arrive at a new approach to the issue which had been engaging his thoughts for a long time, enabled him to achieve a sense of objectivity. According to Robert Bloom, "Cary's greatest failing as a novelist — and his greatest strength as well — is his submission to the variety and multiplicity of experience. In the novels he is only too ready to abandon his own view and assert nearly that there are many views."[5]

Though Cary's inherent power to see any situation from many angles as a detached observer and to powerfully bring out the significance of a problem begins to blossom in his two trilogies, its presence is discernible as early as *An American Visitor*. In this novel, Cary explores the theme of freedom, especially relevant to the African colonial situation, by setting his three main characters as diametrically opposed to each other. They are allowed to represent their views vehemently though not always sensibly.

Marie Hasluck, an American anarchist, who is also an anthropologist looking for the golden age, vigorously puts forth her views about the Birri way of life. According to her,

> 'The Birri are the happiest kind of people,'....we [Europeans] have nothing to give them but disease and lies and poverty and envy and vulgarity. They're doing no harm to us — they're not asking for anything from us — quite the other way. But we just can't help spoiling this beautiful thing' (AV, 89).

The validity of Marie's view is questioned by the materialistic, unscrupulous and pragmatic prospector Cottee whom Marie decries as one who indulges in "the most horrible kind of crime, to debauch and ruin a whole people for profit" (AV, 95). Cottee says, "Natives who wore trousers and went to the cinema instead of hunting lions mightn't be so picturesque as the naked savage, but they'd be happier — they wouldn't want to go back" (AV, 96), and "it does seem rather strange that we won't let these poor devils have any of the comforts and conveniences that we couldn't do without ourselves" (AV, 97). Bewsher, the District Officer, is another pagan enthusiast like Marie, but he disapproves of her excited feelings about Birri life. He endeavours to strike a balance between the two extremes, though in vain. He expounds his own view, which is a combination of both points of view, and tries to prove himself the champion of 'orderly change.' His aim is "to preserve and develop the rich kind of local life which is the essence and the only justification of nationalism" (AV, 133).

Though Cary takes pains to shield his personal reaction, the balance seems to swing in favour of Cottee's revolutionary ideas. The very fact that Cary is rather impatient to alert the readers of the illusory nature of the myth of the 'Golden Savage' by exploding the strong but simple faith of Marie in the primitive cult right in the opening chapter, bears this out. S.H. Kanu, though a little disapprovingly, comments, "The novel opens with Cary's usual assortment of Africans — criminals, drifters and castaways."[6] In spite of Cary's general reputation for indeterminacy, in this novel we find him giving himself away, may be unconsciously.

The jottings, which Cary perhaps intended for his publisher, as quoted by Molly Mahood, capture the essence of the novel. He explains :

> In this story of a modern American girl with the political and religious prejudices of her time and country, we see a passionate love affair and a religious creed growing on the same root as a political idea; each the necessary and complementary expression of the same personality, which is itself characteristic of a national atmosphere. The story of Marie Hasluck is therefore a commentary and

> sidelight upon American civilization and its preoccupations; but as she moves in a British dependency, falls in love with a British official and is involved therefore in local politics, the action raises also urgent and important questions of imperial policy and development.[7]

Though many critics see Marie more as an abstraction than a real character, Molly Mahood attributes the insubstantiality of Marie to an Englishman's lack of understanding : "... since most New Englanders have very strong tribal sanctions, this was a fault of observation."[8] William Van O' Connor also voices the same opinion but gives a different reason : "It seems likely that Cary fails to bring Marie Hasluck to life not merely because he did not know much of anything about Americans but because his own ideas about the Birri seem, in their way, to be almost as romantic as those of Marie Hasluck."[9] But the fact that when Cary published this novel, he was far away from nourishing any kind of romantic ideas as those of Marie and the fact that he consciously took efforts to equip himself with a thorough understanding of the situation with which he deals in his novel, as borne out by the bulk of his manuscripts, do not seem to support the views of the two critics. According to Malcolm Foster, "Marie is a direct descendant of such Henry James figures as Isabel Archer, Milly Theale and Christopher Newman."[10] *An American visitor* is an argumentative novel unlike the later works and so if at all Cary has exaggerated the Americanness of Marie, it is not without a purpose.

Cary begins the novel motivated by his immediate aim to present the case of Africa with the focus on the colonizers and the colonized and to analyze the effectiveness of indirect rule. But he enlarges his objective by including the universal problem of authority and freedom in his arena which enhances the appeal of the novel. In his pursuit of the truth, Marie is used as a tool to bring out the meaninglessness of leaving the Birri to their own fate, full of untold miseries and unexpressed sorrows. Cary questions the ethic of not providing them with the benefits of European civilization under the guise of the preservation of the native culture. The purpose behind the characterization does not end there, as Marie also typifies an anarchist who ironically knows not what freedom is and proves

Cary's point that anarchy need not be a synonym for freedom. Mahood has asserted this view thus : "*An American Visitor* is a political novel, and one of its themes is the captivity of anarchism compared with the freedom of good government."[11]

Marie is seen by the miners as a preacher of "self-determination to bare-arsed apes" (AV, 27). The relevance of this comment becomes clear when one looks at Cary's portrayal of the backwardness of Birri life from the very beginning of the novel. S.H. Kanu aptly says, "... when Cary takes us into Nok, a typical Birri village, it becomes clear that the Birri are, even by African standards, a very backward people.... The life he depicts is one of physical, mental and spiritual confinement."[12] Marie indulges in anti-British propaganda and persuades the native men to remain as they are and not to allow themselves to be corrupted by European education and religion since they have "happiness that whites cannot get for themselves with any money because of their bad education" (AV, 33). But she is jeered at by Henry, a man who has seen a little more of life than the natives. He thinks that Marie, and Obai who stand spell-bound listening to her speech, are "two fools, two savages" (AV, 34). This remark, made ironically by a native about a white woman, shows the growing awareness among the natives of the need for progress and their disgust with those who oppose it.

Marie, being thoroughly frustrated with the offshoots of civilization, comes to Birri seeking a 'Noo Jerusalem' (AV, 91), in other words, a new faith to cling to and she finds the 'Golden Savage' a suitable cult which can give some meaning to her aimless life. She does not miss any opportunity to give full and explicit expression to her belief both in her advice to the black men and her vehement arguments with the white men, especially Cottee. For the first time the very foundation of her belief is badly shaken as she falls into "fits of doubt" (AV, 94) when Bewsher, her idol, is amused to hear her talk about natural system — "a system of natural rights and duties and obligations —" (AV, 90) devoid of any head. Still she holds on to her belief tenaciously, not allowing any kind of thought or incident to disturb her set ideas, shutting her senses to the reality of Birri life. But her marriage with Bewsher brings about a change in her. He becomes her object of "grand passion" (AV, 154), as Cottee says, and her obsession with the primitive cult begins to lose its hold on her.

The readers are given a glimpse of the inconsistency between Marie's thought and her actions in the scene where she trembles at the danger of a delayed allowance in spite of her warning to Obai against the temptation of money. Marie exhibits this weakness more often after her marriage. Saving her husband's life from the snare laid by the natives becomes her primary aim and she is all too ready to sacrifice her ideals. Though she realizes that Bewsher's life cannot be happy without Birri, she has her own doubts about "'...how much of it he's going to enjoy with his Birri'" (AV, 142). When Marie comes to know the plan of the bushmen to attack the Goshi mission, she becomes frantic and sends for the imperial troops without Bewsher's knowledge. The irony of the anarchist resorting to authority cannot go unnoticed. Bewsher's disapproval of her act and his unshakable determination to be consistent in his trust in the people whatever the consequences, causes some ripples in her mind. The Dobsons' unchanging and unquestioning faith in God leaving everything to Him, even in times of danger to their own lives, deepens her changed faith. Under the hypnotizing effect of the Dobsons' religious faith and Bewsher's fervour, she undergoes another 'conversion' without her own knowledge. This conversion almost shocks her and she wonders, "what was wrong with her that she was praying, or rather her body was praying, without any kind of volition on her part" (AV, 177). The Christian religion which she earlier decried becomes her refuge and unfortunately her hysterical decision to stick to it results in Bewsher's death. Finally, she also realizes that Obai and Uli, her idols, "had been talking nonsense like their Greek prototypes" (AV, 193).

> ... she felt in her breast an intolerable longing--she wanted to cry — for the silly young woman who had seen in a little community of naked savages the pattern of an earthly paradise. The same silly young woman who at college had adored the Greeks and wished that she had been born two thousand four hundred years earlier (*Ibid.*).

Cary's Platonic background as revealed by his use of the Greek symbols strengthens his ideological critique of Marie. As a widow,

Marie evokes the sympathy of others. Even Cottee is touched by her pitiable state for a minute, but he cannot accept this woman as 'a tragic queen' (AV, 238).

Marie, the anarchist, who despises authority, ironically remains captive to one belief or the other, enjoying freedom in no sense. This reiterates Cary's contention that freedom is not the prerogative of an anarchist and authority need not be the enemy of freedom. He incisively observes :

> Abuse of civilization is partly a fashion, begun by Rousseau and continued by reformers, by neurotics, and of course by those who, wishing to be unconventional, succeed only in being commonplace; it is partly a genuine reaction of idealists who, having no practical experience, judge society on ideal and abstract grounds; and it is also escapism. Many of those who have gone to Africa and described some primitive native regime as, compared with England, a golden age, are pure escapists (CAF, 111).

The same fate which befalls Marie is also shared by the other pagan enthusiast Bewsher, "Cary's conservative man opposing anything but carefully managed change."[13] He represents the old imperial policy, the contention of which is merely the preservation of status quo in its most unimaginative form. In the essay "Policy for Aid" Cary talks about the two goals of British administration, continuity and balance : "We were not to destroy native rule and economic custom, but to develop them on their own roots; we were to aim at a general advance on all fronts, including education" (SE, 100). Bewsher is guided by the same spirit but unfortunately he is made ineffective as he is unable to survive in a world which is moving fast, irrespective of the nature of the future it is marching towards. As Barbara Fisher points out, "Bewsher is drawn partly from older men he admired in the service. But he represents the Carys, and the Empire as they served it."[14] Cary's tender feeling mingled with admiration for the great administrators like H.S.W. Edwards and T.F. Carlyle who were his predecessors in Africa, explains Cottee's gesture of worship, albeit for a moment, as a sign of reverence for Bewsher's departed soul. But the very next moment Cottee, like Cary, comes back to the world of reality.

Bewsher is seen as a representative of the political administrators who either became megalomaniacs or dull unimaginative administrators.

Bewsher, "a man with a cause" (AV, 39), is no doubt a "Poor old Monkey B" (AV, 39) as Cottee says, but still the readers agree with Gore's view that "Bewsher is one of the happiest men he had ever known" (AV, 39). Bewsher enters the Birri land to carry out his duties as a political officer, but in course of time he becomes so obsessed with the cause of the Birri men that he feels one with them and overlooks their drawbacks. He attempts to champion the preservation of their culture, guarding them against the encroachment of 'civilization.' He tries hard to bring all the Birri sections into one political unit and equip them fully with his favourite schemes of Kifi irrigation, sanitation programme, Ogun Project etc., so that they could progress along their own lines. His deep attachment to his cause makes him feel irritated with the prospectors : "...there is no reason on earth why they should come to Birri and smash up my whole show" (AV, 42). But it is unfortunate that he is reluctant to admit the need for the co-operation which has to be extended by Birri men, without which the 'show' cannot be carried on successfully. Bewsher has been ever filled with the fear that the native men may not always accept him as one of them and what is worse, that they might even look upon him with suspicion. He understands the mood prevailing among them and their preparedness to finish him off at the least provocation. But he decides to continue trusting them. When the Birri are convinced that their lord Bewsher has sold them to the prospectors, they unhesitatingly forget their division and enmity among themselves and join together to take the cudgel against him. Even then, Bewsher refuses to allow the soldiers to march ahead and handle the situation by themselves, as suggested by his well — wishers including Marie. Bewsher touches the heart of the readers mainly by his refusal to violate his own principles at this juncture. He is happy that all the Birri men are united. For he thinks that his long cherished dream of a united Birri system has become true though ironically, to destroy him, "The defender of Birri" (AV, 96). For the first time all have the same objective : "to drive out the Yorubas and the white men, to break the Juju, to kill Bewsher" (AV, 165). Like Conrad's hero Jim,

Bewsher is ready to die for his cause however absurd it may appear to others and his "energy thus goes to promoting what he feels to be the only possible conditions for creative freedom."[15] But in identifying the conditions for freedom and the speed with which they have to be provided he goes wrong. When 'civilization' strikes at a lightning speed as symbolized by the arrival of the miners, he is still talking about the thunder God, advocating natural religion. Bewsher's failure as a political administrator is the failure of colonial administration as it was carried on then. The main criticism against Bewsher made by many critics, including S.H. Kanu, is that, "Bewsher like so many colonial officials in isolated stations, is prone to ignore the code of service and behave like a megalomaniac."[16]

Bewsher's failure arises from his lack of imagination to perceive the existing condition in its reality and respond to it expediently as the situation warrants. In spite of his grandeur as a hero who lives for a cause, he cannot attain a heroic stature like Johnson because of the manner in which he dies. When he realizes that the rebels are not going to leave him alive, he desperately searches for his gun to save himself. He dies an unhappy man, realizing, though very late in his life, the impracticability of his principles. "Bewsher's own feelings as he lay on the ground with two or three spears in his body, though, of course, full of official indignation, was not empty of a kind of amusement as if some part of his mind were remarking to him 'Well, old chap, the joke is on you. You're not going to get away with it, this time'" (AV, 229). When Bewsher is stunned by the sight of Obai attacking him, he reminds us of Julius Caesar, but he does not make us feel aggrieved as he is yet another foolish sentimentalist like Richard II who may be sympathized with but cannot be admired. He can neither be considered as "the first of those creative figures in Cary's fiction,..." as R.W. Noble[17] feels nor as "just another failure but by his own a complete success" as Dennis Hall puts it.[18] Both Marie and Bewsher are theorizers whose views cannot be translated into action as they have no practical application. To quote M. Foster, "Joyce [Cary], in *An American Visitor*, attempted to show the very real and extensive damage such modern theorists and abstractionists could do, in much the same way as Swift demolished their eighteenth-century equivalents in 'A Modest Proposal.'"[19]

On the other hand, Gore, the Assistant District Officer, is shown as a pragmatic Englishman, who can visualize the consequences of a particular action and even warn Bewsher when the occasion demands it. According to Dennis Hall, Gore is more dynamic than Bewsher : "Gore obviously is a member of the administrative class that both Cary and his 'high European official' regard as not only admirable, but also essential if democracy is to flourish."[20] However it is difficult to accept the view of Dennis Hall without qualification. Though Gore is a non-controversial figure, being an unimaginative but loyal pupil of the imperialistic school, he becomes a dull administrator who can make neither himself nor others happy.

The coincidence of the arrival of Cottee with his men and the landing of Marie in Birri is not accidental. For Cary skilfully exploits the situation by making them mutual foils. The novel from the beginning is interspersed with the adverse comments of the prospectors on the enthusiasm of Marie which is channelled in the wrong direction and this serves as a precursor to its fall-out. When Jukes and Allday critically analyze Marie's attempts to impose her ideas upon the natives, the reader gets the impression that these miners are wise enough to view the situation objectively. But Cary's immediate remark that these men are not beyond reproach, adds to the complexity of the situation. "The miners looked at each other as if to say, 'My God, this is the kind of people responsible for our safety, for the Government of the Empire...'" (AV, 27). A sensitive reader cannot miss Cary's subtle dig at the imperialist design to maintain status quo in the colonies in order to survive as their exploiters. However a closer reading of the significant scene of the novel where the three champions with their distinct sets of ideas have a heated discussion, gives rise to a doubt whether Cary too, unconsciously identifies himself with Cottee, betraying his imperialistic bias. The caustic remarks of Cottee like "'We're losing our Empire simply because we don't know how to keep it together...'" (AV, 97) and "We haven't got a system at all — no sort of principles. None of the people we send out have the faintest idea of what they're for," and the sarcasm with which he talks about, "'...Ireland and India and all our other grateful pupils'" (AV, 98) becoming nations, strengthen our suspicion.

The miners play a catalytic role in the novel, for their arrival pushes Bewsher into a complex political situation which demands deft handling. When Bewsher refuses to acknowledge their legal claim to mine, they threaten that they will pressurise him if the occasion demands. The conflict between the commercial interest of the miners and the paternalistic spirit of Bewsher is dramatically treated by giving these white miners an opportunity to corner the white ruler. Bewsher is forced to choose between his superiors in Britain on one side who expect him to obey them and the natives who look up to him as their defender but always eyeing him with suspicion on the other side. His letter to Gore reveals his precarious situation. "If I stick out, I shall be sacked by the S of S.; if I don't stick out I shall be eaten by Lower Nok" (AV, 61). Cary's notes indicate that any political officer who goes to the colonies to serve has to undergo this dilemma at one stage or the other.

In a way, it is the prospectors who throw the stone into the pond of tranquillity for it is their claim which provokes the people to resort to violence. Finally it is Cottee who manages the situation and restores normalcy after Bewsher's death. "It is Cottee the prospector, whom both the Africans and Bewsher oppose, who wins out, for he represents the inevitable revolution taking place in Africa."[21] Cottee plays a crucial role as Cary's spokesman. When Marie tries to convince Cottee that "'It [Birri] doesn't need a government because it's been put on the right lines for ever'" (AV, 9) and accuses him of "smashing up the Birri machinery that really does work" (AV, 91), he makes it clear that it is not the substance of his whole argument. "'All I say is, that it's out of date and ought to be scrapped for something more modern. I want to improve the government, you want to abolish it'" (AV, 91-92). He also attributes Marie's disapproval of any form of government to the primitive "protestant strain" (AV, 92). Bewsher's citing of an interesting anecdote about the Emir and Umoke provokes Cottee to say, "'If he was really nature's gentleman, supposing that such a creature should exist he wouldn't have insulted his host in a particularly cheap manner'" (AV, 93). Cottee especially in this scene, plays a crucial role as Cary's spokesman and his approach draws a just comment from S.H. Kanu that "Cottee's criticism of Marie here centres on the fact that she is opposing civilization without differentiating between its good and bad elements" (46).

Exposure to civilization does not necessarily mean happiness. Like Adam's curse, it brings in its wake unforeseeable disasters, but never fails to bring man freedom. Liberty is the talisman which endows man with 'power' for which he is ready to sacrifice anything including his safety, security and pleasures, for therein lies his 'glory'. The lesson Cary learnt out of his experience in Africa makes him a champion of freedom despite the price one has to pay for it. In *Britain and West Africa*, Cary boldly declares that "West Africa could not even be defended from European culture. But she does not want to be defended. She is anxious everywhere for a modern civilization" and he adds that "She wants it though it might destroy her" (CAF, 194). Cottee's comment on the final situation after Bewsher's death discloses Cary's intention to use it for examining a problem relevant to the whole of mankind. "For even if civilization meant for the Birri a meaner, shallower kind of life, how could any man hope to fight against it when it came with the whole drive of the world behind it, bringing every kind of gaudy toy and easy satisfaction?" (AV, 234). It is a clarion call to the whole of mankind to shake off their romantic illusions and get ready to face what comes up in this ever-changing world. Change is inevitable and so those who aim at the preservation of tradition have no place in the world. "They were to be pitied. For man only had one life and if he wanted to enjoy it he had better suit his taste to his times and not to try to change the times to suit his taste" (AV, 236).

The minor characters in the novel vividly bring out what Cary means by the disruptive force of civilization. Obai who comes under the magnetic spell of Bewsher and Marie, professes that he would do anything to make them happy. His visit to Kanama makes him an important person not only in the eyes of others but also in his own. He becomes their unelected leader and even talks of a united Birri 'nation' because it is the dream of Bewsher, though its meaning is not clear to him, for according to others "He was always catching some nonsense from Bewsher" (AV, 51). Obai, though caught in the trap of civilization and remaining under the spell of it for some time, cannot break the taboo of the tribe and free himself. In spite of his pompous declaration that "'.....we Birri are not beasts to betray our friends...'" (AV, 103-104), he turns out to be one such when he stabs Bewsher. He gets himself killed, without attaining any kind of self-awareness.

Uli belongs to another type. Being caught between two worlds, that of the fascinating Westernized life and that of the natural but irresistible Birri life, he utterly loses his identity. Uli comes back to his village, having learnt some of the new ways of life and wants to impose them on others but cannot. His wife refuses to accept this stranger of a husband and when rejected by the village too, the mission becomes his refuge. He who is considered as the apple of the Dobsons' eyes, is ironically more impressed by the wealth and splendour that surrounds the free world of the Christians than the spiritual gains their religion offers. He is hesitant to come out of the mission for the fear that it "might cause a loss of all comforts..." (AV, 170). But he cannot resist the charm of fighting for his own people and reuniting with them. The missionaries who preached to him about the wickedness of war can no more have any moral hold upon him, for "like all of Cary's primitive converts, he is busy grafting his pagan beliefs to Christian theology, thereby subverting the old as well as the new."[22] He wants to go back to his wife and the Birri life which would make him a real man. "He moved like one joint in a centipede; but to himself he seemed released, free; released from futility, free of boredom; once more Uli of Nok, a somebody in the world, his own world" (AV, 205). Cary's attitude towards the missionaries is rather that of a sceptic. For none of the converts in his novels seems to have grasped the essence of Christian religiosity.

But Henry who has "travelled in the civilization of the great Nigerian world" (AV, 34) knows what he wants and he survives. He so manages that he becomes Marie's cook, but he will never be swayed by absurd ideas. It is Henry who is responsible for the awakening of the people; his fiery speeches rouse them against the white man. He plays an active role in hatching the plot to kill Bewsher and does not hesitate to make some profit out of the disaster. As S.H Kanu says, "He is, in essence, the cracked mirror through which we see the refractory image of a new Birri, torn between its own stagnant traditions and the fluid conditions of creeping materialism."[23] When Henry says, "'... in the great world outside Birri men are not afraid to take what they want, and they would laugh at all these rules which tie you like sheep'" (AV, 163), it becomes clear that the progressive minds among the natives can see only one side of the coin of reality. By means of a cynical remark, Cary seems to exclaim sadly, how unfortunate that the young enthusiastic minds with their undeveloped but immense natural imagination perceive only half the truth : "... in this country [Sudan], according to Henry, everybody did what he liked. Everybody was free and happy and able to acquire riches and to defy all rulers, chiefs, jujus and laws — everybody, that is, with any intelligence and pluck" (AV, 163).

Though critics such as Andrew Wright, Robert Bloom, Dennis Hall and Kinley Robey, have dismissed this novel as thin and uneven, mainly on the grounds of its inconclusiveness, one cannot miss the glimpse of the author who is peeping through his text. This work reads more like a novel of ideas with a specific direction, trying to explore the complexities involved in relations of power which colonialism constructs. Cary gives vent to his longing to cure the mental illness of those who look at any form of government with jaundiced eyes, especially the Americans who "did want an international law but detested 'imperialism.'"[24] Van O' Connor in his study of the characters of Marie and Bewsher, makes a pertinent comment that "In fact, her [Marie's] conduct causes the action to sound like a melodramatic dialogue between followers of Rousseau and followers of Cecil Rhodes."[25]

It is this appeal which transcends place and time that enhances the greatness of the novel as well as of the novelist, as acknowledged by Michael Echeuro : "... the complications of human, political and intellectual situation in the novel does enforce a most definitely humane argument relevant not only to the immediate African world of the novel but to all civilizations and epochs."[26]

A reading of Cary's works as a whole body reveals the semblance between the underlying patterns of his works, though the urgency with which he scrutinizes a particular current problem which was in the air when he wrote each novel makes the approach different. The basic issue raised and analyzed in all his works is what makes man ultimately free in a given situation. In the next novel taken up for consideration, *The African Witch*, the juxtaposition of the immediate political problem and the interminable moral issues which disrupt the orderliness of life, makes it a very complex and fascinating novel.

Cary's African novels generally discuss the diverse effects of liberalism *i.e.*, how the advent of 'civilization' can cause havoc in tribal societies by disrupting the apparent peace which is a mark of primitive life, nevertheless bringing these societies freedom. The native who is exposed to the effects of European civilization either by chance or by the acquisition of Christian missionary education, sometimes even University education as in the case of Aladai, is surprisingly not shown as a man who has the ability to govern himself in spite of Cary's claim that one who has the taste of civilization will never like to go back to his old customary way of life. At one stage or the other such a man is constrained to remain as a free man owing to some causes either accidental or man-made and he goes back to his own fold. This is not the case with Obai and Uli alone for it is true of Aladai also.

In the Prefatory Essay in the Carfax edition of *The African Witch*, Cary explains how his intention behind the novel has been distorted by the critics. The refusal of education to Akande Tom in the novel has aroused a lot of misgivings in the minds of the critics and their sense of disbelief in the writer's integrity of thought. It may be rather surprising to note that the writer who advocates education as an important milestone in the process of gaining freedom denies that to an aspiring youth. But an in-depth study of the novel reveals the fact that this denial adds a new dimension to the novel. In *The Case for African Freedom* where he talks about education, he elucidates the nature of education and its impact on the recipients. He prefers adult education to school education for children, that too imparted in a more informal and interesting manner.

> Education undertaken by grown-ups, in this way, to please themselves, has another great advantage. It does not produce clerks before there is work for them to do. A man who learns to read in order to enjoy a book of tales, or the newspaper, does not

> expect to change his status or craft; he is delighted with his education because it gives him pleasure. But the boy who leaves his village to go to school and who learns writing and arithmetic from a teacher, expects to make a career. He expects his education to give him work, and if it fails to do so, he is embittered not only against his teachers but against education itself. He is ready even to support the nationalist reactionary with the old cry, 'Back to the primitive — down with everything new' (102).

It is interesting to study how far Aladai's reversion to his native life can be considered as the natural course of action as visualized by Cary and how far the author's stand in this context can be justified.

The novel is woven around two central characters, both Africans but strangers to each other in every respect. Aladai, the chosen "one out of a million" (AW, 64) to acquire Oxford education, consciously looks at his own land as alien. Being sensitive to its squalor and smugness he objectively speculates on Rimi life entrenched as it is in the ju-ju. But his feeling that he is a Rimi man never leaves him however much he has assimilated the Western culture. And that is his strength as well as his weakness. On the contrary his own sister, Elizabeth reigns as an unconquered queen of the world of ju-ju with unshakable faith in her latent powers which have been tested and proved. Cary, an adept at expository scenes, brings out the theme of the novel, *i.e.*, war of incompatible beliefs, in the very opening by exposing the readers to the nature of the treatment of the educated, Europeanized black man in the hands of white men.

Aladai, the prospective Emir of the Rimi people, when he attends the horse race at Rimi, is not without some nervousness which is later justified by the reception accorded him. His "dandified perfection" (AW, 11) alone is enough to kindle the wrath of white men and arouse their latent superiority complex as the benevolent civilized rulers of the savages. It peaks their condescension. The Irish police officer Rackham "with a great power of enjoyment" (AW, 12), unfortunately cannot understand the exuberance of the modernized black men Aladai and Coker. He longs to "inflict public humiliation on this pair" (AW, 13). The colour-conscious Mrs. Pratt is scandalized by the behaviour of Judy Coote, the only spontaneous person in the crowd. For Judy indulges in an interesting tete-a-tete with her former Oxford friend provoking Mrs. Pratt to sneer : "'The little fool! — but I always knew she'd do something impossible. I believe she's a Socialist. Most of these Oxford girls are, really...'" (AW, 14). Miss Honeywood, a younger version of Mrs. Pratt in her aversion to the Negroes, is amused by this odd sight and seems to approve of Rackham's comment, "'It's a regular old chestnut, isn't it? — the cannibal chief in the Balliol blazer'" (AW, 15). The typical reaction of Aladai to this shows how in a colonial context, such kind of 'interpellation' in action leads to disastrous effects upon the psyche of the colonized and how they begin to look at themselves in terms of the racist ideology. Fanon's citing of his own experience in a similar vein in his works throws more light on this issue.

Aladai is baffled by the white men's behaviour, and when he is with Judy he sadly exclaims, "'Why do they not like me to wear their clothes — isn't it a compliment? But, of course, it looks as if I wanted to put myself on a level with them'" (AW, 19). Aladai's words betray his lack of confidence, against which every African has been struggling in vain when in the clutch of an inferiority complex..., Judy's reply is very significant; it even raises a doubt whether it is the author's voice which is speaking throught her : "'I think it's because we are such nationalists ourselves — we like to see people keeping old customs and their own dress'" (AW, 19).

The novel is interspersed with many such scenes where the colour of the skin builds a big barrier which separates the white and the black, making it impossible for them to come closer, as in *An American Visitor*. When Aladai does not stop with his shocking entrance at the Scotch club but starts quoting Wordsworth, far from being hailed by the white members of the club, he is made the laughing-stock of the gathering. One by one they leave the place, not being prepared to endure his company. As Charless Hoffman puts it, "Louis Aladai's aspirations are doomed from the start because his education while freeing his mind from the bonds of primitivism does not free his body from the colour of his skin."[27] Cary's picturesque description of such scenes drove the critics to look upon racism as the central theme of the novel, much to the disgust of the author. It is not profitable to join this set of critics, for Cary in a few passages suggests that it is not the colour of the Rimi people but a genuine practical problem which is the cause of friction. For instance, when Rubin with his soft corner for the primitive men, accuses Rackham that "You've got a complex Jock" (AW, 92) and Judy also supports his view, Rackham in a serious tone retorts : "But at present I think you've got to consider the political situation. The blacks out here are not fit to run their own show, and it will be a long time before they learn. Meanwhile we've got to keep the machine running and the only way of doing that is to support white prestige" (AW, 93).

Judy Coote, with her unconventional attitude towards the blacks, is, according to her people, "one of the nigger worshippers" (AW, 42). She is shown as an intelligent, mature being who has a balanced approach to the African situation. She is a combination of Marie and Cottee in her simple adoration of the picturesque Rimi life and in her awareness of the inevitability of change that "a country cannot be kept like a museum for ever" (AW, 52). She exhibits her maturity in handling Aladai, tempering his enthusiasm with practical wisdom. As his friend and don, she takes the liberty to chide him when he enters the Scotch club without prior notice but the next moment gives a pat in order to soothe his feelings. Caught between the fascination of the black prince with his native dignity and love for the people and her genuine love for the white officer Rackham who cannot stand anything native, Judy struggles to find an outlet for her feelings. Yet she manages to champion Aladai's cause till the end. What is interesting to note here is that there are times when Judy herself becomes conscious of the irony of the state of Aladai. Though she tries to convince herself that a black man struggling with his trousers may not be an odd sight in the eyes of the native, she is rather repulsed by it.

> Aladai's trousers had worked up his ankles, showing six inches of bright blue sock and the clasp of his suspender. Even a piece of black leg appeared as Aladai, now rounding up the fugitives, wheeled his horse across their front. Judy burst out laughing 'It's a shame! But what a pity,' she said. 'Royalty ought to avoid such *contretemps*. But I suppose,' she

> reflected, 'natives don't see it like that at all. He looks quite terribly august to them. Oh!'(AW, 50).

This kind of endless ambivalence on the part of the author tells him not to install securely the colonial values, supported by the colonial structure. This, in turn, makes the novel a problematic colonialist discourse.

When the novel begins, Dryas Honeywood is obsessed with her abhorrence of black skin, and in that she represents the white temperament : "I really rather hate black men, I'm afraid. They give me the grues" (AW, 40). But when Aladai is desperately in need of some kind gesture from his rulers, it is her instinctive kindness which prompts her to shake hands with him and stay with him for a while. This indeed saves him from an imminent moral collapse. And Aladai calls it "spontaneous and magnanimous" (AW, 121). In the same way, Rackham who is distinguished by his devastating remarks about this "trousered ape" (AW, 52), undergoes a change when he is disturbed by a sense of guilt after striking Aladai.

Cary, by effectively portraying the complex strands of feelings in many of the characters towards Aladai, implies that he is more interested in the analysis of the psyche of the human mind rather than in discussing the problem of racism in simplistic terms. "Cary has complicated his native and European elements so adroitly in this work that an extremely complex plot meshes almost perfectly."[28]

Fluctuation in attitude is not the mark of the relationship between the white and the native alone. Politics as the shaping factor determines the nature of the relationship amongst the natives also. The "Poor Africa" (AW, 131) with her innumerable problems excites different responses from various native leaders. Aladai emphasizes the need of civilization and he complains to Judy that the British government has failed to extend the advantages of English civilization to the Rimi culture "which is soaked with ju-ju" (AW, 20). Elizabeth, "a conscientious priestess" (AW, 55), will bring blessings upon the people with the help of her juju for "spirits are always at work. Nothing happens by accident in Africa" (AW, 55). Coker, the hysterical religious enthusiast, cries out for blood to redeem Rimi men : "'No man can be saved, save by de, blood of de lamb', said Coker, letting his voice boom and his eyes closed, 'for in dat blood all men washed clean of sin — all men de same — poor man and rich man, white man and black man'" (AW, 128). Makurdi, Aladai's uncle, too, is a serious politician. "He knew better than anyone in the country what could be done with Rimi and Rimi trade by an intelligent emir guided by a businessman of his experience" (AW, 22). The text thus generates 'counter hegemonic views' within itself.

Both Elizabeth and Makurdi wish to see Aladai chosen as the Emir but for different reasons. Elizabeth, "a moving pillar" (AW, 28) in her moral as well as physical stature, is afraid of Sale, the Muslim claimant to the post, the succession of whom means an end to her as a ju-ju queen. Makurdi believes that Rimi will have a hopeful future under the leadership of the progressive Aladai. Aladai who vows that he will put an end to ju-ju and in fact proudly declares that he will not allow Coker's primitive religious ju-ju to enter Rimi, none the less does not want to risk losing the support of his sister by interfering with her affairs. He refuses to go with Doctor Schlemm when the latter frantically seeks his help to avert the disaster which is awaiting the victim of witchcraft, Osi, a beautiful young girl. "Aladai saw the extreme danger to him of enraging the Emir, Elizabeth and the Resident at one stroke" (AW, 129). Aladai does not want to be called a Christian despite his adoration of Dr. Schlemm and his mission work lest he should incur the displeasure of the pagans who form the majority. Sale, who is not less ambitious than Aladai in his political aspirations, indulges in bribery in order to win the race. He and the Master of House plan to cajole Elizabeth to join hands with them through some insidious means and rise against Aladai, but she does not succumb to the temptation. The Waziri informs Sale about the Master's arrangement :

> Then began the negotiations, at once tortuous and circular, always hopeless, by which, since the beginning of time the dependents of an autocrat have attempted to secure themselves in a change of masters by binding the new in some dependable manner before the old is done with. The problem is always the same : to buy trust with treachery; ... (AW, 172).

On the other hand the old Emir, sustained by his ever green thoughts about his glorious past, remains more complacent than ever. According to him, both the aspirants to the post of Emir are silly men : "Sale — that woman-man! Ah! he's nothing. And Aladai, that clerk — he's less than nothing. Eff!" (AW, 176). But he is overwhelmed by his admiration for Akande Tom. The Emir, hence, seeks the help of Burwash, the District Officer, to send Sale to Mecca so that Aladai also can be kept away from the Rimi town. The political expediency displayed by Aladai matches that of the Emir and it reaches its climax when he and his sister decide to exploit the sincere friendship of Judy Coote to their political advantage. Judy is used as a tool by which Aladai's visit to the Rimi town is made legally possible. But Sale outwits Aladai when he declares that he has been named his successor by no less a person than the Emir himself and wastes no time in getting rid of the old Emir. Cary skilfully brings out how, in politics, every movement is well planned as in the game of chess though it need not always yield the desired result.

Burwash is sought after by Aladai after stoutly presenting his claim to be the next Emir. Aladai has lost all his confidence in the white race by now. The political turmoil created by the natives becomes too overwhelming for the District Officer to manage. Burwash whose energy is very often siphoned out by his preoccupation with the proper use of language in his communication with his superiors and whose only obsession in life is to project his image as a peace keeper to those in the homeland, is totally indifferent to the development of the events. Cary here makes a dig at the impracticability of the policies of the older generation of imperialists :

> Experience, therefore, had convinced the Resident that, in a world where it is impossible for the rulers to have personal contact with the ruled, and government must willy-nilly depend chiefly for his data on reports and discussions by letter, the wording of reports and letters is an important matter. Real things — the lives, happiness, destinies of living people — depended quite as much on the literary skill as on the political ability of an officer (AW, 180).

It is not, therefore, surprising that Burwash spends much of his time finding a pretext for using his favourite words like 'impasse' and 'situation' whatever be the nature of the communication. He looks into all the complaints for "the only safe rule is, all complaints must be noticed" (AW, 182). Cary's pungent attack on the white administration cannot be missed in the following passage : "His chivalrous instinct to defend the weak, his British leaning for giving every creature, of any kind of clay, even pure clay, its freedom to exist and go about its own affairs, stirred at once" (AW, 182). Molly Mahood aptly describes this dull, unimaginative administrator whose diplomacy will not be of any use to anybody : "Burwash, whose name with its overtones of wishy-washy, whitewash, purr, blur, and other suggestions of benign ineffectuality was a last-minute inspiration, is a kindly man whose only defects are that he sees no evil and does no good."[29] Ironically the peace-loving man who never likes to swim against the tide is accused as a betrayer both by Aladai and the white men. When Burwash asks Aladai to go to the mission, the latter suspects him of foul intention. Dick Honeywood, "a dull fungus" (AW, 189) according to Rackham, bursts out in fury : "The fact is, of course, that Burwash would see any of us cut up rather than get in the wrong with the black brother. Can you understand it Jerry?" (AW, 188).

The interesting fact to note here is that even the noble Doctor Schlemm, "A man devoted to one course — alleviation of human misery" (AW, 130), gets caught in the trap of politics in his personal and public life. He becomes a hypocrite when he tries to hide the fact that his own pupils including Aladai, have betrayed him and cannot help becoming a trickster once he is forced to play a political game. Even the innocent Dryas who described politics as a bore" (AW, 119), by a mere accident is drawn into it and she turns out to be the central determining force of the events. In *The African Witch* we do not find any character symbolizing a single set of ideas as such. Perhaps a few like Dick Honeywood, the champion of the Empire, are an exception. Witness his impassioned speech : "All your blasted politicals are the same, selling out to Gandhi in India and your Aladai here — what I can't see is, how they think it's going to pay them" (AW, 192). But the whole atmosphere is charged with the air of politics.

The nature of the relationship between the white and the black as shown in this novel is definitely not moulded by racial feelings alone but also by purely personal feelings and emotions, very often motives beyond reason. Andrew Wright holds that

> The truth about the human situation as Cary dramatizes it in *The African Witch* is, always, complex.... And tempting as it is to read *The African Witch* as a colonial novel, it must be considered in the wide context which is always Cary's first interest; the context of men rather than Africans or Englishmen or Africans versus Englishmen.[30]

The point is that the African context is not less important than the universal context but that Cary allows equal play to both. Hence, the significance of Cary's perception of the African experience has a temporal as well as a timeless dimension. To cite a few cases : Judy's earnest attempts to understand Aladai and his national consciousness; Dryas' humanistic approach towards the ill-treated Aladai which helps her to overcome her inherent hatred of black men; Rackham's refusal to accept Aladai as the leader of the natives on account of the former's political belief that half-educated niggers cannot be allowed to run the government, later aggravated by the personal animosity directed against Aladai for having drawn Judy away from him; Burwash whose approval of paganism prompts him to encourage maintaining the *status quo*; Captain Rubin who tries to bring out the affectionate nature of the Rimi people; Mrs.Vowls who advises Aladai not to have anything to do with the white men for they are sure to betray him. Cary thus provides a vast spectrum of attitudes. This nullifies the validity of the stand taken by many critics that this novel is merely an attack on British colonialism and white racism.

Jealousy, the root of all evils, is very often shown as a force behind the individual's irrational behaviour. Cary himself gives a rather obvious clue to this. The flourishing of witchcraft, the monumental destructive force in Africa, is due to the unconquerable evil in man.

> Ibu, though stupid with terror, confusion of mind, misery, cold and hunger, was an intelligent child.

> This quality had probably been her ruin. All intelligent, good-looking persons are exposed to jealous and jealousy is the subconscious source of the hatred which produces injuries — from injuries, fear; and from fear, an accusation of witchcraft. In this way Africa has destroyed, every year, for some millions of years, a large proportion of its more intelligent and handsome children (AW, 84).

However, jealousy is not the curse of Africa alone as irrationality is a trait common to all human beings. Judy, Dryas, and above all Rackham, act under its spell and Cary takes pains to show that he does not identify irrationality exclusively with Africa. Nevertheless, he seems to have faltered, perhaps unconsciously, for the final impression one gets of the novel is what Cary does not want the reader to have and the role of the title is vital in determining this aspect. This proves that even the most gracious and liberal writer may unwittingly reproduce orientalist assumptions though we cannot endorse the view that he is a racist.

While discussing the character of Elizabeth, Virginia U'Ola questions Cary's objectivity.

> His picture of her [Elizabeth] is full of contradictions : he presents her as an intelligent woman sensible and practical yet the god she serves and the tactics she employs for the detection of witches are totally irrational. How does a reader reconcile this fundamental irrationality with her calculated organization of the women's war?[31]

Elizabeth's symbolic act of making Akande Tom crawl upon four legs like a beast and her being not in the least ruffled by the ordeal posed by the alien forces, add to her stature. The former also serves Cary's purpose of emphasizing cruelty as an African trait. Even the rational Aladai is swept over by the irrational wave spread by his sister. Africa, with its juju, is such an irresistible and powerful force that the British prefer keeping themselves away from meddling with it to liberating it, as metaphorically shown by the refusal of education to Akande Tom. Among Cary critics Molly Mahood, who has never been blind to Cary's lapses arising out of the English blood in him, makes the point tellingly :

> A much more serious defect of the book is implicit in its title. Cary wanted to write about the mind's fight against irrational forces, and he chose an African setting for this because the operation of such forces is particularly clear in Africa, both among Africans and among Europeans living there in small, isolated communities. But the title suggests what the book itself confirms that the juju which masters so many characters in the story is to be thought of as a specifically African force. Cary, that is to say, confused setting and symbol when he followed Conrad in identifying Africa and the Africans with the irrational. Such symbolism, still to be found today in the romancing of a South African writer, Laurens van der Post, about the Dark Eye of Africa, is itself part of the very myth of racial superiority which Cary sought to analyze in *The African Witch*. In particular, it is responsible for much confusion in Cary's presentation of Aladai.[32]

Aladai who comes back from Oxford with an enormous ambition to work for the progress of the Rimi people, blindly relies on European civilization as the only means to achieve his end. This grand passion for the national cause weighs him down with responsibility and anxiety even before he becomes their Emir. It is his 'progressive' thinking and his genuine concern for his people which win him a place in the minds of the readers as a prospective leader in the making. But this becomes a mirage once his true mettle is understood. We find him deficient in certain much needed traits and possessing certain unwelcome traits which can block his way and may even dig his grave. From the beginning of the novel Cary throws into relief these qualities . Like an excited child Aladai talks about the impact of English education upon him. "'Such a great people — a great civilization! .... Think of how I felt when I began to read English books and to hear what civilization could mean — it was like growing up thousands of years in a few months'" (AW, 20). His unquestioning faith in the European civilization and his inner urge to have somebody as a source of moral support by his side, prevent him from blossoming into an independent man capable of governing himself and others. His proud declarations like "'If he [Coker] starts any watch-tower tricks or spirit-women games here, I shall stop him — I shall smash him to pieces'" (AW, 21), and his arbitrary dismissal of the Mohammedans — "'About five hundred — in a million — I don't count the Mohammedans, their schools are a joke'" (AW, 21) — amply prove that he has not yet learnt the intricacies and the arduousness of political life. Though he keeps reminding himself and others that his first task will be the abolition of ju-ju, he is always presented as an embarrassed man in the presence of his "magnificent sister" (AW, 33). Whenever some decision has to be taken, he goes to Elizabeth and it is Elizabeth who always leads him.

We can understand G.D. Killam's anguish that "Aladai never has a chance of succeeding in the novel despite the fact that his education, the honesty of his appraisal of the Rimi situation, the moderate nature of the reforms he proposes, make him the logical candidate to succeed to the emirship." But we cannot allege that Aladai fails exclusively because of Cary's racism as Killam alleges : "Cary like Rackham in the novel, recognizes Aladai's quality; like Rackham, however, Cary cannot overcome an antipathy to Aladai which is irrational and racial in origin."[33]

It is worth reiterating here that Cary's purpose behind this novel is that education alone cannot bring the desired effect unless a better, healthy, social and economic background is provided simultaneously. In the case of Africa, he feared that "Education would bring in more violence, more barbarities; it would break up what is left of tribal order, and open the whole country to the agitator" (AW, 312). Cary's approach to the problem is a reflection of the changing trend of the liberal thinking of his day. The complacency of the early liberals that education could easily wipe away the darkness enveloping the world was not shared by the liberals who came later. Cary's belief is that unless a healthy social structure exists to feed and enlarge the creative imagination of man, he cannot be made free. Aladai is the victim of his surroundings. For he is tossed between two worlds — that of the derivative civilized values and that of the magnetic primitive ideas, himself belonging nowhere. This may be the reason which has made the end of the novel controversial. Cary's complex perception of the political reality that in the case of the colonized countries the transference from subservience to equality is not going to be a smooth affair is reflected in this novel.

Aladai, encouraged by his English education, plunges into the white men's world as one among them but only to be chased away like a chicken. Still he clings to that world with the hope of being received by them some day. But once he realizes that the way is completely blocked, he regresses to the primitive world. Cary's political wisdom warns the natives that this kind of regression may not be a healthy sign of nationalism for it is another juju which binds Aladai to captivity. When the white man's juju, namely education, with which Aladai has planned to destroy the overwhelming black juju, fails to sustain him anymore, this new juju, namely nationalism, becomes more attractive and he succumbs to it.

The characterization of Aladai is another milestone in Cary's process of evolving a concept of leadership. The author had taken an English colonial officer as a specimen for his study in *An American Visitor* and examined the cause for his failure in a changing world. In *The African Witch* he deals with a prospective potential leader of Rimi, Aladai and analyzes what incapacitates him from emerging as a progressive leader of his race who would help them become civilized. Cary's contention is that both of them lack political expertise, for they attempt to impose their set ideas upon their people without any imagination and herein lies their tragic flaw. On the contrary, Elizabeth and Musa, the leader of a gang in the locality, have the latent power which makes them natural leaders in their own spheres. Aladai and Elizabeth act as foils to each other. The latter is a natural leader whereas Aladai aspires to be a leader deriving power partially through his education. Cary seems to hold that a man who has both the natural leadership quality and a cultivated sense of authority, will become a leader who conquers the world, as the later novels hint. However, Cary's preference for the powerful spellbinders which is given ample scope in his Second Trilogy, impels him to opt for Elizabeth in *The African Witch*.

In spite of the spirit of rationalism behind Cary's projection of

Aladai as an archetypal African hero, one cannot help noticing the unconscious revelation of Cary's instinctive aversion to the negroes. The repeated use of expressions like 'savages,' 'treasured ape' and 'niggers' to refer to the Africans, especially Aladai, even when it is unwarranted, and the tendency to identify cunning, barbarity and anger with Elizabeth's temperament ['cunning as a savage' (AW, 109), speaking in a 'savage voice' (AW, 130), Fowl with his 'rustic cunning and persistence' (AW, 167), etc.,] support such a view. Even the politically mature Makurdi is not spared by Cary : "Grinning, panting, sweating like a squeezed sponge, he rushed at her, and began to explain, ...'" (AW, 32). Perhaps as Emmanuel Obiechina believes, even though Cary, like many European writers, tried to explore African Culture from an objective point of view, he falls "into projecting a version of African life which will fit into the image of Africa in the popular European imagination" as "'the popular mythology of Africa has permeated European imagination so deeply...."[34] However, what should be admired about Cary is his deliberate attempt to rise above this weakness of European prejudice and creating a completely fabricated construct. In Virginia U.Ola's view "Cary has ... not been very successful in his characterization of Africans, though he is much more successful than his predecessors."[35] It is significant that a non-white like U.Ola acknowledges, although grudgingly, Cary's capacity for dispassion. It represents the best facet of Liberalism in its essence — a capacity for self criticism and disinterestedness which Arnold indefatigably pleaded with the liberals of his day to cultivate. The scathing attack made on almost all English men and women in the novel is evidence enough to counter the charge of racial antipathy. For instance Rackham is referred to as "half woman" (AW, 138). Burwash, the Resident, with his "white-coated belly" (AW, 42), does not fail to provide a comic interlude. In general, Cary lashes out at the white administrators showing them as a body of men not interested in administering the people but living in a world of their own, having their own Scotch clubs and entertaining themselves by playing polo and bagalette even when there is a 'woman's war' going on in Rimi.

However, Cary's reluctance to show even a glimpse of a bright future for Africa, is disconcerting, to say the least. Is it the romanticist in him with a fascination for the picturesque native life who is responsible for his instinctive admiration of the African spirit as embodied in Elizabeth? [In the essay "A Child's Religion" he admits that he himself had been a juju worshipper (SE, 21) and that the child's religion is juju; he also justifies that after all it is the child's natural religion : "...juju was at the beginning of all our religions and it is, after all, a reciprocity of duty and affection" (*Ibid.*, 22)]. Or is it the imperialist in him who is rather hesitant to admit that Africans are fit for civilization and capable of self-government, as voiced by Rackham in this novel? Or is it the natural wish of the ruler in him to remain as ruler without being resented by the natives which is responsible for this ending? It is very difficult to decide on the issue. Cary wrote in candour : "The British Empire for me was the liberal and liberating power which had begotten the free state of Canada, Australia, New Zealand, South Africa and was preparing many more to govern themselves" (SE, 72). If so, how can Cary's stand in *The African Witch* be justified? In *The Case for African Freedom*, he emphatically says, "It struck me that the tribal native is often extremely bored with tribal life. He finds the same attraction as Europeans in change and discovery; above all, in new freedom, even that small amount to be bought for a wage of six pence a day" (CAF, 38). Whereas Cary evinces some interest in projecting such a balanced spirit in *An American Visitor*, it is thoroughly eclipsed in *The African Witch*. Cary seems to be convinced that the Africans are not prepared to benefit from the Europeans.

Though the colonial discourse of Cary generates to some extent the possibility of being its own critique, Aladai's attempt to become a 'mimic man' and the notion of mimicry, in particular has been viewed more as a condition of the subservience of the colonized — a mark of their powerlessness.

Cary is allegedly contradicting himself at various levels and the inconsistency between the ideas expressed in his political treatises and the novels has been fully explored by critics like S.H.Kanu. However, it is his juxtaposition of the inherent contradictions and antitheses in the colonial predicament which adds to the complexity and richness of the novel *The African Witch*; it is what prevents him from realizing his ideal in mere logical terms.

In the essay "Morality and the Novelist," Cary vividly observes :

> But even where ideas are in conflict with earlier impressions and with each other as in Dickens and Dostoevsky, and are assimilated, they do not frustrate the man. For they produce not contradictions but conflicts and conflict is not a logical opposition, a deadlock never to be resolved, but a tension which has to be reckoned with, which must be revealed, which so far from producing frustration and sterility, is a centre of force and power (SE, 164).

What he says about the two classic novelists is applicable to Cary himself. In the ultimate analysis Cary deserves commendation for showing politics in all its complexity. George Steinbrecher Jr. is justified in considering *The African Witch* as "Cary's African masterpiece."[36]

The next novel which we here take up, *Mister Johnson*, comes as a relief to the readers and critics, especially those who have been thoroughly put off by the ambiguities of Cary's earlier novels, and frustrated with their futile attempts to sift the author's 'message.' Cary who perhaps demands too much of participation for readers of a relatively simple taste, provides a piece of cake, as it were, in *Mister Johnson* to be easily swallowed. After his serious experiment with a complex, vast panorama in *Castle Corner* which left him unsatisfied in the end, Cary turns to write a novel about the simplest of characters in a simple background. It is about Johnson "the artist of his own joyful tale."[37] *Mister Johnson* is not only a tale of the joyful artist Johnson, but also a joyful flowering of the exuberant artist Cary, who, for once, is not interested in projecting his hero as a political animal.

B.R. Smith feels that "Although Joyce Cary implies an awareness of the realities of colonialism in all his African novels, he is more interested in the identity of the individual and in the problem of personal freedom than the political and social situation of which the individual is a part."[38] Though Smith's argument is not wholly tenable he comes nearer the truth in the case of *Mister Johnson*. In this novel the hero is shown as a culturally alienated individual in a colonial situation, whose obsession with modernizing himself and his urge to become a white man lead to disaster. "Johnson's idea of a civilized marriage, founded on the store catalogues, their fashion notes, the observation of missionaries at his mission school, and a few novels approved by the S.P.C.K., is a compound of romantic sentiment and embroidered underclothes" (MJ, 16). Johnson has got not only his idea of marriage from these sources, but his entire life is built upon the vague knowledge he has derived from these. However, the social milieu begins to lose its grip over us once we get involved in reading the novel. The lucid manner in which the story of this government clerk is narrated prompts us to see him only as an individual who knows not only the art of living every moment in his life but is also capable of making others live. Johnson for whom every action is a source of glory and enchantment, wastes no time in shedding tears over failures and losses but firmly seizes anything which can feed his sense of glory :

> ... he thoroughly enjoys opening a mail — that is, tearing open large, expensive envelopes and throwing them on the floor. This gives him a sense of the wealth and glory of the Empire and he becomes part of it. Reading official letters is a pleasure to him, for it makes him feel like part of His Majesty's Government, and he even enjoys filing so long as he has to deal with established correspondence — (MJ, 58-59).

"The complicated motives of good nature and glory" (MJ, 62) goad him to take the law into his hands. He authorizes uncatalogued holidays, steals money from various sources, indulges in embezzlement and induces Rudbeck also into it, but is never conscious of the nature of his action and its repercussions, for he leads too excited a public life. In his personal life also, he never misses an opportunity to satisfy his ego as a government clerk, disassociating himself from the fellow natives around him. He pays a high price for marrying Bamu, the "most beautiful, clever (bush) girl you can tink" (MJ, 35). In spite of his friend Benjamin's warning, he weds her as per Christian rituals and tries to turn her into an English wife, cajoling and coaxing her, but always in vain. He remains a stranger to his wife and his half-sister Falla till the end. "Falla and Bamu chatter all day, and whenever Johnson comes near them both look at him with the same expression as if he were a strange dog or an unusual and possibly dangerous beast" (MJ, 119). Johnson throws big parties distinguished by their new English gin, inviting guests only to boost his image as a government official. When Johnson fails to receive any kind of encouragement from his wife and her relations, he seeks it outside and finds it in Ajali :

> Although he knows perfectly well that Ajali is not really his well-wisher, that he is a spiteful and dangerous man, he prefers him greatly as a confidant to the honest and friendly Benjamin. The reason is that Ajali can never hide his wonderment at Johnson's deeds and Johnson needs an admirer far more than a friend (MJ, 67).

And he pays for it. It is Ajali who feeds Johnson's sense of glory by his exclamations of wonder and overt expressions of encouragement whenever he reports his adventures. He tempts him into more and more illegal acts which have deadly consequences. Waziri too flatters Johnson's ego; but both Waziri and Ajali do not hesitate to laugh at his misfortune later.

The occasional compliments of the new officer, Rudbeck who treats him more cordially than the previous District officer, Blore, infuse a new spirit in Johnson. He weaves a wonderful fantasy around this edifice of relationship with the white officer. When Rudbeck's wife Celia arrives, he becomes her guide and takes upon himself the responsibility of looking after her needs, "'I belong for de King — I 'gree for de King. I Mister Rudbeck's, frien' ...'England is my country, dat King of England is my King'" (MJ, 40), proclaims Johnson with a rather ridiculous naivete. As a headman of the road-building crew, he encourages them to work hard with roaring drums, tempting them with gin and his own inspiring songs like "'Out of our way, this is the king road where he flies, the great trees fall/ The sun and moon are walking on our road'" (MJ, 165). stressing the heroic nature of the task in hand. The road becomes his responsibility. He resorts to all kinds of illegal means to see that the road — laying work and his own expensive showy domestic life go on smoothly. When he steals Gollup's money, he is forced to murder him to escape from the immediate danger of being caught by him. He faces the fatal consequence of it but in a glorious way. William Van O'Connor sums up the situation thus : "Mr. Johnson is what he is, a vitality that recreates its environment and refuses to be a *thing*. He is victimized but declines the role of being of a victim."[39]

What gives this simple story of a simple character a political twist is the politicization of an ordinary relationship between a native clerk and a white officer which is made extraordinary by how it ends. "Rudbeck, new to the service, has treated Johnson, his first clerk, with the ordinary politeness which would be given to a butler or foot-man at home" (MJ, 26). Johnson takes it as a gesture of friendship and it makes him feel drunk with joy and excitement whereas Rudbeck does not even take notice of him as a human entity. He does not even remember his name when he sees him the next time and to him Johnson continues to remain 'a comic' (MJ, 102) and to his wife Celia 'a perfect quaint' (MJ, 102). But Johnson is too full of life to remain neglected for long. Later Rudbeck becomes his friend and he shares with him "the power of refusing to notice unpleasant things until they force themselves upon him" (MJ, 87). In course of time Rudbeck submits to the power in Johnson though he is not aware of it, for the drive which he is lacking is provided by the buoyant native clerk. Johnson suggests to Rudbeck who has a "passion for roads" (MJ, 51) the laying of a 100 mile-long North road to connect Fada with the main Kanou road. It shows Rudbeck the way to channel his energy and he simply follows his clerk.

Rudbeck, not a man of circumspection, by temperament fails to prevent Johnson from falling a victim to his exuberant imagination and crooked actions by not checking him as an officer ought to have done in normal circumstance. Instead, Rudbeck is rather amused by his behaviour : "'Why damn it all, Johnson. I didn't know you were a bloody thief'" (MJ, 89). And he is surprised to hear Johnson talking about stealing from his own treasury. "'But it's an idea — yes, it is an idea. Of course, it's impossible — but it's an idea" (MJ, 91). When Rudbeck is forced to realize the magnitude of the situation, it is too late and he can neither save his pitiable clerk nor himself. He is asked to draft a charge sheet against Johnson which leads to the tolling of his knell. Johnson who is capable of finding glory even in a disaster, knows how to turn this dreadful end of his into a glorious act. He pleads with Rudbeck, his idol, to shoot him and not to hang him as decreed by the court. The guilt-stricken Rudbeck cannot decide how far his report has been responsible for the sad end of Johnson. Although he does not yield to Johnson's demand immediately, he eventually shoots him. On the spur of the moment he allows his sense of friendship to overcome him and pulls the trigger adding glory to Johnson's life. Rudbeck commits almost a murder in the technical sense but feels as though "he is growing ever more free in the inspiration which seems already his own idea" (MJ, 251). As R.W. Noble remarks, "Rudbeck is essentially a passive person whom Johnson inspires to exercise freedom from external restraint first to help widen their world, then to cut Johnson off from it."[40]

Mister Johnson may be considered as a tribute to the friendly and generous nature of the Africans and such a reading is supported by what Cary says in the Prefatory Essay : "... I remembered him [a poor clerk] when I drew Johnson. He reminded me too of something I had noticed as a general thing, the warm-heartedness of the African; his readiness for friendship on the smallest encouragement" (MJ, 8). But his novel has taken another turn which might not have been anticipated by Cary, mainly by its controversial ending. Critics have been given ample scope to give a political twist to this novel and the swelling racial feeling in the recent past has furthered its intensity. A text which was intended to be simple has developed 'a figure in the carpet.' Molly Mahood has noted how "the mid-century's obsession with race relations still distorts the book for black and white readers alike."[41] Cary has unfortunately, or shall we say, fortunately for the text, left the ground open for the African critics and readers to accuse him of having treated the black man with the least concern for him as a human being. For Johnson has not been treated "any more than a faithful hound" (MJ, 168) by his superiors in the novel. For instance Ngugi wa Thiong'O gives vent to his offended feelings in the following passage :

> In this novel he [Cary] offered an idiotic African as the hero. Mr. Johnson is the dancing, fun-loving African full of emotional vitality and the enduring

> human warmth of a child. In the novel he is condemned to death. What was his dearest wish? To be shot dead by the European District Officer. The District Officer grants him that wish. Don't we do the same for our horses and cats? The point is that in the novel the reader is supposed to admire both the District Officer and Mr. Johnson, they have established a human contact; that of the rider and the horse, the master and his servant.[42]

Some of the English critics have also attacked Cary's novel on the ground that it is a 'patronizing' book. Frederick Karl who disagrees with many of Cary's ideas, has made a caustic remark that "Yet he [Johnson] remains an innocent, a pawn in the hands of a European culture which makes use of him and then after having tempted him must kill him."[43] Arnold Kettle in a similar vein says, "Rudbeck shoots Johnson as he would shoot a suffering dog to whom he feels a special responsibility and although the horror of this act is conveyed it is somewhat blunted by the underlying paternalism of Joyce Cary's own attitude."[44] However, sincere these critics may be, their view cannot go unquestioned. J.Z. Kronenfeld acknowledges Cary's attempt to treat Johnson "in terms clearly thought of as universal;...." but with some reservations. "Cary is caught in the liberal's dilemma, he wants to be understood as saying all men are basically alike; this however, makes it impossible to explain the limited possibilities of some men by taking into account the cultural contexts and special situations that might make their behaviour unique."[45] Cary might have been myopic in not realizing the seriousness of the situation where a black man is shot dead like a dog by a white man and it may be the paternalist and the imperialist in him which prevented him from thinking along these lines. But the critics also prove the same in not accepting the probability that it is Cary's single-mindedness in giving full expression to the genuine relationship between a white and a black man transcending the barriers of colour and race. Robert Bloom hints at the subtlety of this relationship :

> Rudbeck's sympathies are, in a sense, both there and not there. We have a mere flicker of fellow feeling in a man who can barely explain himself

> without causing us to smile at his insensitivity. Yet, the gesture of human community and involvement has been performed unhesitatingly. Africa, its inaccessibility and its customarily nonhuman juxtapositions of white men and black, has been triumphed over.... One of the least promising of Cary's colonial officers has been forced by Negro love, naivete and distress to an act of unpremeditated tenderness and regard.[46]

Above all, it is very surprising to note that the critics and readers who can take the death of the white administrator Bewsher in *An American Visitor*, in the hands of his beloved Birri men as a matter of fact, should be so offended by the manner of the death of Johnson because he happens to be a black man. We would do well to remember that Bewsher lived for the cause of Birri men, and he is speared to death by the black. It is reasonable to expect Cary to decide on the same for Johnson of whom he is rather fond. Cary seems to stress in the case of Johnson that "tragedy, disaster and suffering are the inevitable consequences of the many sided conflicts arising out of man's creative imagination.[47]

Cary had intended this novel to be a simple novel about a simple character and we may add, without any political theorizing. But paradoxically, it has been seen exclusively as a portrayal of the disintegration of the tribal life subverted by its disruptive forces. Cary has failed to achieve his purpose, maybe because of his choice of Africa as his setting for the novel. But the text generates its own dialectics despite the author's simple intention. Since his Africa was ruled by white men, the novel's milieu called for the introduction of a team of white officers.

Cary's obsession with his favourite theme, change and tradition, makes him a captive, as he is not able to go outside of the familiar arena of the administrative set up with its tussle between progressive and conservative officers. But it turns out to be a blessing in disguise for the text and its readers. Blore, the District Officer, who "likes all old things in their old places ... dreads all change, all innovation" (MJ, 25). He reminds us of Bewsher and Burwash of the earlier African novels. Rudbeck who welcomes change belongs to Cary's progressive type. His wife Celia is a replica of Marie in her exaggerated, excited, remarks about everything in Africa. But unlike Marie she is fed up with her "acting a part" (MJ, 103) in life and very soon her fantasy melts away, for "... to Celia Africa is simply a number of disconnected events which have no meaning for her at all" (MJ, 103). It is not the setting alone in *Mister Johnson* which resembles that of the earlier novels but even the theme seems to be of the same kind. Cary's attempt to present in a very serious manner his favourite debate whether civilization, here as symbolized by the road, brings in havoc or prosperity and happiness to Fada people, also seems to divert the attention of the readers from focusing on Johnson as a typical Caryan hero. But in reality it thickens the apparently diluted political stuff of the novel. Blore "considers motor roads to be the ruin of Africa, bringing swindlers, thieves and whores, disease, vice and corruption, and the vulgarities of trade, among decent, unspoiled tribesmen" (MJ, 51). Waziri considers it as a "misfortune" (MJ, 95). Both the Emir and Waziri hate the road for they say that it will "bring all kinds of rascals to Fada-spoils dis bush people" (MJ, 116). But Rudbeck and Johnson think differently. Johnson tells Waziri that "The Emir is a old savage fool — he has no idea of civilized things. Roads are a most civilized thing. When this road is opened, Waziri, you will be surprised" (MJ, 95) and he adds that "the markets will be full everyday of every kind of thing — there will be heaps of money for every body, all you in Fada will be rich" (MJ, 95). Rudbeck believes that it will undoubtedly bring prosperity to these backward people. But as it happened in the case of Bewsher, Rudbeck's enthusiasm does not remain unabated for long. Doubts and uncertainties begin to creep in. The road itself seems to speak to Rudbeck : "I'm smashing up the old Fada...; I am bringing wealth and opportunity for good as well as vice, new powers to men and therefore new conflicts. I am the revolution" (MJ, 186). It poses itself as a challenge to Rudbeck. Cary's serious involvement with the road as a symbol may remind us of Dickens' *Dombey and Son* and Ben Okri's, *The Famished Road.* The way Dickens has used it symbolising the power of the Industrial Revolution and the general post-colonial tendency to reconfigure the same symbol — roads and road-making, as part of a cripping colonialist legacy problematize the text.

A Bakhtinian reading of the novel also makes it clear that the temptation to indulge in a comic portrayal of English administrators has been irresistible for Cary and so this novel is full of sarcastic remarks about them [Vide the last chapter]. Rudbeck decides to build a road not motivated by certain specific expectations but because ". . . from Sturdee he has caught the belief that to build a road, any road anywhere, is the noblest work a man can do. He has also found it enjoyable" (MJ, 52), and

> He is on the road everyday, simply to enjoy it. He can't keep away from this keen new pleasure. He is like thousands of Englishmen who every year, from some accidental source, get the idea to make a garden or build a summer house, and labour night and day in it, neglect their business and their friends for it, risk double pneumonia for it, and when you say, 'There is going to be a war,' answer, 'Impossible,' because they have just planted tulips or ramblers. (MJ, 93).

The resident Bulteel's main task is to bring out the sad plight of the white colonial officers. He sympathizes with Rudbeck's policy though the latter has violated the general rules. Bulteel bewails to Tring, the new A.D.O. :

> 'After all, I suppose we're meant to be trusted — that's why they give us special conditions — and, really you know, Tring, we've got to be trusted or the whole thing would come to bits. I know we wouldn't have had even the Dorua Road, if we'd stuck strictly to the rules' (MJ, 127).

Later he cautions Rudbeck saying, "'Stick to the rules, as near as you can. That's the way to get on in the service, my boy, and you know you want to get on. As a family man'" (MJ, 161). Cary's apparent inability to come out of the colonial Africa with its myriad problems, the handling of which had landed him several times in embarrassing situations, has in fact turned out to be a boon. For his African novels when read in the post-colonial perspective with a historical hindsight, reveal themselves to be profoundly probing and even prophetic. They become sites for competing cultural powers.

Mister Johnson has been rated by many English critics as one of the best novels of Cary. In 1952 the *Time* magazine called it "the best novel written about Africa.[48] For Kinley Robey, "page after page of the novel dances with life and energy."[49] Its technical perfection and its splendid narration which makes it almost a lyric, have even earned the author the Black Taits Prize. But paradoxically, it has left several critics in doubt about his reputation as a liberal humanist who strives hard to overcome the pull of the imperialist in him and to represent the cause of the betterment of Africa with a genuine concern for its people. And the credit for this distortion goes mainly to the African critics. For, ironically, when Cary's real political novels escape being seen as political novels, *Mister Johnson*, with its least political and social theorizing, has captured the attention of the critics. It may not be a political novel but it is the most politicized novel.

English critics who have paid Joyce Cary high tributes for his excellent comic vision of life, a natural facet in him as an Irishman, have been rather hesitant to accept him as a serious writer. The problem of overcoming his own inner conflicts as an imperialistic Englishman intending to see Africa humanistically, has proved to be a little too much for Cary at times and the loopholes and incongruities in his novels are its natural outcome. The belligerent critics of Cary have seized and gloated over this fact and have waged a war against him, on this ground. Some others have decided to keep away from any discussion of his African novels and yet others have focused on them as patronizing novels; and the result of all this is that Cary continues to remain a writer whom the critics have been reluctant to understand.

"The tribal life has almost vanished and it will never come back," wrote Cary. "The peoples demand education and with it a new standard of life, for education gives a richer power of enjoyment and those who have learnt how to use their imagination will never be content with the narrower existence."[50]

Cary wrote so in the fifties and it may not be a mark of his far-sightedness and originality of thought. But he must be given credit for visualizing the change and dealing with the world and its problems as they are now and as early as in the thirties when he wrote his earlier African novels. The Nigerian novelist Chinua Achebe facing the present crisis, notes :

> But things happen very fast in Africa. I had hardly begun to bask in the sunshine of reconciliation when a new cloud appeared, a new estrangement. Political independence had come. The nationalist leader of yesterday (with whom it had not been too difficult to make common cause) had become the not so attractive party boss. And then things really got going.[51]

Cary is second to none in showing how the empire colonized the imagination of the colonized and forced the colonized subject into the internalization of the self as the other but he had the intuition to perceive that the world is in a perpetual creation and the Africa of the imperialistic imagination is not a permanent state. The signs of disintegration and its consequent unforseeable effects both for the good and the bad, depicted so effectively in *An American Visitor*, cannot be easily ignored. Cary no doubt suffered from a few doubts and uncertainties but that was natural when he wrote his African novels in the 1930s and 40s.

On the other hand, the readers and critics who belong to the Africa which had captured the thoughts of Cary, have begun to take up the cudgel against him in the post-war times. African critics have been somewhat biased in their approach to Cary. For their readings of Cary take away part of the dialectical richness of the textuality of his African novels.

The African writers who have been resisting western representations confounding national specifics contend that they, and they alone can and will project the real Africa. Caryan portrait of African life is audacious and supercilious, according to them, and so he has become the central target of their attack.

The African writers have not reacted so violently to the early African novels of Cary (which had as their central concern, the policies to be adopted in Africa). There have been indeed a few, who have objected to Cary's obsession with the filth of Africa and its violence. But his last African novel *Mister Johnson* has invited a lot of criticism. The reason may be what Molly Mahood mentions, although in a different context, in the following observation :

> Right or wrong Cary's insistence on food before votes has become as irrelevant as his concern with the rival merits of direct and indirect rule. In tropical Africa, colonial rule with all its accompanying anxieties about how and when power should be transferred to the subject people is a thing of the past.[52]

The Africans have now lost interest in such novelistic discourse as they believe that it does not have any relevance to their contemporary life.

The present-day problem of the Africans is how to decolonize their mind and so their grievance in general is against the presentation of Africans as archetypal characters marked by barbarism, irrationality and violence. Above all, a negro's apish imitation of the white man which makes him a laughing-stock is something which justifiably arouses the wrath of the African critics. Cary's Johnson is one such typical character and so more than any other novel of Cary's, *Mister Johnson* has generated a lot of heated argument : "However, delightful, even splendid,the character of Johnson may seem to the British reader, to the African, Johnson is a European monster, a culturally vacuous stage Irishman dressed in black skin and voiced with a bad approximation of West African pidgin English."[53] Yet it cannot be refuted that the innate urge in the black man to become 'white' which means 'power' and 'glory,' by coming closer to the white man, emotionally or physically, has been widely acknowledged, though to the dislike of the Africans. A reading of the famous critic of colonialism and racism Frantz Fanon's book *Black Skin White Masks* (1952) confirms that Cary has after all not distorted the African reality of the twentieth century as alleged by the Africans. Fanon's citing of Myotte's case powerfully brings this out :

> ... what Myotte wants is a kind of lactification. For in a word, the race must be whitened; every woman in Martinique knows this, says it, repeats it. Whiten the race, save the race, but not in the sense that one

> might think : not 'preserve the uniqueness of that part of the world — in which they grew up' but make sure that it will be white.[54]

An exhaustive study of what kind of men and psychological models imperialism has created, makes Fanon come to certain conclusions. His path-breaking book *The Wretched of the Earth* (1961) talks about the two opposed worlds, the rational beautiful world of the white men and the other darker irrational world of the black men and he sees the colonial structure as a manichean world. Reading Cary's African novels against the insights provided by Fanon into the African psyche, one finds that Cary deserves praise for his liberal attitude which enables him to see both the white men and black men as human beings who share the same weaknesses and for his resolve not to treat them like water-tight compartments. Cary very powerfully though subtly acknowledges, for all his liberal sympathies, that colonization was bad for the black and the white alike. In locating the ideological impasse in a vivid historical and moral situation, Cary turned his novel into a site for a debate on the implications of post-coloniality for the colonized as well as the colonizer.

There is hardly any white character in his novels who has not fallen a victim to his tongue-in-cheek treatment as we have already discussed in this chapter. It is unfortunate that the African writers fail to notice this and feel sorely offended imagining that only the black characters are treated in ludicrous terms. Starting from Bewsher with his crooked legs, and the lame-legged Judy Coote, to the unimpressive Rackham, none of Cary's white characters looks smart or behaves very majestically. Paradoxically it is this kind of comic portrayal of the English characters as against the patronizing treatment of the Africans which might have turned the English critics against him. Cary's characterization indeed reminds us of Fanon's words : "The negro enslaved by his inferiority, the white man enslaved by his superiority alike behave in accordance with the neurotic orientation"[55] In spite of realizing this truth in fictional terms, Cary cannot gain the good will of the African reading public. Chinua Achebe considers Joyce Cary's much praised *Mister Johnson* as one of the "appalling novels about Africa,"[56] and his own novel *Things Fall Apart* is a reaction to it.

Chinua Achebe however, in the same essay, has acknowledged that European civilization has offered the Africans, "education, paid jobs and many other advantages" (65) and he explains how they are living at the crossroads of culture : "But still the crossroads does have a certain dangerous potency; dangerous because a man might perish there wrestling with multiple-headed spirits, but also he might be lucky and return to his people with the boon of prophetic vision."[57]

It is however disheartening to note that Cary, who has tried his best to understand the Africans as human beings, has failed to depict even a single African character who can guide his people with a prophetic vision. It is ultimately this failure which leaves a mark of dissatisfaction in the admirers of Cary. Euro-centric criticism has read Cary's sympathy for the Africans as patronizing thereby miserably failing to understand the seriousness of his novels. On the other hand Afro-centric criticism has focused more on the projection of Africans and Africa in his novels as stereotypes and has refused to see him as a humanistic writer. And thus Cary still remains a victim of prejudice from both the sides. But when the patina of prejudice is removed his credibility as a political novelist will come to be better appreciated. The rapidly growing image of Cary as a major writer of the forties and the immense interest that some of the African writers and critics have in recent times shown in his works indicate the continuing relevance of his thinking to our times. This, however, calls for a proper re-historicising of his context. We see a glimpse of it in D.R.C.R. Goonetilleke's objective criticism of Cary (1991) in a comparison of him with Conrad :

> He [Conrad] has certain conventional attitudes towards negroes ... and knew little about them; consequently he cannot portray negroes as Joyce Cary can .... Cary shows a fine, open-minded interest in African culture, a culture very different from European civilisation and at an earlier stage of development .... Cary is lucid, concrete and assured even when presenting African realities most unfamiliar to civilised men, such as the human sacrifices in *Aissa Saved* and *Castle Corner* or the ju-ju in *The African Witch*.[58]

Such examination of past texts which perpetuate or discuss the latent assumptions of colonial discourse prove that the inherent contradictions and resistance are not an evidence of Cary's personal failure but a reflection of the cultural and liberal dilemma.

4

White Imperialism and the Celtic Peasant

It is difficult to see any work on Ireland not ensnared in political complications, as no one can escape either politics or history as they are writ large upon each and every aspect of life in Ireland. But one of the major problems faced by Irish writers is the political necessity to present the Irishman as the embodiment of goodness and as the victim of external political forces as W.B. Yeats opines :

> Ireland, since the Young Irelanders, has given itself up to apologetics. Every impression of life or impulse of imagination has been examined to see if it helped or hurt the glory of Ireland or the political claim of Ireland. A sincere impression of life became at last impossible, all was apologetics.[1]

In spite of this general claim, the examination of Cary's novel the *Castle Corner* proves that he with his keen sense of objectivity, is able to do justice to the reality of the Irish situation. It may be stated at the outset that in this novel, Cary does not treat the Irish situation and Irish cause from the point of view of a single political vision. In other words, it is not an apologetics, to use Yeats's term. He has allowed the dialectical play of forces without any partisan feelings to hamper it.

The novel *Castle Corner*, which was published before his most successful production *Mister Johnson*, has been regarded as slight by many critics, mainly on account of its lack of organization and Cary's failure to handle the material as a skilled craftsman. Dennis Hall, for instance, refers to it as "an interesting failure, in that it shows him [Cary] aware of the possibilities of a wider canvas, but its principal value is that it causes him to return to the path on which he had set out and continue along it."[2] Hall seems to allege that a vast complex fictional matrix was not Cary's forte and none knew it better than Cary himself after the writing of *Castle Corner*. Cary's own confession that "I had not fully realized that the very virtue of art, of which the power is that it can give experience, on that same account, limits its scope in argument"[3] adds weight to the above criticism. Yet, contrary to this view, one may say that the novel acquires significance for the simple reason that it strives to encompass in its canvas the entire domain of Cary's experience of life as an Anglo-Irish man, tied to both Ireland and England by birth and sentiment, and bound to Africa by his enriching vocation as a political officer.

Cary's enchanting childhood days spent in Ireland and his Wordsworthian ecstasy over the natural scenery around him remained with him even in later years. But the horrors he witnessed in Ireland which was passing through anarchy and civil war in a series of social, political and religious conflicts, remained a familiar but unfelt experience with him till the end. As a result, his response to the Irish situation seems to be conditioned by his mixed feelings towards England as a liberating force as well as a force to be resisted rather than by his individual involvement in Irish affairs. He admits :

> My earliest memories are of Donegal, its wild hills and the great sea loughs of Foyle and Swilly. I loved the country and the people, spoilers of children. But my heroes were the great men of English history, many of them Anglo-Irishmen like myself; and English history is world history. My imagination played on a world stage. I was engaged for England; I triumphed in her glories and suffered in her defeats and shames (SE, 72).

It may perhaps be due to the fact that the Irish cause did not engage his being as seriously as the African that he fails to create a poignant Irish political novel as he does manage to do in the case of Africa and England.

There are only two novels of Cary which have Ireland as their setting and of the two, *A House of Children* stops at the level of being a rich evocation of his childhood. On the other hand *Castle Corner* presents a highly chaotic world, enhanced by its frequent, sometimes arbitrary shift of setting involving Ireland, Africa and England. The reader has to play the typical Caryan role of a creative artist and impose some kind of order and give it meaning although at the expense of objectivity. One kind of pattern emerges if Ireland is taken as the focal point. In one sense it is also true because the Irish are the main concern and Africa and Britain happen to be part of the canvas. The Irish go to Africa for survival, searching for money and gold (*e.g.*, Felix). Again, without the intervention of Britain there cannot be a permanent political solution. When viewed this way a discussion of imperial policy and political intrigues, becomes meaningful.

Castle Corner is primarily an elaborate artistic representation of the turmoil undergone by both the landed gentry and the Irish tenants, whose lives are more determined by the politics of their class and race than by their individual merits and demerits. Cary, being a victim of the cruel injustice meted out to the Protestant landlords, needs no conscious training to capture the tragic plight of the members of the castle in this novel, who are driven like leaves in a storm. Cary expresses his anguish as an injured man in one of his essays : "... it is precisely the resident landlords, who have been born in the country, who have lived and worked all their lives in it and put all their capital into it, who suffer most" (SE, 64).

At the same time Cary as a true liberal humanist, could render a touching portrait of the helpless tenants groping in the darkness. Notwithstanding all this, Cary's predicament as an Anglo-Irish member of the "Garrison group" is betrayed throughout the novel. Robert B. Eckles and Richard W. Hale Jr. describe this group as follows :

> They formed an aristocracy both like and unlike the English landed gentry. In times of quiet all went well; when stress came, as it came too often, Protestantism meant loyalty to the King, Catholicism meant revolt, revolt meant reconquest, and a new set of 'planters.' So as wave after wave of English

> upper-class settlement came in, the 'Garrison' evolved its special attitude toward life. Its members kept a watchful and suspicious eye on the very tenants with whom they were on terms of warm friendship. A curious relationship of mutual confidence and mutual distrust grew up, comprehensible in full only by Irishmen.[4]

The parallelism between Corner's family and Cary's own is obvious and *Castle Corner* might have remained another autobiographical piece of writing, if it had not been dotted by serious political discussions.

The opening scene of the novel provides a clue to the paternalistic aspirations of the easy-going, self-complacent landlords who have begun to be openly challenged by the tenants, thereby revealing the brittle native-settler relationship :

> For old John, at eighty-three, brought up in the eighteen twenties, God the Father was the ruling conception of life. God was Father of creation, the King was father of his people, and he, John, was father of his tenants, both English and Irish, especially the Irish here at Castle Corner. He found them helpless and foolish children (CC, 9).

But when he interferes with the private plans of Padsy and Con by ordering them to vacate, it creates havoc. The children start running to and fro helplessly like frightened chicken and the sixty-year old Mrs. Foy takes command of the whole group as their proper leader : "To see her on the clamp beating the huge, gaudy drum with canes, her knuckles already bleeding, was like seeing one's mother take command of armies" (CC, 14). Con "screamed like a mad man" : "'They say I can't marry and they say I can't work. Why don't they cut us like stirks and sell us to butchers?'" (CC, 16). However, the Foys' determination to fight against their powerful master (who would not hesitate to resort to force to get his work done), to save themselves from being reduced to the level of wage-earners, is not shared by the group of people who serve in the kitchen in Castle Corner. The latter discuss such a serious matter as the eviction of the tenants "with the detachment of Chinese philosophers regarding the moon" (CC, 20). Their fatalism which is pitted against the challenging spirit of Mrs.Foy and Con adds to the pathos, and our sympathy is naturally drawn to the poor tenants.

John Corner, on the other hand, has his own reason for standing in the way of his tenants : "The worst thing that could happen to the tenants is the dividing of the farms. If we allow that, they'll all want it and then we'll have the same misery and poverty here that ruined Connaught" (CC, 24). Should any one raise questions about the consequences, his answer would have been this : "'God will provide,' or, 'we are all in God's hands — I can only do a plain duty'" (CC, 25).

Old John, however, seems to handle the situation tactlessly by inciting the tenants all the more by using force. His two sons, the peace-loving and pleasure-seeking John Chass who resides at the Castle Corner and the highly philosophical but dreamy 'Home Ruler' Felix, prove to be in no way better than their father. It is interesting to note that at this crucial juncture, Bridget, guided by Kitty, the would-be wife of Con, regards Mary Corner, John Chass' wife, as her last refuge. With her "domestic view of the matter" (CC, 11), Mary is ironically enough revolted by the idea of hurting her servant Kitty and her people. Love is her creed and she leaves politics to men.

Cary excels in the evocation of an atmosphere which brims with pathos, anger, love and blind faith and the artist in him revels in the luxury of the picturesque. R.W. Noble feels that "Cary begins *Castle Corner* by delineating two households [Castle Corner and the Foys] which represent the conflict in Ireland. His description, because it touches the particulars of people and places, is far more evocative than historical exposition or political argument could be."[5]

If the eviction scene evokes our sympathy towards the poor tenants, the knowledge of the miserable state of the Corner family counterbalances it. Felix, who returns home after twelve years, is forced to think of selling his dear castle in spite of his worship of the land. Slatter who "was one of those who made fortunes by buying up the estates of landlords ruined by the boycotts and rent-strike of the land wars" (CC, 29) is the first one to greet him. Felix knows well that it is foolish to invest in Ireland when there is talk of Home Rule which may mean disaster to many upstarts like Slatter. Felix's only solution in hand is the Mosi Company in Africa, "a company providing universal wants" (CC, 31). Since the case is lost both for the landlords and the tenants, he advises the tenants on the one hand to go to America, a fit place for the workers, and Slatter on the other to invest in Mosi Company. His urge to sell the castle before Home Rule is implemented baffles his father and brother, but he is certain that change is inevitable and its consequences are bound to be bitter :

> ... unlike Slatter he understood why nothing could be left alone, why all over the world the same changes were taking place, smashing up all the old ways of life good and bad, customs, religions, economic systems, by a force as irresistible as that of a moving mountain; and he knew that this tremendous blind thrust, released by education and science, would go on until the whole world, as seen by Slatter, was overwhelmed and new forces had come to a new equilibrium (CC, 30).

Felix's response to the on-going changes in the Irish socio-political scene is an instance of the way Cary has assimilated Bergson's idea of the flux of life. Felix, a Fabian socialist who starts as an ambitious Oxford young man with a keen interest in philosophy, achieves no success in his studies thanks to his involvement with his pamphlet "Schopenhauer and Darwin : The will to live" (CC, 28). He becomes a savage instead in Africa who is "going native" (CC, 245) : "Even Mosi traders were shocked by Felix' dirt and idleness" (CC, 245). His unwarranted excitement about his career, his exhilarating obsession with the concept of "an artery of commerce" (CC, 54) and his Napoleonic pride in undertaking such an enterprise, reduce him to the level of a comic personality though his zest for life seems to have appealed to the imagination of Cary. William Van O' Connor sarcastically remarks on Felix that "He goes out to Africa 'on business,' and soon, in the process of losing most of the family's fortune, finds his main business to be in 'satisfying' the frequent needs of his black servant-wife."[6] Yet, it is not easy to dismiss him as a mere addition to the bulk of characters.

Occasionally he seems to be voicing forth out views which are close to Cary's heart. In his imaginary conversation with Cleeve, while discussing "authority and freedom, tradition and progress, democracy and efficiency, change and security," he says,

> These everlasting conflicts have produced all the miseries, tyrannies, revolutions and pogroms in the world — they have smashed up every nation, race and church since the beginning of time. But there is no reason why they should do so — the fundamental problems are quite simple (CC, 320-21).

And he concludes that "It simply boils down to the question of good life" (CC, 321). Felix finds 'good life' in his identification with the natives and his blissful life with Dinah. "He was simply living his life as it came to him" (CC, 245) and nothing can interrupt his sensuous enjoyment of every moment of life. But in the hedonistic and elitist societies of London, the same Felix is looked up to as a wise man and a successful father. Cary's choice of him as his mouthpiece to convey his views on the permanence of indestructible ideas like peace and security and the predicament of a liberal in his time is worth consideration. The dual role played by Felix as a serious thinker and as a sensuous romanticist can be considered to some extent as a reflection of Cary's own divided self.

Above all, Felix's submission to Dinah and his son Cleeve's entanglement in an affair with the Irish native girl, Bridget show how they have fallen from their standard of being rulers to that of passive victims of the charm of primitivism, thereby, sounding the gradual downfall of imperialism. While in Africa, Felix is challenged by the native men when he defends the unwed but pregnant Bandy, and he is condemned as a source of corruption. Barbara Fisher remarks : "Thus English Liberals see their gospel message questioned. The very name, Felix invites such questioning."[7]

If Felix represents one set of rulers who almost forget their position and 'go native,' John Chass symbolizes the other who leave everything to Providence. Chass takes the least effort to check the growing threats from the sensitive, active natives who have been awakened from their slumber by the fiery speeches of the nationalists. Chass is a true version of an Irish landlord, as he has all the qualities which Cary attributes to any typical Irish landlord while discussing his uncle Tristram Cary.

> ...he was a typical Irish landlord of the old school — a sportsman, a good fellow, hospitable to the extreme, and a very careless economist.... Above all, he was a gambler. He did not plunge, but he loved to bet, and he slowly wasted a fortune on horses and cards (SE, 33).

John Chass is shown as a frivolous man who keeps up "the spirit of the pioneer" (CC, 148) by taking part in the tandem race.

Rifty Egan's exaggerated boast that "Ant Sukey has a thousand pounds saved — she's richer nor John Chass himself — he couldn't raise two for a tinker's wake" (CC, 297) shows the irony of the situation where the landlord is cast down to the state of a poor miserable man whereas his servant can command some respect from others and such reversal of roles is not uncommon in Cary's work. In spite of the impending danger, John Chass dismisses the serious affair of the election as part of his routine. He refuses to canvass when Joe Giveen tries to evoke a positive response from the people by promising them that "'he'll drive the Queen out of Ireland in a month'" (CC, 347). He does not address the Unionist meeting and is giving a party when the nationalists are holding three meetings a night. In Annish there is euphoria over the passing of the Irish Councils Act, which will facilitate the setting up of district and country councils. But John Chass with his extravagant glorification of Harry's conquest of Daji and with his talks about the ruling race, only provokes the nationalistic feelings in them. The *Annish Gazette* makes use of his speech to persuade the people to vote against him : "Let us see that Mr. John Corner, at least, shall not pollute the chair of the new democracy with the blood-stained shibboleths of the Saxon imperialist or sit upon the new council with such tried patriots as Mr. Joseph Giveen" (CC, 345). John Chass dismisses this as "'A fine piece of MacJefferson Brick'" (CC, 345) and continues to be indifferent to the rising chaos over which he has no control. Slatter's cry :

> ... if we're all rooned, every man jack landlord of

> us in Ireland, it's because of the likes of you that would rather be playin yourselves than fightin traitors and rebels like Joe Giveen that lives by England's trade and slanders the hand that feeds him" (CC, 347)

is the outburst of an energetic man of some political consciousness over the triviality of a passive fatalist. Even after his defeat in the election John Chass "seemed more like a man on holiday than a deposed chief" (CC, 352) and continues to buy Mosi shares. John Chass indeed "loved people, sport, good company and probably he loved Castle Corner too, without noticing it; as a man loves an old coat, and does not know his love until the coat falls to pieces" (CC, 12-13). And so it is not surprising that he has neither the time nor the sense of responsibility to realize that the Empire itself is breaking into pieces.

Slatter, the enterprising aspirant to the castle, acts as a foil to Chass's passivity and ineffectuality. Slatter is an ardent worshipper of the creed of materialism but his energy and enthusiasm are indications of his prospects in the future, though in the novel, he is made to lose much in the bargain. According to James Simmons, "Slatter is confident, ignorant materialism incarnate, the very symbol of Ulster. All his 'betters' laugh at him, but like Mortensgaard in *Rosmersholm* and Lopachin in *The Cherry Orchard*, the future is his, 'he is capable of living his life without ideals.'"[8]

Castle Corner, in general, raises many universal political questions. But the seriousness of the novel is heavily marred by the lengthy descriptions of non-political matters and irrelevant details. Enid Starkie's assault on Cary for his tendency to be carried away by the personal appeal of favourite characters and incidents, is indeed formidable :

> There are too many loose bits, very good intrinsically in themselves, which have not coalesced, and the action dashes without organic necessity, from Donegal to Oxford, to London, to Africa and back again, and all the passages are included because they happened to be in what he once called his 'rag

> bag,' where he stuffed, haphazard and higgledy-piggledy, all sorts of related material.[9]

Enid Starkie may be justified in her accusation to some extent. But now fiction is not expected to have a well-knit form and this change in the assumptions of the readers and critics robs such criticism of its strength.

Cary started writing this novel with great ambition. Barbara Fisher, aided by the study of Cary's manuscripts, traces the motive behind the novel thus : "This novel was, in fact, to do for politics what Tolstoy had done for war. 'Shew political novel of ideas parallel with the private, cf. War& Peace.'"[10] She further makes a comparison between the *Iliad* and this novel. However Cary could not realize his purpose fully well, for he had not yet learnt the art of striking a proper balance between the study of individuals and that of society. The excitement with which he handles the sensuous, adventurous incidents slackens once he starts concentrating on serious matters. Cary had intended *Castle Corner* to be a novel with answers for universal political questions, but it became something between a political novel and a chronicle. If it were a chronicle only, it had no need to involve itself with some political ideology. But the novel does hold a core of political interest.

The pattern underlying this novel becomes discernible if one ignores for a moment the uneasy feeling caused by the redundant, arbitrary passages. The Irish characters in this novel, though many in number, generally fall into four groups — the first as represented by Con, who has no more patience to put up with the alien landlords and who can think and feel only in terms of ruler-ruled bias; the second as represented by Kitty to whom politics is a myth and love alone has no barriers; the third aligned with Sukey who is resigned to the situation but gives vent to her frustration by screaming at others; and the fourth constituted by the more imaginative and creative people like Bridget who know how to make something out of the existing situation however gloomy it may be. Corresponding to them lie the four groups of English people — firstly, the fatalists like Old John Corner and John Chass; secondly, the upholder of human values as the ultimate end in life like Mary; thirdly, the rebellious and race conscious men like

Harry Jarvis; and fourthly, the creative men of imagination like Felix and Cleeve.

The tragic factor common to both the Irish and the English characters in the novel is the intensity of the forces which compel them to flee the country for survival, despite their deep love for their soil. Of Felix who returns to Annish after twelve years, the author remarks, "It seemed to him tragic that anyone having been born and brought up in a country so beautiful, so worthy to be loved, should not be able to live in it" (CC, 28). On the other hand, Padsy Foy's love for his land does not allow him to go to America even though money is provided to him. Kitty's "love of Annish and her love of the Virgin were parts of one love in which Annish was the holy place of God, as much nearer to Heaven than America as the miles of ocean between them" (CC, 303). Her return to Annish after her brief exile in America brings her back to life in the real sense. The way the Annish people sing the farewell song when their dear ones are leaving them for strange lands, moves one's heart : "The discordant voices were like cracked flutes, shrieking fiddles, flat bassoons; a hurricane of despair that made one's nerves shake like twigs in a gale; caught the breath in one's throat; squeezed the tears out of one's eyes" (CC, 65). The song, indeed, expresses a common sentiment which has stood in the way of the progress of many tenants.

The same despair that fills the adults assumes a different shape in the case of young children. They are drawn to politics even before they know what they are talking about. The discussion between Harry Jarvis and Philip well reveals this tragic dimension. Philip who is not even certain whether he is a Home Ruler, rebukes Harry when he calls Parnell "a bloody traitor" (CC, 63). Philip's friends, including Breedy and Padsy, "liked him and trusted him and he was eager to deserve their trust" (CC, 54) and so he supports their cause. The way the Irish Foys provoke Harry makes it clear that even children cannot remain immune to politics for long. Their use of his nickname 'Cocky' enrages him so much that he retorts, "'Why shouldn't I be here on my own ground?'" Witness the growing resentment : "'Your ground is it?' : one of the boys said, in a quiet relishing tone. 'I thought it was Egan ground. I'm tould all Annish was Egan ground, and Inishhowen, too, before any of you Englishmen knew how to cook your meat'" (CC, 66). As the rejoinders are vollied in this vein, with Breedy yelling, "'To hell with King Billy'", all Harry's excited feelings rush out of him in a new direction : "'To hell with the Pope'" (*Ibid.*).

The burning anger and hatred towards each other expressed in the passage above, had gone deep into the psyche of the people in Ireland. It is this which made a distinct group of Liberals oppose Gladstone's Home Rule which in their opinion, would only intensify the existing rupture between the Catholics and the Protestants. Matthew Arnold, for instance, proposed some kind of adjustment in the attitude of the British towards the Irish as a way out of the impasse.

> The Irish desire it [Parliament] so much because they are so exasperated against us. The exasperation is good neither for us nor for themselves. The thing is to do away with the sense of desperation by removing its causes, to make them friends. The causes of the exasperation are not in our political tie with them, but in our behaviour and treatment by all means.[11]

Cary however does not develop the social milieu in *Castle Corner* in such a way that the readers can feel the tension originating from different sources, but effectively renders the impact of it on the young minds. Manus Foy, "the glory of the Foys in Dan's house" (CC, 57), "knew the whole of his rosary" (CC, 16). He "was ambitious to be a priest, and when, in chapel, he watched the priest in his vestments going to the altar, he had felt wonder that everybody did not want to be a priest;..." (CC, 16). But he cannot march towards his goal, for like many of the boys of his age, he becomes a victim of politics. Many children-gangs like that of Manus Foy's Ivyleaf Boys, become part and parcel of Irish life and the riots caused by these groups become a menace to the English lords in the novel as was the case in Irish history.

> Father MacFee and the papers said that the country was disturbed. To people in towns and in places like England this seemed a far-fetched metaphor. But to anyone who lived in Annish and heard the bushes

> muttering at night, saw lights like eyes flash suddenly from a mountain top and close again, it did not seem like a metaphor at all (CC, 75).

Even after the Home Rule Government is defeated, the Irish boys are unwilling to subject themselves to the healing effect of the time. They would still cherish the hatred against the priests who killed their champion, Parnell. "To Manus it was the worst treachery to desert the chief because he had been defeated in death as well as life. He felt such hatred now for the traitors that he knew he must kill them" (CC, 115). While the other people are having a jubilant get-together in the castle, Manus with his comrades is waiting to murder Joe Giveen. He finally manages to hurt him with Philip's gun.

Philip, the apple of his uncle Slatter's eye, turns out to be a rebel of another kind. His accidental meeting with Padsy turns a new chapter in his life. He who has been torn between his father who wishes him to become a priest like him, and Slatter who aspires to launch him into a more profitable commercial world, finally decides that serving the Annish people is his mission in life. Inspired by Felix's socialism, he grows to be enamoured with the latter's idea of education as a key to their liberty. He makes vehement speeches about the need for education and the abolition of poverty. "Poverty's got to go and it will go — quick and soon. For if they don't abolish it by law, there'll be a revolution. People are getting tired of such nonsense" (CC, 103). He reacts sharply against Darcy's misfortune but surprisingly it is not appreciated by the peasants themselves and "they had long made up their mind that young Feenix [Philip] was up to no good" (CC, 109). Cary portrays with subtlety the obdurate mentality of the Irish peasantry.

> They did not know the word Socialism, but they recognized the creed and they disliked it very much. Annish farmers were landlords and conservatives in all their instincts. They wanted Home Rule to give them more land and better markets, but they didn't want any innovations.... (CC, 110).

Therefore, they cannot easily digest Philip's "speeches against the landlords and the rich" (CC, 109). They feel that "The Dunderry boys might break windows for Holy Ireland, for that was a religious act; but this boy's talk was dangerous and probably immoral" (CC, 110). Felix's concern for this talented young boy makes him remark that "'It's a pity if Philly breaks his head on a brick wall — he's the best of the young ones round here. But its a bad time for the young ones — a third rate age all round'" (CC, 112). Slatter's description of Philip's endeavour as "romantic nonsense" (CC, 112) is thought-provoking and it is disheartening to see how, many a boy like Philip are wasted mainly by their mania to distinguish themselves somehow, sometimes without any motive at all but to have some excitement, especially, when the country is passing through bad times.

Cary further develops the theme of chaos created by civil strife by revealing how even the institution of religion begins to be politicised due to the prevailing political imbalance. The tenants have always looked upon Father MacFee as a living God. But "Padsy was a Parnellite, and for the last six months he had been suspicious of the priests" (CC, 69). Father MacFee also cannot remain free from politics. His conscious attempt to keep himself at a distance from John Chass makes the latter rue, "'politics-politics-the ruin of everything'" (CC, 71). Ironically Father MacFee himself is not sure why he should shun the Protestant landlords for now that the Catholic Church has been "emancipated, respected by the British government; more rich and powerful than ever before...." (CC, 71). He, however, continues to be deeply concerned about the spiritual welfare of the people and his sincere anxiety over the weakening faith in God among the Protestants, especially due to the ill-effect of Darwinism, is an indication of this. He "grew hot and red with anger when he thought of the enormous power of atheism and the ignorance and weakness of the faithful. Every newspaper from England and America, every book carried poison, heresy, atheism and temptation, and every year there were more to read them" (CC, 71). Father MacFee does the same job as Feenix, Philip's father, who is then preaching against Darwinism trying to save the people from its trap with the following argument :

> 'For as we know, my friends, to use the great shibboleth of these confused times, what is called progress has been founded solely upon the struggle

> for existence; upon pure selfishness. What, then, has the scientist to say of this scientific ano-maly, my friends, of altruism. For ob-serve, even the smallest good act-the least por-tion of unselfishness in any act, is to-tally inex-plicable upon the scientific hy-po-thesis of the struggle for existence' (CC, 95-96).

But those who are caught in the muddy stream of politics are not ready to see religion in an unbiased manner and the result is chaos and confusion. Even Manus Foy, who is a "proof against infection" (CC, 72) according to Father MacFee, is enraged by the news that the priests have murdered his hero. He spits upon Father MacFee's umbrella and derives some pleasure out of it. He even goes to the extent of throwing a direct challenge to him. Like Philip, he too "had got into some narrow place and couldn't get out" (CC, 73). His inability to strike a balance between the two forces — politics and religion — breaks his heart : He was checked on all sides, and even in his love of the chief and his hatred of those who had broken his heart, he was held back. He could not strike at Father MacFee. Holy Mother Church stood between them" (CC, 73-74).

It may be observed how Cary's identification of religion with politics becomes valid in the Irish context. One may recall here Blake's famous utterance : "'Are not Religion & Politics the same Thing? Brotherhood is Religion,/O Demonstrations of Reason Dividing Families in Cruelty & Pride!.'"[12] It also becomes clear how, as an Anglo-Irishman, Cary has never been able to see them as separate issues. It is interesting to note at this juncture that mixing of politics and religion was not then peculiar to Ireland alone. Paul Arthur considers it a world-wide trend :

> Switzerland's Sounderbund War (1847) was fought between Catholic and Protestant cantons; Germans endured the Kulturkanph; and certain British and North American cities experienced sectarian riots between 1830-70. ...Internationally, a proselytizing evangelical Protestantism reacted against Catholicism's ultramontane movement and, paradoxically, the rise of nationalism failed to blur religious differences in Switzerland and Germany.[13]

Against this background the celebration in the novel of the Golden Jubilee of Queen Victoria's ascending the throne assumes significance, for it brings out the feelings of the confounded people of Ireland towards the Queen. John Chass who is highly excited by the very thought of it, starts painting the picture of the Queen and even makes himself a laughing-stock by overdoing it. He orders mugs and beer for the gathering and this event brings the Irish characters together. Padsy is paid to drink to the Queen's health; "though he abused the imperial glory; he took his share of it" (CC, 176). He refers to London as "the robber of the whole world" (CC, 177), and old Egan proudly claims that it is the Irish soldiers who won the cause for the British : "Who does the fighting for them? Where would they be without the Irish soldier? Isn't the Irish regiments well known to be the bravest in the whole army? Look at the Connaught Rangers and the Fusiliers!" (*Ibid.*). Old Dan heartily agrees with him : "Didn't the Irish bate the whole world in the days of Finn?" (*Ibid.*). Finally, Padsy declares that it should not be called the British Empire for "'It's the Irish Empire'" (*Ibid.*). The commemoration of the British Queen becomes subverted when it becomes the glorification of the intrinsic worth and valour of the Irish and to those who are present, it is the British who are in reality dependent on the Irish for their prosperity.

We have more instances of the dubiety of the Irish attitude to the Imperial regime. "Big Giveen, the grocer, and the nationalist committee had refused a subscription to the jubilee fund, giving an example which had to be followed, so that the total was smaller than expected" (CC, 178). But the enthusiasm of John Chass who is the chairman of the committee for the Jubilee celebration is shared by the people in general. For "The Annish people were nationalists to a Catholic; but as Catholics they were not jealous of rank nor did they think that self-respect forbade them to be polite. They would have greeted the Shah of Persia or the King of Siam with equal cordiality" (CC, 207-208). However, "the twin threats of Catholicism and nationalism," to use the phrase of Paul Arthur,[14] are keenly felt when Con sneers at the Corners as "the biggest robbers in Annish." He asks, "why wouldn't they rob ye when ye let them'" (CC, 209) and the others seem to agree with him. The sensation caused by the sight of Chass's only son Shon, "a princely beauty" (CC, 209) who decides to have a part for himself in the imperial glory, and his subsequent death, serve two purposes. They not only evoke our sympathy but also symbolize the eclipse of the Empire.

In a sea of turmoil like this, Cleeve and Bridget are floating like lotus leaves, to bring in an Indian analogy. In his preoccupation with these two characters Cary seems to go off the tangent. Cleeve, who lives every moment of his life like his father, loves Annish and makes love to appealing girls. Once he is exposed to the Bohemian world of Helen Pynsant, his love for Annish is replaced by that of London society. Cleeve becomes an aesthete and writes to his father that Walter Pater and Oscar Wilde were the only great men of the age and he would not be long in Oxford. Cleeve along with Cobden to whom love is a "religious profession" (CC, 276) and "Helen a cult" (CC, 276), testifies to the rising prestige of aestheticism. The portrayal of the London society with all its ramifications, woven mainly around the romantic Cleeve and Cobden, and especially Helen Pynsant as a queen surrounded by a set of younger lovers, can in no way bring credit to Cary; it cannot be taken but as a sign of his inability to stick to the mainstream of the novel. Cary himself has said once that to get the "sharp and strong feeling, the reader must not be confused by side issues. All the scenes and characters, all the events in the book, must contribute to the total effect, the total meaning" (AR, 5).

Cary's unconscious violation of his own norm in this novel has led to a lot of criticism. Charles Hoffman points out that :

> Life at the castle goes on, but its symbolic significance becomes diffuse as the action moves to Africa or England as the character development shifts from the Corners to the Pynsants or the Chorleys, as the battle of ideas changes from land economics to aesthetics or the Boer War and pacifism. The overall plan of revealing the revolution, as it affects the lives of many characters in different ways, defeats the symbolic purpose of Castle Corner.[15]

Cleeve and Bridget as typical Caryan people of creative imagination, impress us but they do not seem to belong to the novel except as symbols of their respective classes. The talk of a marriage between Cleeve and Bridget interests us, for it indirectly suggests the union of the opposing sects of the ruling Protestants and Catholic tenants. John Chass's polite refusal to accept Bridget as a member of the family on the ground that "... — it mightn't be just the right thing for Bridget — to be taken out of her class and religion, too" (CC, 218), reflects the attitude of the men of the ruling class who still believe in sustaining their "instinctive confidence in the rightness of things, as established by natural providence" (CC, 208). The mention at this juncture, of a novel which is begun by Cleeve "about Annish, in which the young master of the castle fell in love with a beautiful peasant, and their marriage, by uniting a protestant and catholic, made peace in the land" (CC, 140), clearly suggests what Cary's views are.

In coming forward to marry Bridget despite her condition, and with a definite motive of acquiring some status in the society, Rifty Egan recalls Chester Nimmo of the Second Trilogy. "The bargaining therefore was soon over. Rifty accepted eighty pounds with a heifer, a sow in farrow, and the tenant right of twelve statute acres on Knockeen; a fortune which would put him far beyond the reach of laughter" (CC, 221). As a married couple, though Rifty and Bridget exasperate each other, they make the best out of it : "...their marriage was a success because their idea of marriage was of a joint stock union for work and duty..." (CC, 297).

In the same way, Cleeve's winning of the hand of Stella towards the end of the novel, despite his knowledge of her deep love for his cousin Harry Jarvis with whom unfortunately she cannot see eye to eye in matters relating to politics, is highly political. Cleeve, after losing his dear Lucy who becomes captivated by the genius Porfit, and Stella who loses her lover Harry Jarvis who is tied more to his cause of Empire, are drawn towards each other by the force of circumstances. Cary exhibits his keen interest in depicting how even relationships take on political overtones. But it lacks in complexity and variety when compared to the later novels.

On the whole, should we ask how efficient Cary has been in handling the Irish material, the answer would be definitely in favour of him, for he portrays the Irish sensibility and scenery with a certain personal excitement. But if the question is extended to assessing his achievement as a writer of an Irish political novel, we cannot be affirmative in our response. For, he has neither been able to provide a deep view of Irish society and history nor has he seized on the landlord-tenant conflict and that of Home Rulers versus Unionists as the crux of the Irish problem. The novel also suffers from a lack of any serious ideology relating to Irish political conditions though Cary's awareness of Irish history cannot be questioned by anyone. Being himself a member of a declining Anglo-Irish class, we feel that he could have done better in capturing the political unrest and the vitality of the period.

Cary, no doubt, seems to be deeply concerned with the tragic plight of both the Irish landlords and the tenants. But the disillusionment and the wrath of a true liberal at seeing the disintegration of something precious is missing. For instance, John Bright, the famous Liberal politician of the nineteenth century, during his speech in the House of Commons delivered on 2nd April 1849, angrily asked :

> What is that in Ireland worth to you now? What is Ireland worth to you at all? Is she not the very symbol and token of your disgrace and humiliation to the whole world? ....We have had a union with Ulster, but there has been no union with the whole people of Ireland, and there never can be a union between the Government and the people whilst such a state of things exists as has for many years past prevailed in the south and west of Ireland.[16]

The reason for the lack of a comparable passion and heightened sensitivity on the part of Cary becomes clear, if we understand his personal attitude towards the Irish problem. He himself confesses that :

> If there were tensions I knew nothing of them, and I do not recognise them now. All those deep, richly-felt contrasts and conflicts remained simply as experience, the more vivid for its light and shade. But it is possible also that they gave me, even as a boy, a certain critical feeling (rather than judgement)

> about the more complacent views of politics and history which were then common form (SE, 20).

In terms of our concerns in this book the full power of his critical sense is evident in the thought-provoking African and British novels. The absence of an emotional involvement with the Irish predicament stands in his way in making *Castle Corner* a masterpiece, whatever might have been the intention. At the same time, it enables him to have an objective view. The fact that he wrote this novel, long after Ireland became a Free State, deprived him of the chance to render a case for the freedom of her people as in the case of the Africans. Moreover, Cary seems to be somewhat overwhelmed by the intensity of the conflicts within himself. As a settler he still nurses the injustice meted out to him. As a humanist he identifies himself with the miseries of the poor tenants. And above all, as an upholder of the British Empire, he seems to have faith in its "liberal and liberating power" (SE, 72). All these make it difficult for him to visualize a clear political approach to the Irish problem.

Despite his uncrystallized ideological position with regard to Irish politics at the point of writing this novel, Cary's portrayal of London society as a seat of political debates gives him ample scope to analyze certain political issues especially, the colonial policy of Britain towards Africa. It reminds us of the earlier African novels he wrote. He very effectively seizes on the question of Imperialism and it assumes greater significance because of the period during which the novel *Castle Corner* was written.

Cary in his own tactful manner brings out the irony of the two basic human sentiments, love of peace and nationalism, working against each other. The general tendency among the great nations to keep off war and the way it is being challenged by the rashness of the committed imperialists, is well brought out through Harry Jarvis. Laka district in Africa remained undisturbed for a long time. But a peculiar situation arose due to the confrontation of many conflicting human interests :

> France, Germany and England were all enchroaching on this rich country; but in a manner peculiar to the time. No one wanted war, and each knew that war

> might come at any moment over some frontier clash in Africa, yet each continued to advance as if by some mysterious compulsion.
>
> They were, in fact, compelled by many forces; by national feelings in the people, released by popular education; by ambitions and weakness of governments, by the ambitions of colonial soldiers and officials; and of course by the imperial idea of national glory (CC, 160).

In the last century the whole of Europe seemed to be in the grip of Darwin's theory of the survival of the fittest at all levels and the glorification of the cause of Imperialism was one of its offshoots. The doctrine of the "Survival of the fittest" first put forth by Herbert Spencer and later accepted by Charles Darwin, spurred the ideology of colonialism. Darwin's discussion of 'high' and 'low' races and of 'stronger' and 'weaker' nations, is a pointer to the developing graph of Imperialism. Cary exclaims in *Castle Corner* :

> It was so strong that it ruled even statesmen who had been brought up to believe in another one, in a quite different providence which was supposed to have designed all things for brotherhood instead of competition. It compelled Gladstone to send armies to Zululand, Afghanistan and Khartoum, he had to obey its command expressed through its millions of slaves, or he would have been driven from government (CC, 161).

The split in the Liberal party towards the end of the nineteenth century, which was mainly the outcome of the divided opinion among the Liberals in their approach to colonial expansion, resulted in the emergence of two distinct groups, namely Liberal Humanists and Liberal Imperialists. In his speech at West Monmouthshire on 31st May 1899, Sir William Harcourt summed up the Humanist thrust of the policy of Imperialism which could bring greatness to the Empire :

> It is a policy which has its first regard to the consolidation of the vast dominions, the countless

> millions, and the varied interests which compose our unequalled Empire, the development of their resources, the lightening of their burdens, the fostering of their natural growth, the relief of distress within it, and the raising of the standard of all sorts and conditions of men who are the subjects of the Queen.[17]

The Liberal Humanists in general concurred with the view of William Harcourt. But in course of time, due to the rapid growth of the sense of nationalism and competition which were romanticized all over Europe, some of the Liberal Humanists began to think in terms of colonial expansion as a required political move, if the prestige of their homeland had to be preserved. This slowly led, for example, to the Empire's involvement in land speculations and organization of syndicates to protect their rights over the booty of the colonies by checking the intervention of other big powers who were eagerly waiting for their turn. The emergence of this new feeling in them turned them into Liberal Imperialists. However, they remained cut off from yet another group of men who aspired for expansion at any rate, regardless of the tragedy of the loss of men and means. The worst group of Imperialists were motivated only by their private gains.

Castle Corner attempts to translate this political reality into the novel form by crowding it with characters who embody the spirit of Imperialism of all kinds. Harry Jarvis who heads the list has much in common with the Liberal Imperialists. His disillusionment with the British Government for its lack of enthusiasm in expanding their domain, actually springs from his sincere belief that only Englishmen can save the natives from their oppression. To him, his mother country is a great liberating force which cannot be challenged by any other power on earth. Harry Jarvis starts his career in an Irish regiment but is transferred to Africa by choice on account of his insubordination to his superior. He was provoked by the remark of his superior that "the Irish though fine soldiers were children in all practical affairs" (CC, 113). Hence, his offensive conduct. However a new vista is open to him when he envisages the possibility of visiting the Laka chief in the self-assumed capacity of a messenger from the Queen. While his interception of the slave raiders on the Northern Mosi gives him more confidence, he receives the news about the "talk of a treaty with France to fix the limits of each nation's sphere of influence" (CC, 316). The view that France may receive Daji infuriates him. Not dampened by the "cowardice of the Government" (CC, 166), he marches towards Daji with the minimum number of men and the limited means at his disposal, to the surprise of Pooley who stands bound by the British command "to avoid a clash with the French and to keep out of Daji, ..." (CC, 319). Harry's partriotism is such that he is ready to risk even his job and reputation to maintain the prestige of his mother land : "It seemed to him that something precious and even holy, something immeasurably more important than trifles like his life or Pooley's was being sacrificed by this Englishman's stupidity, the honour of an Empire which was also his own honour, and his own glory" (CC, 322). Cary praises Harry Jarvis' act as follows : "His feat was as much beyond headquarters' reach of idea as Cezanne's pictures in that same year were beyond that of the Salon Jury. Both were original and simple acts of imagination" (CC, 324-25). This remark reveals Cary's instinctive admiration for such heroes. Harry's conquest of Daji, which is inspired only by his urge to show the Empire's power, makes him 'The Conqueror of Daji' and he is "compared with Clive, Wolfe, Kitchener, Lugard" (CC, 344). Benskin, who is looking "for imagination, for the imperial spirit" (CC, 147), makes use of this opportunity and projects Harry as a glorious hero in the eyes of the English public.

Benskin, a South African millionaire who knows the value of the African booty as well as the strength of political 'power,' can appreciate the approach of the British towards the colonies : "Benskin was one of those, like Rhodes himself, for whom at that time the Empire was a sacred cause" (CC, 147). In Benskin's view "The Empire brought peace, prosperity and free institutions wherever it went" (*Ibid.*) and hence his argument that the status quo should remain. As a man fully aware of the golden chances in Africa, which had made him powerful enough to buy everything and everybody, Benskin manages to enlarge his business by including in his circle men with the imperial spirit. In course of time, he buys up even the representatives of the Empire, John Chass and Felix.

When General Pynsant dies, Benskin, a "real schemer" (CC,

80), is proposed for the vacant post, but Jones, the editor of the Porriton Gazette, attacks him by calling him "'One of the worst of the Kaffir drivers'" who "thinks money can do anything" (CC, 225). Chorley, his partner in business, suffers from a 'deep division' in his mind, torn as he is "between Church and State Liberals like Pynsant and Benskin and the chapel Liberals like himself and Porfit, a religious and fundamental difference" (CC, 199). Yet he defends him saying that "the important thing for Liberals was to pull together on the big issues like Free Trade and Home Rule" (CC, 225). The Nonconformist "Porfit's campaign against what he called the landlords and randlords had been embarrassing to Chorley who was a friend of both Pynsant and Benskin" (CC, 198-199), but what unites them finally is their stand against the Boer War and their whole-hearted opposition to the war speeches of Harry Jarvis, who is supported by Benskin.

Harry Jarvis is "astonished like most serious young men in their twenties by the inefficiency and carelessness of nearly everybody" (CC, 82), and feels strongly that "the Government was feeble, the War Office hopelessly inefficient; and that the resources of the empire were being wasted by selfishness and lack of imagination" (CC, 83). His conviction that their religion is "good enough for export" (CC, 89) makes him feel that it is a disgrace on their part to leave the heathens in Africa and India to remain as they are. Harry's conviction echoes the hegemonic notion of the times that "the exportation of their [European nations'] various economic, political and religious institutions was...a necessary step towards a higher form of human organisation in the rest of the world."[18] Harry's sentiment even towards Castle Corner, a smaller version of the British Empire, is the same. He laments that "everything precious and unique, the old ways at the castle, the castle itself, was going to the devil; because no one would take the trouble to keep them up" (CC, 92).

Harry delivers a heart-rending speech in Porriton, overwhelmed by the warm reception given to him by the people :

> ... I know if any of you had been in Africa with me, you would have done as much as ever I did to save these people from their oppressors and to give them some of the freedom and peace and justice which

> we all enjoy as a birthright, ... We ought to be thinking of the men who are meeting, perhaps this minute, the attack of the Boers upon our peaceful colonies in South Africa. And so I say God bless our soldiers, God bless you, and god bless the Queen (CC, 367).

Porfit calls the Boer War "'The greatest crime in history...'." He adds : "It is a crime that can't be hid under a bushel. The whole world sees it and knows it for what it is, the foulest betrayal since Judas sold his soul for gold" (CC, 368). Harry's speech, no doubt, makes a strong appeal to the crowd but equally effective are the anti-war speeches of Chorley and Porfit. The latter discusses politics using the phraseology of religion. When Cleeve protests that it is the Boers who started the war, Porfit rebukes him saying that "'Ah, but that was the real triumph of Judas, ... that his treachery did not appear, that he did not need to offer violence. It was the betrayed who first unsheathed the sword. Judas was not seen'" (CC, 369). Chorley sarcastically remarks that "'Even without comparing Kruger with Christ I should have thought our position was obviously impossible. We're going to murder these people, men are being killed at this very moment, and what for? Gold'" (CC, 369). We only have to recall how the Boer War provoked vehemently opposed reactions. In Kipling's view "it was a war undertaken for the cause of democracy;" but to Conrad it was "an appalling fatutity."[19]

Nussbaum, who is a staunch believer in the Liberal doctrine of free competition and in Darwinism as the eternal guide, "did not believe in the Empire any more or less than he believed in God, but he considered that both deserved the support of intelligent men; like the police force and the gold standard" (CC, 371). In general, he is sceptical of any kind of eternal security and peace and so according to him even Rhodes' imperialism is a myth. The fact that "He did not think of the world in the first place as a complex of powers, but of cultures..." (CC, 276) brings him closer to Cary with his donnee 'war of cultures.' And it looks as though Cary gives himself away in his portrait of this ugly Frenchman. Cary seems to imply that if at all the Empire survives, it is due to the efforts of the money-grabbers like Benskin who rely on the Empire for their sustenance and prosperity rather than those of the romantic idealists like Harry Jarvis who lose everything in the end but cling on to the illusory glory of serving the Empire.

Cary tellingly reveals in novels like *To be a Pilgrim* and the second Trilogy how one's attitude to war determines one's political career. But, *Castle Corner*, only hints at this and that too, towards the fag end. Stella hates politics as a muddle "which had suddenly produced such confusion, had turned her friends into lunatics so that Chorley contradicted himself and Lucy hung upon Porfits' words; which had thrown a shadow even on the triumph of Harry" (CC, 367). To put it in a nutshell, "In a week of war, dozens of reputations had been lost and made as if by luck; not only of the soldiers but of the politicians" (CC, 367). Cleeve alone stands apart from the crowd, watching the whole scene, scoffing at men playing tricks with the game of war but cannot continue so for long. Felix's remark at this point arrests our attention and it looks as though Cary himself speaks to us through him.

> ... the reason our Liberal friends are in such a muddle is that they're always obsessed by this idea of a moral providence — it messed up their economics and it always messes them up in a war. Liberal democracy collapses in the presence of violence because it has never faced the problem of force. (CC, 376)

Cleeve's accidental introduction to politics exposes him to the ugly side of it within a short time. He realizes that "The first thing to do is to smash the Liberal imperialists — people like Benskin — they're the worst" (CC, 396). Stella also joins him and her love for Harry makes it all the more disgusting for her to see him excited about the war "against a few poor farmers" (CC, 396). Cleeve's angry remark that "'Anybody can see that it's a mean war — what would you say if the Germans said they wanted our coal mines and therefore they had the right to conquer us'" (CC, 397), and Harry's inability to answer him, can be taken as a clue to Cary's own stand. The author, as usual, pits the two opposite views, one against the other, in an unbiased manner. Harry Jarvis and Cleeve Corner represent the dividend self of the author as swayed by the spell wielded by the imperialist Liberals on the one hand and pacifist

Liberals on the other. This gives a polyphonous texture to the novel. To quote Barbara Fisher, "The conflict within the Liberal party is a major clue to this novel, and to both trilogies. So is the tragic gullibility of youth."[20]

Above all, the way the novel ends disturbs one's mind (CC, 418). After all the commotion in the London society as to whether the Boer war is a crime or a noble cause, we hear Sukey groan in the kitchen in Ireland : "Me feet, the Judases" (CC, 418). It may be that the touching end of the novel reflects Cary's anguish that people should invariably treat politics either as a gamble or as a hobby, leaving the poor people like Sukey to suffer in their unknown corners of the world. Cary is not an idealist to hope that the world is going to change for the better. Amidst the sea of conflicting waves of movements, there is found one constant, one dependable thing, that is love. People like Mary, and Padsy remain steadfast in their everyday life and are not carried away by the changing tides. Practising the politics of love and humanism, they sustain their individual ideals even if the money-grabbing politicians and idle speakers tend to tear the world to pieces.

Being a relatively early novel, *Castle Corner* pins its faith in the liberal ideal of individual sincerity and love. Even so we cannot say that Cary's liberal values are naive abstractions. For already in this novel, we have the bitter taste of political expediency, both at the individual and the Governmental levels, which sullies the purity of the romantic liberal ideal of the benevolent imposition of alien systems on an anti-thetical ethnic people. As such the political interest of this novel has the twin thrust of the subjugation of the Irish peasantry and the conquest of the land and riches of Africa. However, unsatisfactory the fictional organization of the novel may be, the work is significant for the lead it gives us into Cary's political pre-occupations. In fact the novel is a crucial link in the developing canon of Cary's works.

5

The Liberal Dilemma

> Liberalism in Britain has always had a very different character, rugged, restless and stubbornly anti-establishment, reflecting its origins in religious Puritanism and provincial radicalism. The nurseries of Liberalism in this country were not smart salons and pavement cafes but solid and severe Nonconformist chapels and temperance halls. Its finest exponents have been not so much clever philosophers or, smooth talking intellectuals as straightforward, practical men and women with firm convictions and with fire in their bellies.[1]

The focus of this chapter lies in how effectively Joyce Cary captures the spirit of Liberalism in its totality in his later novels on British politics and how he perceives Liberalism as a principle of government as well as a matter of attitude simultaneously. Though his attempt to achieve this distinction reaches its peak only in the Second Trilogy, it meets with partial success in *To be a Pilgrim*, belonging to the First Trilogy.

To be a Pilgrim demands attention mainly because of the panoramic view of the age provided by the protagonist Tom Wilcher, a man of adequate discerning capacity, though seemingly on the verge of insanity. His glorious past enriched by the various powerful people like Edward, Lucy, Sara, Amy and Bill, is captured through the telescopic consciousness of this seventy-year old conservative lawyer whose obsession with the thought of becoming a 'pilgrim' gives the novel its title. Although many critics have chosen to focus on the inner turmoil of Wilcher as an individual, it is Wilcher as a symbol of his generation, torn between the Victorian complacency and Edwardian cynicism especially among the younger lot, which is going to be highlighted in this study.

In Cary's view, "he [Wilcher] has grown up, like many English men, Liberal by conviction, but Conservative in heart. In him, that is, the attachments of sentiment, which are the perpetual root of Conservative feeling, are stronger than the drive to adventure."[2] Wilcher's own description of himself as "Mr. Facing-both-ways" (TP, 236) sums up not only the essence of his singular character but the hundreds of Liberals of the time including Cary himself. Fred Reid in his essay "The Disintegration of Liberalism, 1895-1931" elaborates how the novelists and playwrights and poets along with their contemporaries "often wavered ambiguously between anxiety and optimism and their mood cannot readily be understood within an historical framework which heavily emphasizes stability and smoothes out crises."[3]

Some critics have chosen to ignore the contemporary state of affairs and treated Tom Wilcher as a simple character. The *Time* magazine described *To be a Pilgrim* as "the record of Tom Wilcher, one of Sara's employers and lovers, an uncomfortable, comfortably-off lawyer with the lust for life and an itch for salvation."[4] Fred Stockholder commented that "Wilcher's constant involvement in the management of the things of the world that belong to other people is actually disinvolvement. He is always aware of it; this makes him a stodgy fool — a comic type...."[5] Such is the negative impact this novel has made on the critics. We should, however, turn to the other side of the scene.

Wilcher, living under the care of his niece Ann, aged twenty eight, is forced to come into contact with the younger generation. A person living most of the time in the world of memory but brought into contact with living people, enjoys the advantage of being able to compare and contrast two generations. Talbrook for Wilcher is still charmed by that special 'power' possessed by his dear ones, Sara, Lucy, Amy, Bill, Edward and his own parents. But the change which is slowly brought about by the lifeless, cold, cynical Ann and Robert disturbs him. Wilcher cannot understand why the younger generation should turn indifferent, consuming their anguish, but he realizes that it is inevitable and comes to finally admit that "'In fact, I have been ungrateful to these young people, especially to Robert. For he has at least set me free...'" (TP, 299).

The novel is interspersed with Wilcher's devastating comments on the attitude of Ann and Robert and the younger generation in general. Wilcher who has seen the least educated but the most lively people, finds it difficult to digest the fact that a highly educated girl like Ann should struggle at every stage to cope with life and treat everybody, including himself, as a commodity. This makes him doubt the value of education and he alleges that "Ann, whose education is like a set of boxes, all neatly arranged in a filing cabinet, has put me in a box labelled 'Exhibitionist'" (TP, 183). When Robert and Ann treat every aspect of life very casually, not even their marriage excepted, he cannot help commenting : "It is no good talking to children like Ann because they have no education; only information. They are like waste-paper baskets full of exploded newspapers and fraudulent handbills" (TP, 207). Wilcher's reference to education, made in a serious tone, reflects Joyce Cary's interest in the nature of education as a key aspect of Liberalism. Cary's conviction that education alone cannot give any special power unless the individual has the inherent power to assimilate it, is made plain by his depiction of the Freudian scholar, Ann, as very dull and unimaginative. Cary declares in *Power in Man* :

> Man, therefore, is not only unique in the possession of a natural liberty, and desire for truth, but in his separate character. All his teachers and his state can do is to enable him to make the best of it. They can give him the power to realize himself in his own unique nature and they can stultify and deform it; but they cannot change its essential quality (24-25).

It is indeed a fact that Cary has hardly shown any character in his novels to have been the beneficiary of a sound education which gives him 'liberty.' Ironically, young men like Richard in *Except the Lord* and Edward in *To be a Pilgrim* who are recipients of the so-called higher education get stuck in the middle of their lives, unable to proceed further, whereas the less educated people with their inner drive have marched a long way in life. The conviction of the radicals that education by itself cannot increase one's power but a better social and cultural atmosphere created by the state with the help of the people alone can save them, may be recalled here.

Joyce Cary's use of the term 'power' has always a large context and its recurrent use in it gives *To be a Pilgrim* a new dimension. Cary so adroitly delineates the characters that though the current situation is morbid enough to drive them to distraction, they remain steadfast. Thus, they prove Cary's point that "The powers of imagination and enjoyment are not limited by necessity; political and economic powers are limited" (PM, 34). Ironically those people with immense innate power are exclusively 'private people,' people without any political direction. Bill and Amy are a very happy couple, though they cannot brag of the finer things of life and capture the admiration of Wilcher. But they do not escape the criticism of others. Edward, for example, feels that their conversation on any subject, but especially a political subject, explained to him the history of the Greek word 'idiot.' "'They are the most private citizens I ever met, even in a village pub'" (TP, 327). One may say that the raw power in them gushes forth rather in an unrefined manner, bringing them closer to the primitive simple people. Lucy's so called courageous act of following Brown may reflect her adventurous spirit but it is still an impulsive act. Though she scrubs the floor and tortures herself, she cannot admire the Benjamites. The girl who declares that "'... I should hate to be a Benjamite'" (TP, 190) turns to be one later. It is clear that Lucy, whose power always overwhelms Wilcher, is overpowered in turn by a bigger power in the form of Brown. Sara is always portrayed as a character who lives only as an emotional being and never bothers to think even for a minute. On the whole Brown alone emerges as a spellbinder, he having the capacity to translate his ideas into action, however irrational they may be. Very often he refers to God's voice. If the nature of these characters is considered deeply, we begin to doubt whether it is Cary's own inclination as a romanticist that impels him to admire the passionate, rustic, simple men, and make them magnificent.

Edward, on the other hand, is very different from the impulsive and emotional characters mentioned above, with his intellectual bent of mind. He commences his career in a very energetic manner, but finds himself unable to proceed further once he starts following the dictates of his emotions. He has something in common with the representatives of the younger generation, the cold Ann, the robust Robert, the cynical John, and the corrupt Glady. They have all been in touch with reality and naturally have been moulded by circumstances. They are not impulsive like Lucy and Sara and so they encounter doubts and uncertainties which turn them cynical and indifferent to the precious things of life. When Ann blames Tom Wilcher for spoiling her career as a pathologist by making her a wife by tricky means and the mother of a child, she reveals her inner conflict, born out of her cognizance of the existence of more attractive things outside her world. Robert, on the other hand, though a high-strung young man, exhibits some spirit and partakes of the inner drive of his parents in pursuing his end. His preoccupation with his first corn harvest,when Ann is in pains, is in no way more whimsical than his mother's behaviour. If he cannot share any of Wilcher's sentimental attachment to Talbrook, it is because he is a man of action rather than a sentimentalist. "To Robert Brown, Lucy's son, Talbrook is a farm to be run, a practical proposition."[6] If the first set of people are in the state of savage men, the second may be compared to those who have been compelled to face the mixed consequences of civilization.

Cary does not fail to point out the weakness of the Victorians as represented by Wilcher. However, critics, in general have agreed that Cary's balance swings in favour of the first generation in the novel. Andrew Wright points out that this novel was reviewed in 1949 as a "Vote for Victoria" by the *Time* magazine.[7] But he has rightly perceived that "Against this self-contained, conservative world is set the present, the creative and therefore destructive younger generation of his niece Ann, a doctor of the newest school, and his nephew Robert, a farmer with new ideas."[8] For Cary admits by implication the fact that people are not mere dummies and men must move with the times. That may be inferred from Wilcher's acknowledgement that Robert has indeed brought life back to Talbrook : "But he does not destroy Talbrook, he takes it back into history, which changed it once before from priory into farm, from farm into manor....Robert has brought it back into the English stream and he himself has come with it;..." (TP, 485). Cary has obviously reckoned with the dialectics of the generation gap in this novel.

Wilcher thus represents thousands of Carys who were ripped between their love to see England kept intact as a supreme power and their wish to see the emergence of new nations with their distinct culture and dreams which inevitably entails the destruction of the old. "Like E.M. Forster's *Howard's End*, Talbrook Farm is a symbol of England, and as in Forster's novel the question of who inherits the land becomes the question who shall inherit England."[9]

In *To be a Pilgrim* the political views of the old Liberals chaperoned by the Prime Minister Gladstone, who championed the cause of weak nations cannot win the sympathy of Wilcher and his brother Edward when they are young. They are even surprised that such a man could have been the idol of the mass. "To Edward, and therefore to me," says Tom Wilcher, "Gladstone was an old-fashioned Whig, and already an obstacle to progress. We condescended to him as the Grand Old Man" (TP, 287). But Wilcher's father, "a devoted Gladstonian, disliked all the ideas of the young radicals led by men like Lloyd George" (TP, 286). Himself now an old man, Wilcher is not in a position to swallow the views put forth by the present generation and they in turn do not appreciate the hard labour of his generation. Ann indeed feels sorry about "the awful way the people are wasted — even brilliant people like Daddy — knocking himself to pieces on those old politics" helping to make "'A revolution — to get rid of the poor old Lords'" (TP, 362). She dismisses it as "'[a] lot of noise about nothing'" (TP, 363). The injustice of one generation to another, as Wilcher puts it, is given a tragic dimension in this novel.[10]

Cary has always endeavoured to rise above his prejudices, often successfully, sometimes in vain. He, no doubt, acknowledges the need for change but like Wilcher, his heart bleeds to see both the good and bad things being destroyed at the same time. Enid Starkie who knew Cary well as a person, also espouses a similar view : "I always felt this pervading sadness beneath the gay and gallant manner. Wilcher, in *To be a Pilgrim* seems to me to reflect him more fully — especially his attitude to life — than Gulley Jimson, in The *Horse's Mouth*."[11]

To be a Pilgrim is a good example of how Cary skilfully yokes the micro and macro aspects of politics in the predicament of Wilcher and the fortunes of Talbrook. This novel is a milestone in Cary's exploration of his favourite theme of family as a microscopic replica of the state. Wilcher's father whose "idea of religion was that of Confucius, rules of conduct, carefully taught and justly administered" (TP, 197), runs the family as a strict ruler. Parallel to this we have "the complicated politics of our nursery" (TP, 210). It is not the elders alone but also the children who have "their own ethics, logic, politics — all no less complex than that of adults."[12] Lucy who tries to exploit the loophole in the nursery law and begins to relish her power, and later the young Wilcher, who plays the same trick when he is sick and feels a sense of glory in being indifferent to the unwritten code of law, bear evidence to this fact.

Even after growing up, they vie with each other in making use of each other. Edward does not hesitate to pass on his beloved Julie to his brother Wilcher when it suits his convenience and though Wilcher, pretends to be rather reluctant in the beginning, uses her as a means to achieve his own end. Wilcher, again as the master of the Talbrook House, is ready to take Sara as his servant in spite of her bad conduct certificate and she in turn does not grumble about working without due payment. Nor can she resist the temptation to steal and sell trivial household articles, at times to help her former husband and her children. As Edward Galligan comments, "One can only conclude that this mad financial juggling helped to make it possible for Sara and Wilcher to make love grow between them, to fabricate a creative, liberating relationship."[13] Above all, the diplomacy Tom Wilcher employs to maintain the morality of the family members when Ann and Robert come under the same roof, is a matter for consideration. Using his will as a bait, Tom Wilcher strives hard to keep Ann and Robert together when their marriage is almost broken. He later persuades Ann to be religious at least for the sake of the child she is carrying, by promising a bribe in the form of 'a deposit of 200 a year' on the child, which will be put in a trust. He baits her saying that "'he would have a very good claim to Talbrook....'" (TP, 248). He even reminds her of the provision he has made for her : "... she was to have a thousand pounds on my death, and a hundred and fifty more for every year

I should live after her undertaking the care of me" (TP, 248). There cannot be a better instance to highlight Cary's intense political consciousness even while depicting a family situation.

The attitude and the propensity of every individual in Wilcher's family is moulded and to some extent conditioned by the existing political trend. Wilcher's father loses his temper when he sees Edward's radical stand supporting the old-age pensions scheme of Lyold George "'Pauperising whole country....'" (TP, 286). When Wilcher talks about moving with the times, he shouts at him : "'yes, moving where. Ruin. Turning good English workmen into parasites. And look at the price of corn — what's going to happen?'" (TP, 286). But when Edward continues assailing his colleagues, his father suffers a heart attack which leads to his death. The open-minded Wilcher who is not a man to be weighed down by responsibilities and conflicts, who considers even Talbrook as, "'Not a bad billet' or 'not a bad camp'" (TP, 184), betrays his split mind in his ability to decide whether Lucy has to go back to her husband. Here too, it is the political trend of the age which seems to influence and determine the behavioural pattern. He, to whom "the Church of England, the Presbyterian and the Wesleyan stood apart as churches of the true God" (TP, 222), considers the Benjamite sect as the worst of all other free sects and so "'Brown's work isn't God's work. It is devil's work'" (TP, 222). Yet he leaves the decision to his daughter when Brown comes asking her to go back with him. Tom Wilcher comments. "Our father had two contradictory views about women; one, that a wife must cleave to her husband at all costs; the other, that a woman, as a living soul should have all freedom. Many of his generation held the same contradiction; they were Christians as well as Whigs" (TP, 260).

Lucy the "nursery rebel" (TP, 192) also turns to be a victim of the prejudices of the time. "She had the genius of a leader in revolt, full of malice as well as rage" (TP, 192). Her decision to marry the 'puggy' Brown and her behaviour are analyzed as follows by the two brothers, Wilcher and Edward. It is an act of courage and faith from Wilcher's point of view and he concludes that if Lucy and Brown live together in spite of their torture of each other, it is because "They were both people of power; life ran in them with a primitive force and innocence" (TP, 263). Edward, on the other hand, ascribes to it a political motive : "She has turned herself into a char because she feels that her own class is finished. She doesn't feel grand enough as a mere lady. She has flown to the arms of Puggy to give herself the sense of nobility" (TP, 241). But the same Lucy behaves in a ruthless manner when it comes to the question of her children mixing with the lower class children. Among the critics of Cary, it is Cornelia Cook who has placed the situation in the context of contemporary British politics :

> Lucy's scorn of the lower middle class, scathing in the Jones episode, and her insistence that Robert be raised a gentleman, reflects the egoism of these nonconformists which enables them to humble themselves with pride. Such individualism within the grass roots support of the Liberal party, together with the detachment of its upper strata, brought the party to disarray before the organised ideological challenge of the post-war socialists.[14]

Amy and Bill also share with Lucy their "want of sensation," to use Ruskin's apt phrase,[15] though they have the innate energy to face life with all its miseries without groaning and moaning. The following conversation (as cited by Lucy and recollected by Wilcher), substantiates this : "...when Bill left Amy for the first time, her last words, called after the railway carriage, through her tears, were, 'Where did you leave my bicycle pump.' And that Bill answered at the top of his voice, 'Don't forget you're punctured behind'" (TP, 271). Bill, a soldier by profession, is the least interested in the politics of his time and even when Wilcher discusses the impending war rather seriously, Bill cannot "discuss the war danger except from a professional point of view" (TP, 392). John, Bill's son, who "too appeared to be a private person" (TP, 395), takes it lightly : "There always seems to be a war somewhere, doesn't there?" (TP, 392) and so begins to concentrate on his new boat and the sail just like his parents who are busy with their garden and newly built house. He is almost surprised when Wilcher talks about responsibility, which is strange to him. "A boy of your age should take an interest in things. And European politics are going to affect your whole life. Very much so" (TP, 394). After a little reflection John answers, "'But I suppose the political people are looking after this'" (TP, 395). As a contrast, Edward tries to channel his nonconformist energy in a more sensible and constructive manner by involving himself in the struggle for social change though his battle is not decisively won for a few reasons which will be discussed later.

Julie and Glady who live in a cosmopolitan world with their own sense of morality, belong to a different class. They witness others like Edward and Wilcher and later John being dragged into their world without any resistance from them. Their cynical frivolity in general can be attributed to the following factor :

> In the years after World War I the middle classes suffered severely because of the economic revolution..... As a result there was an intellectual and moral revolution.
>
> This revolution, by which 'the Bright Young People' took over leadership, was outwardly shown in dress and deportment. Women's dresses were no longer designed to conceal feminine charms.... Smart young men wore 'Oxford bags' — shapeless and **bolloonlike** trousers, which covered the entire shoe — or golf knickerbockers....[16]

In the novel, Tom Wilcher's repeated reference to the way of dressing of the young people may be understood better in the light of this comment.

Cornelia Cook observes how John turns out to be "a typical post-war peacetime casuality" and "Ann the stereotyped career girl of the 'thirties steeped in psychology and intellectual independence" (TP, 124). Ann is all too ready to bear the cross and move about with a solemn look on her face provoking Wilcher to remark, "But all these girls nowadays, after their first twenties, have that look. Sad and responsible" (TP, 181). Robert just like his mother can be harsh towards people who are dear to him. Ann ascribes this to "Time spirit" (TP, 370). "'The truth is, I suppose, that he wasn't a born brute, but he thinks he ought to be a brute. He's like these Nazis and Fascists, who behave like beasts on the highest principles, ...'" (TP, 370). Sidney Monas feels that "Ann and Robert represent the younger generation, with trappings of America and Europe sprangling their surface, but the weight of their own English tradition unconsciously giving them gravity."[17]

Cary thus creates a whole galaxy of characters in the novel, almost a microcosm of English society demonstrating that it is very hard to remain unaffected politically in an 'epoch of expansion,' to use Matthew Arnold's, famous phrase. Cary infuses the novel with the spirit of war feeling, focusing not only on the impingement of war on lives of the common people but also the plight of the politicians who almost gamble with the cause either for the selfish motive of winning the hearts of the public or out of conviction to save the humanity from disaster.

We may recall that one of the main issues early in this century on which there was divided opinion which led to the split in the Liberal Party in Britain and to various re-adjustments among its members, was the question of war. It was generally accepted that it was the pressure of circumstances, (German folly, Austrian disintegration, Balkan turbulence), which compelled Edward Grey, the Foreign Minister who was noted for his peace-seeking diplomacy to indulge in preparation for war. However Edward Grey's decision to enter the First World War, did cause a lot of sensation among the public. Cary gives a graphic description of the war-time atmosphere digging deep into the distinct motives for and against the war.

Edward, the representative of the political world in this novel, decides to play with the feelings of the public, with the cause of war as a bait, mainly to realize his personal ambition *i.e.*, winning the election. Tom Wilcher's sincere pleading with Edward to be more considerate and humane, goes unheeded. Edward very light-heartedly dismisses it saying, "'That's the great attraction, ..., at least to certain energetic minds. The engineer, for instance, he likes to start afresh from a blue print. And the artist, he likes a clean canvass'" (TP, 381). He also insists that "'We 've never allowed for the artistic temperament. The Kaiser has it — and it flourishes in Vienna'" (TP, 381). The serious conversation in which Edward and Wilcher engage themselves during their stay in Julie's flat, throws light on how and what factors impel a nation towards war, besides the foreign policy adopted by a particular nation and the unforeseeable events that strengthen it. Cary seems to catalogue almost a list of the people who contribute to the war mood. Firstly, the young, sporting ones who "'... are energetic and have so much time to give to politics....'" (TP, 385); secondly, the group of people like Julie "'... who feel that the world is wicked — that it deserves punishment'" (TP, 386); thirdly, the people who "'... are ready to take any risk to themselves so long as they can get their revenge on somebody else — often some purely abstract enemy, like Germany or France or England'" (TP, 386); and above all, the large number of "'people who are dissatisfied with their lot — the failures'" (TP, 386). According to Edward, if the war had not been so expensive and demanding, people would be at war all the time and Julie too subscribes to it : "'But we know there is an evil will...and the evil will delights in all evil'" (TP, 386). Tom Wilcher alone cannot be moved by any of these sentiments and he is very firm in his stand that the war has to be stopped at any cost and if not, they have to own the responsibility. He even joins the local radicals and opposes the new Navy Bill and advertizes in the paper that "the Government policy was leading us into war; that we should offer friendship to Germany and not provocation" (TP, 391).

Whereas Tom Wilcher is disgusted so much with this war fever, fanned by public men and frustrated souls, the most private people like Amy, Bill and John remain unperturbed. Wilcher's attempt to induce some kind of political consciousness in these people ends in vain and he confesses that "But now I was frightened by the privateness of such as Bill and Amy and John" (TP, 395). Wilcher's anxiety over their attitude of cutting themselves off from public affairs, as though, it is none of their business, is expressed vigorously in these lines : "'And who is looking after the political people? Did you never hear of democracy or imagine that it had duties as well as rights?' ..." (TP, 395). He insists on the necessity to protest if warranted : "...'its the only government for us in England — in fact, it's the only reasonable government anywhere, because people can agitate and make nuisances of themselves when they feel like it.'" As pointed out by Randall Stevenson :

> Some of these historical changes, such as the First World War, [Wilcher] sees as the result of 'the enormous power of evil . . . evil will.' This strong and often pessimistic moral sense makes his narrative

> throughout an anxious elegy for the 'decline of religion' and the shifts in public and private ethics which threaten 'the life of the spirit' in the twentieth century.[18]

However, it may be noted that Cary does not consider war necessarily as a product of the evil in man :

> The majority of people in any democracy not corrupted by local vice or cowardice hate despotism and cruelty in any part of the world. It will therefore, if it has liberty of speech, protest against them. If this protest leads to war, the majority will suffer, many will die for their faith in goodness, in justice. These men are worthy of honour and so is the state that bred them (PM, 151).

But at the same time Cary condemns 'war for the sake of war' : "All peoples hate war. The only war-seekers are found in certain youth movements, among neurotics, and among some abstract thinkers" (PM, 154). One can find that in *To be a Pilgrim* not only does the author deal with the question of public versus private men, but he also reveals how inter-related their worlds are.

The juxtaposition of the private people with the public men leads to the next question of private and public morality. The Second Trilogy which has brought Cary the discredit of being the worshipper of an opportunistic rogue like Chester Nimmo, demands a juster reading. The portrayal of Edward as one in the making of a politician provides the author an opportunity to voice his strong, bold comments on the morality of a public man, though not as explicitly as he does later in *Prisoner of Grace*. Tom Wilcher who struggles to make a judgement upon his brother's demeanour and attitude towards life is rather baffled in his attempt. Edward a nonconformist in spirit is rather attracted towards the Benjamites but not in the way Tom Wilcher is. Perhaps the support Edward extends to the Benjamites may be due to the selfish motive of getting their votes, as hinted at by Wilcher. And also as a man with a different set of ideas, he cannot approve of the Prime Minister Gladstone's views. His enthusiasm to give the nations their rightful power builds up his reputation as a young Radical fired with imagination. Wilcher, like others, realizes that "Edward is exceptional" (TP, 338) but he cannot understand how a political genius like him can be so careless and irresponsible in his personal life. "'Edward is a great man in politics...but in finance he is simply a dangerous lunatic'" (TP, 347). He does not hesitate even to borrow from his poor brother Bill, a father of four children, to satisfy his whims and fancies as a dandy.

> 'I am furious with him, and my fury is the expression of my uneasiness for Bill. It is the revenge of the private citizen, the humble idiot, upon what is called a public man, with his special immunity. I want to break that shield of pre-occupied egotism' (TP, 331).

He shouts at this idol of a men Edward : "'you great public men may be very important and all that, but merely private people do have some rights'" (TP, 331). But Cary lets the same Wilcher comment after some time, "I reflect that Edward has, in fact, important responsibilities. That one must not blame him for a certain carelessness in domestic relations, since public men suffer special disabilities, etc., and so on" (TP, 331). This opens for the reader a new vista. Cary seems to imply that the various problems confronted by a public man like Edward makes him different and naturally the morality of his world is alien to others.

Edward uses pro-Boer business as a primary issue in his election campaign and Bill accuses him of treason. "The savagery of that election" (TP, 315) at Ragworth where both the parties try to appeal to the baser instincts of the mass and "quite ready to organise violence" (TP, 316), is a surprise to Tom Wilcher but Edward takes it as a part of political life. "'Politics isn't church work — it's a battle of wills'" (TP, 316). In his work *Brave New World Revisited* Aldous Huxley talks about two kinds of propaganda namely 'rational propaganda' and 'non-rational propaganda.' He helps us to understand what power "words" have and what a major role it plays in a democracy. Edward's tackling of people, considering the nature of the special group of men in front of him every time, and Chester Nimmo's deft handling of people in the Second Trilogy prove this point.

Once Edward becomes a public man, he pretends to satisfy the demands of the public. Edward becomes the junior minister of a young ministry but he "had made himself popular and feared, and so he had increased his actual power" (TP, 356). He has the uncanny knack of feeling the pulse of the public. "'A government has to show energy and do something, and that means making changes.... And of course, the expectation is always beyond what any government can do. People want a new heaven and a new earth before the end of next week'" (TP, 356-57). So he talks of "the importance of the scientific approach to politics....; a new world at all costs" (TP, 358). Wilcher is astonished at "Edward's prestige, achieved so easily and unjustly. For what has he done... except talk and make the right friends ...'" (TP, 358).

In spite of his initial triumph Edward cannot remain a successful politician for long. His own words, "'Any one can make a beginning in politics — it's the finish that kills'" (TP, 235), come true in his case. "His vein of rashness and cynicism" (TP, 316), his tendency to give vent to his feelings in the form of pamphlets now and then, and his inability to resist the temptations of being a private man, make him a disaster as a public man. Edward's absence from England, enhanced by his complete submission to his newly married wife at a critical situation when his power has to be asserted in his homeland, turns everything topsy-turvy. After his return, he "wants to play at politics again" (TP, 382), this time by stirring up "war fever" (TP, 382). Wilcher is enraged by his brother's attitude but he understands that "'he is a typical party politician; no sense of responsibility. He is blinded by ambition, by that secret demon which infects all politicians, whether they like it or not'" (*Ibid.*). However, this time the goal is out of his reach. He has courage and conviction but not the 'grace' in Caryan sense, a quality which aids Chester Nimmo to resuscitate the inner springs of his life whenever he is in danger of losing spirit. Edward cannot remain a politician in all walks of life. Cary who very ambitiously launches himself on a study of the leitmotif, private versus public life, leaves the question of morality rather unanswered. In other words, it looks as though he would agree with the mitigating, evasive response of Wilcher : "I shall not blame Edward. I will only say that he's too much for me, that I don't understand these politicians. I am only a private person" (TP, 349). The author takes up this matter more seriously in his Second Trilogy which turns out to be almost a treatise on this subject.

The novelist who shows quite a sensible but cynical politician in Edward, presents another type of a spellbinder in Brown, a politician practising the art of religion : "His head was extremely big, and he had the face of so many great orators and preachers, advocates and demagogues, a political face; short pugnacious nose, long upper lip, huge thin mouth, heavy but shallow chin, deeply clept; hollow deepset eyes" (TP, 260). The frightful power he wields over others including the strong-willed Lucy, is something which Cary seems to find irresistible. This 'power' indeed is the prerequisite of any successful politician. Wilcher is even afraid to stand near the congregation held by Brown :

> ...I was afraid of Brown; I thought he could convert me, and I was enjoying life then as never before, in my years at Oxford. Why was I afraid of Brown, I was a clever young man who was reading Kant. Brown had no arguments that did not fill me with contempt. But when he sang these verses from Bunyan, ..., then something swelled in my heart as if it would choke me, unless I, too, opened my own mouth and sang (TP, 188).

Cary's portrayal of the scene where the old couple Joneses are made to fall at the feet of Brown, adds to this effect. Perhaps, it is the fascination such characters with vitality but not much rationality hold for Cary that leads the critics to label him as a celebrant of Life Force. However, Cary has vehemently refuted it.

> I'm no life-force man. Critics write about my vitality. What is vitality? As a principle it is a lot of balls. The life force is rubbish, an abstraction, an idea without character. Shaw's tale of life force is either senseless rubbish or he really means — Shaw as God's mind. The life force doesn't exist, show me some in a bottle. The life of the world is the nature of God, and God is as real as the trees.[19]

Ian Bradley's assessment of Liberalism helps us to evaluate Cary's plight. "The fact is that liberalism is open and sympathetic to all aspects of the human personality, physical, emotional, spiritual and the downright irrational just as much as intellectual and rational."[20] The problem with Cary is that he seems to be fascinated by the physical, emotional, spiritual and the down right irrational, sometimes more than warranted. However, it cannot be denied that he is much concerned about the reality of social life, in spite of his worship of the spirit of nonconformity among individuals and the novel *To be a Pilgrim* justifies it.

"Possessions have been my curse. I ought to have been a wanderer, too, a free soul" (TP, 184). This earnest urge in Wilcher to be a pilgrim like Sara with her "living faith" (TP, 179) and Lucy with her "spirit nourished in faith" (TP, 218), is expressed throughout the novel in a heart- breaking manner. Wilcher's final resolve to accept the continuity of history with its inevitable changes, gives a religious tinge to the novel. The title indicates Cary's inclination to read the flux of history in this light. However, what invites commendation is the skill displayed by Cary in connecting the tormented soul of an individual with the soul of England itself, giving a political turn to the novel. Sidney Monas aptly remarks that "Wilcher represents the Protestant tradition, Protestant drive, with a taint of madness because it imposes such fearsome responsibility on the individual, with no provided outlet, 'not even a confession box.' He adds that "The conflict between love of property and the Protestant drive 'to be a pilgrim' is seen as fundamental to English history" (468-69). Witness the loud declaration of the hopeful Wilcher :

> I am a Wilcher — I am like Bill and Lucy; like my father who spent half his life in camps and lodgings. It is in my blood, which is all English... But the English soul is a wanderer, a seeker. You find it in every corner of the world, dressed in some local imagination; studying Chinese antiquities, or ready to assure you that salvation is in the Hindu yoga. The English have taught every nation to admire its own culture .... (TP, 458).

Wilcher's optimism, however, buckles before the intransigence of the reality. He sees the nation being "fascinated by some dark unknown sea, draw nearer and nearer to it, walking on the very edge of war and destruction" (TP, 468). He notices that "When Chaucer wrote of pilgrimage, in England, then every man knew where he was, and where he could go. But now all is confusion and no one has anywhere to go ...." He adds : "A pilgrim is not a lost soul, I thought, nor a wanderer. He is not a tramp. But these are lost souls who don't even know that they are lost" (TP, 470).

At the personal level, Wilcher suffers from a lack of conviction which enables Sara, Amy and Lucy to "cut out their own destinies" (TP, 221) through their faith and courage. Wilcher frankly admits that :

> I thought I could be an adventurer like Lucy and Edward; a missionary. I shouted the pilgrim's cry, democracy, liberty, and so forth, but I was a pilgrim only by race. England took me with her on a few stages of her journey. Because she could not help it (TP, 498).

But as an embodiment of irresolvable conflicts, he evokes some serious questions which are to be pondered over. It is worth recalling Aldous Huxley's view at this point :

> Given a fair chance, human beings can govern themselves, and govern themselves better, though perhaps with less mechanical efficiency, than they can be governed by 'authorities independent of their will.' Given a fair chance, I repeat; for the fair chance is an indispensable pre-requisite. ... Again, no people in precarious economic condition has a fair chance of being able to govern itself democratically. Liberalism flourishes in an atmosphere of prosperity and declines as declining prosperity makes it necessary for the government to intervene ever more frequently and drastically in the affairs of its subjects.[22]

To be a Pilgrim centres on a few nonconformists who govern themselves without the 'fair chance' Huxley is talking about. Lucy who gives Wilcher a sense of power all through his life evokes a sensible remark from Wilcher in the end : "'... you are a spoilt obstinate vain woman who has made a god out of herself. Yes, you think you are a martyr to religion, but you are only worshipping yourself and sacrificing to your fearful pride'" (TP, 454). As a man who has lost the battle, Edward confesses that "'You [Tom Wilcher] gripped something. I hit the air'" (TP, 440). On the other hand, Amy and Bill and also the young John as noted earlier, insulate themselves with a privacy and insensitivity which provokes Wilcher to comment in sheer disgust :

> I feel again a deep oppression of weakness, as if the whole of the civilized order about me, in which Bill and Amy walk so confidently and so rashly, and the young John carries his grief with so much dignity, is nothing but an appearance, a dream. And from the dream, our unhappy people, especially Bill, Amy etc. are about to be awakened (TP, 350).

Cary's main concern is to show how these people who epitomise the nonconformist spirit, lack in a reformatory zeal which is the pre-requisite of democracy where one has "duties as well as rights" (TP, 395). Whereas the next generation, devoid of the zeal for life itself, still holds a grudge against the old generation, thinking, "'The war was a bad joke played on us by a lot of old fools'" (TP, 417). Tom Wilcher laments, "It was the cynicism of the young which shocked and frightened me. It was as though the spring leaves, deliberately, for some secret and devilish purpose, distilled poison in their own sap and withered on the twigs" (TP, 417).

Cary has rightly chosen Wilcher as the spokesman to admonish the younger generation, at the same time betraying the flaw in the liberal outlook. The novel therefore may be considered as a study of democratic history as the correlative of the Protestant nonconformist trend. In his letter to the critic Mark Schorer, dated 13-10-51, Cary remarks, "... others lately (one especially in the New Zealand) who called me a protestant novelist but of course my theme is far wider than any religious construction. It includes aesthetic and political freedom, the whole problem of the created symbol."[23]

To be a Pilgrim indeed raises many questions connected with a liberal society which is conducive to a democratic set-up, but answers them only partially whereas his Second Trilogy is a deep study of these issues in their more magnified form, including some more aspects within its ambit.

Cary's *Prisoner of Grace*, more than any other novel, deals with "the difficulty of 'managing people' as the ultimate problem of democratic politics" (PG, 144). The relevance of an individual as a "political problem" to be handled adroitly and the predicament of a man whose political expertise is put to test by the need to manage people, are one of its main concerns. It is doubtful whether any of the political writers such as C.P. Snow, George Orwell and Aldous Huxley, have so successfully brought out life itself as a canvas with intricate designs, visualized with one's political sense.

In the view of Ernest Barker, "The first and primary democracy, in which debate and compromise are used to settle differences, is the institution of marriage."[24] Cary too has perceived marriage as a political institution, if not always as a democratic institution, and this notion has been given subtle expression in most of his novels, especially the later ones. As mentioned earlier, *To be a Pilgrim* comprises a heterogeneous group of such units with their distinct policies and attitudes. But *Prisoner of Grace* treats the matter with more seriousness and poignancy.

Prisoner of Grace is the story of Chester Nimmo who is a politician not only by career but is an individual to whom "the lingo of politics was as natural as the air he breathed."[25] And "he did see life largely as relations which (like those between nations) were subject to all sorts of 'strains' and 'diplomatic action'" (PG, 131). Chester actually starts his political career with the help of a bargain, in the name of marriage with Nina whose 5000 pounds is the price for the marital status he gives to her, an unwed prospective mother. But in twenty-five years of time, this poor lay preacher does come up to the position of a Cabinet Minister, to the surprise and pride of Nina. When he is so intoxicated with his triumph in the Battwell election, Nina exclaims :

> He had an expression that I had not seen before, naive and chidishly frank. "I can tell you what no one else knows — that I promised myself this when I was Bing's office boy in second-hand trousers. I did n't know how it was to be done, but I said I

> should do it if it cost me my life. And I don't know quite how it has been done. But I do know what to do with it — you'll see" (PG, 108).

Cary's *Prisoner of Grace*, becomes partially a tribute to this power (which costs both Chester's life and his soul), the power which enabled a Hitler to twist the world around his finger. Cary, during his conversation with Lord David Cecil, remarks :

> And Hitler, d'you see, is fascinating to the crook Bonser; because he says 'Look at the way Hitler gets away with it! Look at the way he runs the people round!' Now Hitler did that : people wouldn't believe that Hitler was dead; and he was such a great prophet, you see; a prophet of evil.[26]

Cary adds, "But he had such power, he made such an impression, that is to say, people live in creative imagination; they need it, you see; and the man who gives it to them always get this frightful power over them." The above passage expresses vividly the author's ambivalent feelings towards such great spellbinders. There is wonder and awe on the one hand, and a sense of uneasiness on the other hand that after all evil springs from the fountain-head of such sources. Placed within this authorial horizon, Nina's dual attitude towards this dynamic and ambitious man, Chester Nimmo, perhaps becomes less of an enigma.

Cary's genius in weaving the material of domestic and public politics into an intricate web cannot escape the attention of a critic even if he is highly hostile and this mode may be considered as a distinct contribution of Cary's to the genre of the political novel. His achievement reaches its peak in the Second Trilogy, the credit mainly accruing to *Prisoner of Grace*. Elizabeth Janeway in her article "A Great Man Who was My Husband" aptly puts it thus :

> Now in *Prisoner of Grace* he gives us man as political animal as seen by the woman he married. Yet this book — one of his major creations — is much more than a 'political novel.' It is a fascinating exposition of the political attitude that is involved in the very act of living, particularly in this most remarkable marriage and this most remarkable man..[27]

Like Chester Nimmo, Nina also becomes "a good political wife" (PG, 56) when she finds "on her hands a political job, in handling a husband so different from herself in ideas, in character, and in taste."[28] Nina, who "loathed politics, which seemed usually to put aunt [Latter] in a bad temper — it was the enemy of all peace and comfort" (PG, 18), begins her political life along with Chester. The complexity of Nina's marital life begins to sprout on the very day they are together for the first time. His prayer for God's blessing on their union seems to her "so comic" (PG, 23) that she feels like laughing. Chester with his class obsession, a major practical problem by itself, further aggravates the situation by turning it into a suitable weapon to beat her down :

> Then he detested Italy (which I adored-it was so warm and full of colour), and was shocked by the poverty of the people, which to me at that time seemed as 'natural' as the richness of millionaires; that is, simply the customary state of things and certainly not a good reason for spoiling a honeymoon (PG, 24).

Not only does Chester reveal his Protestant bias (PG, 145) but he also lays the foundation for building up his case against Nina's class : "wherever it [Roman religion] had power you found ignorance and oppression and dirt and poverty" (PG, 24). But the same Chester proclaims the very next moment his respect for Nina's feelings." "'I know you have been brought up to have different religious ideas, and I hope you will be true to them and never pretend to agree with me unless you really feel agreement....'" (PG, 24). It is such grace, however false it may be, and the speeches he delivers in his "'thrilling' voice" (PG, 40) which begin to wield great power over her, in fact to the extent of making her feel guilty. "I felt, too, as everyone seems to feel when accused of being in a superior class, very uncomfortable and even guilty, and so I was very eager to help him" (PG, 31). His repeated sexual assaults which are borne by her rather mechanically in order to be nice to him, in spite of her repulsion of him, is a sign of his complete victory over her. As Giles Mitchell notes, "This same marriage is also a political triumph for him; the sex act is an especially gratifying political triumph, that is, a victory won over class barriers."[29]

Nina does not take much time to understand what marriage is and how to make the best out of it.

> I had learned already how much, in such a complicated and 'political' (I was soon to understand what Balzac or perhaps it was what Vauvenargues meant by calling matrimony a political education) relationship as marriage, one should be grateful for simple thoughtfulness (PG, 27-28).

Starting from the refusal to admit the fact that Jim it was who fathered Nina's Tom, Chester indulges in a series of prevarications. Nina does indeed respond to the call of her conscience which very often reflects Chester in his true colours but she always ends up listening to his voice. "Chester's voice was one of his great gifts — it made him a power" (PG, 40). Nina finds herself being completely converted into a different person, "a thing dreaded even by wicked and unhappy people" (PG, 25). Even so she consciously tries to be an individual capable of making judgement, but emotionally she is entirely enslaved by the power wielded by Chester over her steadily and even calculatedly. She becomes a split woman : "It seemed that I was two women, one of them quite furious still and watchful of every move by this cunning enemy, and one of them so close and sympathetic to him that she felt all his feelings like her own" (PG, 40). Every time he praises her for her Christian charity and expresses his need for her, she undergoes a "conversion" (PG, 43) and they begin their life anew all over again. This conversion, she admits, is a common experience to all young married women, but in her case, she finds it more acute and frequent. "I knew now and never could forget that Chester, with all his affection, was playing a kind of political game with me. He was taking up a strong position and thinking of his career" (PG, 43). The various strategies he employs to conquer her gradually — the "confidence trick ... with a little bit of trust in God added" (PG, 91) he plays at the railway station almost numbing her senses and incapacitating her thinking, the "putting off trick" (PG, 96) which he resorts to in restoring her spirits after this crisis in their life, and the "time trick" (PG, 300) he performs to bring Nina back to him using Jim as a trump card — have a very strong impact upon her but not without leaving in her a sense of rancour.

From the very beginning Chester uses his marriage only as a political weapon. And Nina in turn does everything which is expected of a "political wife" (PG, 56) Nina accompanying Chester Nimmo during the election time is a political necessity which brings him closer to her. Nina sardonically acknowledges, "If he wanted a special favour from me, like going out to a very dull dinner (I did not like dinners just then when I was so big), he would begin, before any mention of the invitation, by bringing me flowers or chocolates" (PG, 131). She adds, "Of course, many husbands do so; what I mean is that for Chester these attentions not only expressed gratitude and affection — they formed part of a complicated 'politique'" (*Ibid.*). But once he reaches the stage where he finds "'the world at his feet'" (PG, 168) he becomes more confident and ironically even overcomes his obsession with "class." What is more, he becomes one with the aristocrats. When Nina requests Chester not to spoil Tom's tender mind with his emotional radical speeches and even coerces him to give the child a better education, overlooking his public talk against the privilege of the upper class, he finds her no small problem. Nina's "wicked and cruel" (PG, 176) attempt to kill herself adds to his discomfiture and his conduct towards her changes completely.

> He treated me more like a problem and less like a cherished possession; you might say that he used a different diplomacy. I was still the conquered country and one quite unfit for responsibility — but all the more capable of making a dangerous nuisance of itself (PG, 176).

One cannot help thinking of the imperialistic implications of the image of the conquered country in this passage. Cary in his self-conscious effort to portray marital life as a political problem revels in political phraseology to describe the intricacies of this life "'which need the equivalent of 'understandings' and 'spheres of influence'" (PG, 282). The long series of ruptures finally leads to the separation of Nina from Chester when the latter, by a political manoeuvre, stops the Committee meeting supporting the Lugas' Rights. Nina's lover and cousin Jim who is serving in Luga,

Nigeria, was then fighting for the cause of the Lugas who "were in the greatest danger of losing then independence (hundred years old) as a tribe being joined in with a foreign race (Mohammedans living in the plains) under a chief whom they hated and then having an immense new trade road driven right through their farms" (PG, 275-76). He is supported in this movement by Nina and Aunt Latter in England]. However, Chester's decision to bring her back makes Nina realize later that "'He was, in fact, far wiser and deeper in his 'political' idea of human ties than I had been in my romantic one ...., I found myself bound to him in a relation which was still 'spiritual.'" (PG, 311). Charles Hoffman aptly remarks that "... he married her for her money and social position in order to further his political ambitions, but he is nevertheless fond of her and he needs her."[30]

This is the reason why Nina's separation from Chester Nimmo after the great disaster of 24 (his defeat in the elections) cannot put an end to their relationship. Her endurance of Chester Nimmo's unwarranted interference with her may evoke varied responses but her understanding of it is as follows : "... it was no good pretending that I merely tolerated an old man's whims because he was pitiful — I did not love Chester and I had never loved him, but now, more than ever, at the end of his life, I was in his power" (PG, 396). She is also aware that if she does not encourage Chester Nimmo, she is "committing a mean crime against something bigger than love" (PG, 398).

Nina's contempt for Chester Nimmo's crookedness on the one hand, and respect for his political genius on the other, which constitute her dual attitude, are no doubt reflected throughout the novel, but the question of her captivity and freedom still remains a matter of debate. Michael Echeruo, for instance, protests that "Nimmo is able to triumph over her because she is the prisoner of her own grace, because she would never be 'political' on her own account."[31]

Barbara Fisher opens a new vista by making Nina the symbol of suffering womanhood.

> When Nina writes of 'that great man who was once my husband,' she could well be trying to explain,

> for future generations, how our generation made a Hitler our bedfellow.... just as many women like her, forced to marry to 'keep up the family,' had doubtless had to adjust to similar situations. Perhaps this is the chief source for the idea that women should suffer.[32]

How far the above views are valid can be settled only by a thorough scrutiny of the nature of Nina's role in the political game.

If politics had been confined to Chester alone, the novel would have merely ended as a simple study of artful villainy tinged with 'grace.' What actually adds to the appeal of the novel is the projection of almost all the characters in the novel as excellent performers of their roles in a political manner. If the private life of Chester can be considered as nothing more than a bundle of tricks played upon the nerves of Nina, her handling of the situation at all crucial moments also reveals an equal capacity for conceiving political stratagem. In Cornelia Cook's view :

> Through the brackets Nina can show that while Chester's moral force — his grace — overwhelms her, she understands the role of expediency and compromise in any moral or political situation. Thus Nina's narrative itself explains her skill as a manager of people, a politician in her own right.[33]

Nina need not be considered as a prisoner of her own grace, as some critics have contended, trying to establish her as an embodiment of goodwill, silent suffering and sacrifice. At the same time, she is not a mere prisoner of Chester's 'grace' also. Dennis Hall is convinced that :

> Throughout her life she does nothing but what is likely to give herself the greatest possible satisfaction. She cannot have everything she would like, of course, and sometimes she is obliged to accept the smallest evil rather than obtain the greatest pleasure, but she is not a victim, nor is she anybody's prisoner.[34]

Though there is some truth in this statement, Hall has been somewhat lop-sided in his criticism of Nina. Nina, no doubt, is a woman who knows how to use any situation for her own profit but never disregards the needs of others whom she sincerely wants to help, if the situation allows her. The earnestness with which she tries to understand Chester and her conscientious act towards the end of the novel of not deserting the old man, make Dennis Hall's attack on Nina unjustly caustic. For Nina well knows that her continued association with him is not going to pay her in any way. Nina's earlier act of leaving Chester has been looked at as a sign of her selfishness and she herself might have known it. Hazard Adams observes that "... Bootham and Sally [Chester Nimmo's clerk and Nina's daughter] have a point if they want to pursue it, for Nina did divorce Nimmo after it appeared certain to her that his political career was over."[35] But her reunion with Chester when he is out of power nullifies whatever truth in it.

Nina's marriage to Chester initiates her into an unfamiliar world full of intricacies and complications. But very soon she finds that "Nothing is more exciting than to be mixed up with a beginning of a public career . . ." (PG, 31). She realizes the nature of the political world where :

> The lies were mixed up with some truth (like Chester's belief in a class plot), and the selfish calculations (like Goold's planning to make trouble at Lilmouth) melted at the edges into all kinds of 'noble' ideals (like Chester's passion for freedom and free speech) (PG, 56).

So she becomes a judge with a more flexible yardstick to measure Chester's moral fervour, ironically, applying the same to her own behaviour also. Though she is convinced that Chester "plays political tricks even with his own feelings" (PG, 128), Chester's sincerity in believing what he does is the right thing, touches her heart. For instance, whether he is for or against war, he finds a real purpose in his pursuit and there lies his 'grace' as conceived by the liberal tradition, and Nina's 'grace' in turn lies in responding to this 'grace.' Actually speaking, both of them are the prisoners of each other's 'grace.' George Watson's analysis of liberalism as perceived by Lord Acton throws more light on this type of predicament :

> Acton called liberal morality the doctrine that 'lets God work,' though God here might as reasonably

> stand for the moral convictions of the honest doubter and enlightened infidel.... God's chief means of action on man is grace, and grace is individual. Expose the individual to that alone. Do not bury the conscience beneath the ruins of crumbled ages, and set the thrones on sepulchres — snatch the sceptre from the grasp of the dead. So God might be called the supreme Liberal in this view, his demands being always on the individual; and the moral sense in the end can only be a matter for the single conscience.[36]

Nina's simultaneous management of two men, offering them what they desperately need while extracting from them what she thinks can fulfil her needs, is a mark of her superb political genius. She faces the problem of uttering falsehood consciously when she enters into some sort of agreement with her son Tom. She promises Tom that she would hide from Chester Nimmo the information about his engagement with Julie on condition that he finishes his school before entering into the profession of play-acting. Nina admits that her relationship with Tom for quite some reason, has something secretive about it and "it was like a conspiracy" (PG, 201). From now onwards she immerses herself in "a mass of lies and tricks" (PG, 206) to such an extent that she finds domestic politics unbearable. Perhaps her own experience of handling her marital life as a political problem, from the beginning to the end of her life, makes her more tolerant and understanding towards Chester.

If creative deception is Nimmo's strength, Nina also proves to be rather good at this art. Nina wants to believe that Chester Nimmo is a god-sent hero with a definite purpose of managing the people just as he wants to believe in her trustworthiness and accepts her children as his own. For instance, when Nina and her son witness from the back seat of the car, how the people become intoxicated and overwhelmed by the impassionate speech of Chester, defending the pacifists, they try to assure themselves that "he meant every word" (PG, 253) : "(Tom and I would always remind each other at such times when we felt the pressure severely that Chester, though he had to 'play politics,' was really a sincere, good man)" (*Ibid.*). Later if Chester with his evangelist's force in the use of words can convince her easily that it is his moral duty not to resign from the war cabinet, it is mainly because she wants to see his "ratting" from his viewpoint. Cornelia Cook upholds Nina's stand thus :

> Her understatement about Chester's seeming — hypocritical actions both parallels the felicity with which Nimmo could, in the practice of politics, reconcile himself to compromising situations and demonstrates Nina's aware acceptance — a political compromise on her part — of her husband's motives.[37]

Cary does not spare even the minor characters making them active political performers. Aunt Latter regards marriage between Chester Nimmo and Nina as the solution for their problems and her management of the situation is commended by Nina herself : "How bold, then, Aunt was in seeing what 'could be done' with both Nimmo (given my five thousand pounds) and myself. It was really a triumph for her and her 'political' sense,..." (PG, 21). But this politician herself in course of time becomes a "political problem" (PG, 144) to be managed carefully. Even the glorious report about Jim's service to the Luga community is the result of her manoeuvre : ".... the book had been Aunt's plan and her success" (PG, 230). In spite of Chester's insults poured upon Slapton's family, she does not hesitate to make use of him. When she hears about Jim's trouble in Africa, she comes closer to Chester much to the surprise of even Nina : "Again I was surprised by the way these two, who really detest each other, came together" (PG, 231).

Goold, another close associate of Chester Nimmo turned enemy for some time, movingly laments about the fate of Chester's soul : "'... how little it profits a man to gain the world if he loses his own soul'" (PG, 217). And he blames the London society for spoiling Chester. Ironically, the speaker himself is a young evangelist who shuns all the vanities and luxuries of life, but now owner of "a tall hideous new Gothic villa" (PG, 214). Cary's circle of politicians includes even native village girls like Daisy. Daisy's private life is free from any kind of political intricacies unlike that of Nina. But she too is not without a tactics of her own with which she manages to get what she wants, for instance, a carriage.

On the whole the Second Trilogy, especially *Prisoner of Grace*, seems to have reduced human life to a struggle for survival where the ends always justify the means, however crooked they may be. One may feel rather stifled by the pressure of the politically contaminated air that surrounds the novel. But the author seems to have a purpose in mind. Despite his innate enthusiasm for life, if Cary has confined the Second Trilogy, especially this novel, to the level of a mere grim study of man as a political animal, it is to show how politics has its reign in every household whether one is conscious of it or not. This perception in fact, has enabled him to demonstrate that if it is difficult to manage people at home, it is even more formidable a task for a public man to manage a bigger, that too, a heterogeneous crowd, which always looks up to him as a demi-god. As a democrat, Cary believes in liberalism as a mode of behaviour. Liberalism invites us to transcend our limited notions of good and bad, and view the immense complexities of life, private as well as public, in a dispassionate spirit.

While discussing the Second Trilogy, Malcolm Foster explicates Cary's aim as follows : " ... how can a politician achieve that elusive balance between morality and practicality? This is the trilogy's subject, yet it was obscure for many readers."[38] It is interesting to know what Cary himself has to say about his controversial hero Chester Nimmo who has many things in common with Lloyd George, although not intended to be so. Barbara Fisher has made an exhaustive study of Chester, making a comparison of Chester even with Middleton Murry and D.H. Lawrence. Cary's working notes as cited by Michael Rosenthal suggest :

> 'Story of important political man — *eminence grise* — his relations his loneliness — *his responsibilities* as a Christian. Battle *between principle* and his political duty. He *must be a hypocrite not to lose his influence* with devoted, followers and *supporters with money*.'[39]

Chester Nimmo, the consummate artist in politics, emerges from a very poor background like the real politician, Lloyd George. The pro-Boer agitation gives a good start to him and in no time he becomes a national hero with his fiery speeches against the war-makers and the troops whom he labels as 'murderers and cowards'

(PG, 48). Like Lloyd George, who by risking his life made the people discover his "tremendous bravery and self-sacrifice" (PG, 44), Chester too embraces danger by organizing a meeting at Lilmouth with a definite purpose. He causes some sensation but convinces Nina that "'... we have no right to consider a personal risk — the matter is too serious. This war is a crime'" (PG, 48). Later the same man who projects himself as the prophet of peace decides not to resign from the Parliament. Subsequently he becomes a minister in the war ministry. This is a major "ratting" according to others whereas his defense goes thus :

> ... he "confessed to being deeply misled" and to never having believed it possible for any civilized people to be guilty of so dastardly a crime (the invasion of Belgium) against the very basis of civilized religious liberty, which was the sanctity of the pledged word. And so, with a reluctance which those who knew him and his record could understand, he had been compelled, as an act of conscience, to support the cause of truth, which was also that of peace and freedom, against aggression which he could only describe as devilish (PG, 263-64).

Another notorious instance which mars his reputation is his involvement in the "contract case" which no doubt recalls the famous Marconi case, but it happened three months earlier. This case not only finds him guilty of misusing his power but also strengthens the criticism against him that he once attacked the landlords as "baby starvers" (PG, 65) and "blood suckers" (PG, 135), but turns to be one of their kind. However one finds Nina's defense of him in terms of the imperatives of his life quite convincing.

> He did not do anything that any clever business man would not have done, and won great praise.
>
> But owing to the very special conditions of politics, and the way the people treat politicians, looking for a chance to find the smallest fault with them, and quite ready to invent faults that don't exist, it would have been *quite misleading* for Chester to have told

> the whole story of Banks Rams. It might have produced a *great injustice*, that is, the ruin of Chester's career (PG, 210).

Many more aberrations of this kind in his political career can be cited, but they are less serious when compared to the above which strikes us as a peculiar amalgam of good and evil.

In spite of the contradictory reactions to Cary's treatment of Chester, many critics are on the side of Robert Bloom in his merciless attack on Cary as a quibbler :

> By writing with an unyielding relativistic, ultimately indeterminate, objectivity, by refusing to clarify Jim's inadequacy and sanction Chester's behaviour unmistakably in the trilogy itself, Cary becomes guilty of a kind of novelistic dereliction of duty.[40]

The force of Robert Bloom's indictment may be countered by a remark made by Cary in a letter :

> What I believe, ... is what Nimmo believes, that wangle is inevitable in the modern state, that is to say, there is no choice between persuading people and shooting them. But it was not my job to state a thesis in a novel, my business was to show individual minds in action and the kind of world they produce and the political and aesthetic and moral problems of such a world. In short (in the trilogy),the political situation as I conceive it in my world of the creative free individual.[41]

It does not mean that Cary is prepared to brush aside the value of morality as some critics allege. Cary himself admits that he has been accused of "advocating universal dishonesty" (SE, 230). However, if the readers take some effort, they can discover that Cary's characters indeed reap the reward for their falsities. Chester's sterility and his gory death are symbolic of the condemnation of his soul. Cary while discussing political and personal morality declares that "...political action is always the expedient action, the most honest statesman cannot always keep up his promises or fulfil his programme" (*Ibid.*, 228).

It is the typical mark of a liberal not to believe in absolutism but judge everything critically with his eyes open to the hidden layers of truth, penetrating the paraphernalia. One may recall how Cary justifies Stafford Cripps' political compromise made in a particular situation to save the occasion :

> [Sir Stafford] Cripps [Chancellor of the Exchequer in England under Prime Minister Clement Attlee] was one of the honestest men who ever went into politics, but when he was asked if it was proposed to devalue sterling, he answered that there was no immediate intention to do so. At that moment it was already arranged to devalue sterling within a few days.[42]

Cary's argument regarding the latitude allowable to morality in political and personal spheres becomes clear if a passage from *Prisoner of Grace* is recalled. Nina tries to judge private and public morality by the same code of law and pronounces a verdict upon Chester Nimmo which undoubtedly is Cary's too. She quotes an incident in her childhood days which involved Jim and herself and compares the behaviour of Jim, (an ordinary man then) and that of Chester the public man :

> No one would dream of calling Jim a hypocrite for pretending to himself and me, in the middle of a violent storm, that we were doing something reasonable and possible. And no one has any right to call Chester, who had ten times more imagination than Jim, a hypocrite for pretending in the middle of a political storm (which went on all his life; he was never 'in harbour' — there is no such thing in politics) that he had always meant this or that, when, in fact, he had only taken note of it as a 'way out.' (PG, 226).

There is an urge in Cary to make an earnest appeal to the people to be more understanding and tolerant towards the public men so that they will be in a better position to work for them without fear of violent public criticism. Indeed only this kind of mutual trust and co-operation will work in a democracy and if the public is waiting for a chance to pounce upon the men who govern, it will only hamper the efficiency of the government. Cary lived in an age when people were in a fierce mood to hurl stones at any spellbinder. They strongly felt that it was their art of rabble-rousing which led to the war and the consequent set-backs and sufferings. And they started worshipping the Labour leaders and Socialists as their idols who claimed to work and die for the sake of the common man. Bramsted and Melhuish point out :

> ... in the twentieth century humanitarian liberalism has seemed pale and ineffective to many people. Groups who regarded themselves as underprivileged expected little from the mild zeal of liberal reformers and much more from radical socialist or communist methods. After 1918 it was not liberal individualism but the belief in a collective — whether class or nation — which seemed to carry the day.[43]

Gladstone and later Lloyd George, and Roosevelt, no doubt became the butt of criticism, but the truth is that they and their policies had only a minimal role in moulding the destiny of their nations. According to Cary, the world is in perpetual turmoil and its movement cannot be curtailed by human force. As Michael Echeruo points out, the main purpose of *Except the Lord*, the next novel in the trilogy, is to prove this fact. *Except the Lord* is "an acknowledgement of the tragic limitations of all reformist zeal, the very impossibility of a millennium on earth."[44] Cary gives vent to his feeling of sympathy for these public men in the following passage albeit in the context of discussing Britain's colonial policy :

> Administrators are criticised, even by their own countrymen in Parliament, for acts described as surrender to violence, appeasement. They work under a continual fire from both sides, one lot saying, 'Get on and get out, in the name of all that is reasonable and right, that is, nationalism and the people's will;' and the other crying, 'Hold fast in the name of all that is good and sensible, that is, justice, honest administration and the people's welfare.'
>
> But the first are living in the dream world of anarchist catchwords, the second in the past (SE, 102).

Cary is not content with the mere exposition of the fact that wangling is a part of political life, as shown in *Prisoner of Grace*. So he writes another novel *Except the Lord* where he shows how a man who starts his political life with genuine sincerity is slowly corrupted by power, and the problems which accompany it. This novel is not a defence of a single man called Chester, but that of every other politician whose fate is that he is misunderstood and almost lynched by his contemporaries.

> If I draw back now the curtain from my family life, sacred to memory, I do so only to honour the dead, and in the conviction that my story throws light upon the crisis that so fearfully shakes our whole civilization.
>
> It is the story of a crime, of a soul, my own, plucked back from the very edge of frustration and despair (EL, 5).

Referring to this bombastic opening speech of Chester's, Alan Kennedy observes : "He makes his motives sound so high that we are immediately on our guard for insincerity."[45] Yet, the truth underlying the confession of Chester assumes more significance, if we bear in mind the fact that it is a Radical who has seen the decline of his political career along with his Party, who is addressing us. Moreover, certain fundamental questions raised in the novel, which pose a challenge to his sense of righteousness at various stages in his life are confronting humanity as a whole. The way Chester responds to them is typical of any imaginative man with some resourcefulness.

Except the Lord is a record of a series of episodes which forces a poor boy with a good evangelical background to understand what a muddle 'politics' is. To start with, his own father, the elder Nimmo illustrates how impossible it is to escape from its clutches. Even when Chester is very young, he comes under the spell of the religious power wielded by his father, an Adventist, who has pinned all his hopes on the Second Coming of Christ as a panacea for the ills that assail the whole of mankind. Ironically, he cannot be under his father's hold for a long time. The glamour of it begins to fade once the stark reality peeps through. The behaviour of the drunkard, who almost blackmails his father to give him 10 $ on the ground that he is a Christian and so he cannot refuse it, acts as an eye-opener. It is indeed the first bolt which explodes the crystal — clear mind of the young Chester Nimmo. He recollects this incident after a very long time : "How cruel is that charge, of the selfish against the Christian, often poorer than himself, 'you profess Christ, therefore you have no right to refuse me anything.' In fifty years of politics, I have not known worse — it wounds so deep" (EL, 6). The elder Nimmo might have forgiven the poor man as one morally weak, but to the younger Nimmo this is nothing short of blackmail in the name of religion.

Chester Nimmo, though poor has been revelling in the "enchanted world of affection" (EL, 8). But the shifting of the family to the strange place, Shagbrook which treats them rather contemptuously and the terrible sickness which grips his mother, bring it to a sudden end. Responding to the new locale, he remarks, "What amazement fell upon me to find myself in a mean cottage, one narrow slice out of a terrace in Back Lane, Shagbrook, with only a muddy road in front and a muddier yard behind. For days I wandered in a trance, which was too bewildered to be misery" (EL, 12). Mrs. Coyte, their new landlord, who "preferred Wesleyans to Baptists, and both to the church" (EL, 13), teaches them what is meant by 'power.' They also learn from their father's congregation how this 'power' is superseded by a bigger 'power' *i.e*, the power of a spellbinder. Chester's experience of the magic of the art of rabble-rousing starts with his father's avocation : "Perhaps it is impossible in England for any man of prophetic force to want followers, and some of these new recruits were men of importance; . . ." (EL, 16). Here one recalls Aldous Huxley's view of the 'power' in a man to move the masses :

> The driving force which has brought about the most tremendous revolutions on this earth has never been a body of scientific teaching which has gained power over the masses, but always a devotion which has inspired them, and often a kind of hysteria which has urged them into action....[46]

However, the elder Nimmo's children very soon come to know how limited this power is in its utilitarian value. It is Georgina, who adores her father, who wakes up to the reality earlier than others. Despite the general anguish in the family that the precious life of their mother could have been saved if they have had the money, no one except Georgina looks at it as a sign of injustice. As against her conviction, the elder Nimmo's passive resignation that "'it is not for us to question the work of Providence, the Lord gives and He takes away ...'" (EL, 39), begins to look rather shallow.

On the other hand, Shagbrook people who find the Nimmos alien because they cannot identify themselves with the knowledgeable mother of Chester's and the nonconformist father, find fault even with the names of the children and look upon their tragedy as a punishment sent by God. "For in such primitive communities, the smallest difference of habit, of education, is enough to bring suspicion and hatred" (EL, 9). By his portrayal of the Shagbrook life, Cary makes it clear that even a small village like this cannot remain outside the purview of politics. The deceptive simplicity of the life of this hamlet belies the "highly complex and delicate balance of personal relations between families and persons,...." (EL, 24). Cary goes on to comment on this feature :

> ...some degree of quiet and decency could only be maintained by a reciprocity of obligation and reprisal, a balance of powers in which true charity and fellow-feeling, conscience and self-respect — in short, Christian tradition and example, more or less recognized as such, was mingled with what I must call real politics, a system established over years of trial and error (EL, 24).

Malcolm Foster elucidates how Chester's perception of politics is moulded by the village set-up along with his own family situation : "... the elderly Nimmo, speechfying crook or not, still contains within him the idealistic young man. For that matter, the young man, who knows the *absolute necessity* of compromise in his household and his village, is learning the art of politics."[47]

Chester Nimmo claims that though Georgina now and then hints at the injustice, they have never been envious of the rich. "The real rich belonged to a world as strange and romantic to us as fairy tales. We had perhaps even less desire to enter that strange and elaborate world than hope" (EL, 40). But the death of his mother and the ensuing funeral which becomes an arduous task for their father due to financial constraints, usher in a tremendous change. Chester himself acknowledges how the class sense in him, which later leads him to many devious acts, should have stemmed from the injustice and poverty of his younger days : "There was a time within the next years when the hatred of social injustice and of the fearful inequalities of our society became an obsession with me and Georgina, a pressure that tormented us even in our dreams" (EL, 40).

Earlier we noted how Nina in *Prisoner of Grace* becomes the victim of this slowly nursed hatred towards the upper class. Cary has, in fact, graphically portrayed the collapse of the middle class in the context of the First World War, through the declining Wilcher's family in *To be a Pilgrim* and Lord Slapton's family in the Second Trilogy. He projects Chester in the Second Trilogy as the representative of the emerging working class in a period when the social and economic forces tilted the balance in favour of them. A recollection of the changing attitude of the members of the Slapton family towards Chester in *Prisoner of Grace* substantiates this point. Jim's cousin Wilfred begins to cultivate him "because Chester had suddenly become a man of power and his friendship was more valuable than the collective goodwill of a declining family like the Latters" (PG, 165-66). Nina becomes his prisoner and Aunt Latter turns to him as her final refuge. Golden Larsen incisively remarks that "Her [Nina's] isolation and Jim's self-exile to Africa to work among the Lugas represent the isolation of their class as a whole — a class without purpose."[48]

The process of Chester Nimmo's achieving prosperity as an artful politician which starts with his family background, gives ample scope for Cary to develop his favourite theme of family as a political unit in *Except the Lord* also. The pathetic condition of Georgina who is forced "to take a mother's place without a mother's natural authority" (EL, 44) and the consequent emotional crisis, compel her to be diplomatic in her relationship with others. This not only enlightens Chester of the dark side of life but also the readers of how much one has to be political in the management of people. Her first lie to her father that she did not talk about G. when she actually mentioned his name to Richard creates for the first time a wide gulf between the father and the daughter in fact, altering their relationship : "But from this time he became to her a person who, like ourselves, sometimes needed to be handled, managed, who could not be trusted to know his own advantage" (EL, 52). Later, her decision to leave G.'s shop and join the Green Man, the inn, run by G's wife Bella shocks her father, a tee-totaller. "Yet like a wife,... she was still firm in her own line of conduct when she thought it justified by family duty" (EL, 52). She knows well that their need for money justifies her action whether approved by others or not. No one better than her dear father knows "how much her happiness in a cruel world depended upon the cast of her soul" (EL, 58). The resemblance between the predicament of Georgina with her series of adjustments and that of Chester whose political career is full of compromises and justifications, is indeed striking. Whereas Chester's acts become the source of his guilt, Georgina's compromises elevate her soul and it is interesting to find out wherein lies the difference. One may concur with the view of S.H. Kanu on this matter : ". . . Chester's keen personal sense of guilt ... derives, in part, from the full knowledge that as a politician, he has frequently gone far beyond Georgina's kind of necessary lie to the lie which twists the human mind." [49] Georgina becomes a strange person to all those around her. "Georgina to us became now still more peremptory; in despair of our liking, she seemed, like other autocrats, to find pleasure in abusing her subjects" (EL, 59). However, the children know how to tackle her. Chester Nimmo very tactfully tries "to involve her in a promise while she was still in the mood of excitement produced by the elephant" (EL 62), informing her of the Lilmouth Fair. He also succeeds in extracting her promise by his "cunning diplomacy" (EL, 63) and all the children by their small contribution to the cause of the striking miners make it a reality. Georgina indeed points out that they may not be justified in spending so much on entertainment when the miners on strike at Ramstone have been starving themselves. But Richard manages to affect that they are not on the wrong side by arguing that, "If the strikers were suffering it was their own fault" (EL, 65). Chester, on the other hand, cannot be so easily persuaded. He is much bewildered by the economic problems behind it. For, the father's emotional involvement in the fate of the miners has always exerted much pressure upon the children's conscience.

The freedom given to the Nimmo children to decide on such matters on their own, unlike many other children, adds to their problems. Chester feels, "In fact this freedom of choice made our problems more difficult — we were always faced by a conflict of duty and inclination" (EL, 70). The children in their own little world feel themselves left in a turmoil which needs a lot of management skill.

The decision to go to Lilmouth Fair and the ensuing problems, emotional and financial, underscore the fact as to how the politics of childhood is as complicated as that of the adult world. The rupture in relationship among the Nimmo children caused by their varied opinions and the necessary adjustments made by them in order to maintain the amity among themselves, provide adequate material for an interesting study. The conspiring of the children finally to go to the Lilmouth Fair under the guidance and help of Cran, making use of the absence of their father, is in no way less diplomatic than the activities of a professional politician. Georgina who treats the whole scheme as something extraneous to her, later turns to be one of the visitors to the Fair and indeed regains the intimacy of her brother Chester within a short time. Chester remarks that :

> Such sudden changes of allegiance are, of course, common enough in family life, where daily co-habitation provides in a few days incidents and emotions enough to furnish out an ordinary friendship for years. The allies of yesterday are implacable enemies of to-day, and after a long history of events friends again to-morrow (EL, 97).

They are indeed bound together more by their guilt of having yielded to the enticement of evil.

The author who has shown the nature of the working of the psyche of the children belonging to the declining middle class family in *To be a Pilgrim*, here deals with a set of poverty — stricken lower class children exposed to the seamy side of life. The former are driven by cynicism which makes them rather rebellious in their own way, turning for example, Edward among them into a radical, and Lucy into a Benjamite. Here, the deprivation and the consequent violation of faith in the existing system impel them to plunge themselves into non conformism, with Georgina seeking a commonly disapproved means of earning and Chester becoming a revolutionary.

The attitude of the Nimmo children, especially Chester and Georgina, towards their father, compels the attention of the readers. Georgina, with her readiness to sacrifice her absolute ideals for the immediate family cause, is pitted against her father whose faith in God's justice is so unshakable that he lives true to his belief till the end, despite harsh realities. Chester is placed in the centre, and he could observe their actions more objectively from two different angles. Ironically while the elder Nimmo stands steadfast adhering strictly to his principles, some unseen forces catch him unawares, pushing him down into the world of reality. This shatters the hopes of his children at every stage, causing some kind of uneasiness in Chester's mind in particular from his younger days. Georgina's decision to work in G.'s shop and later in the Inn, adds to the gravity of the situation.

The visit to the Lilmouth fair gains symbolic significance when read in this light. The very atmosphere of the Fair is marked by "the sense of lawlessness, the pushing and shouting, and yet the good behaviour of most of the people" (EL, 79). It seems rather strange to Chester in the beginning, but he quickly perceives in it the basis for freedom. One cannot miss the presence of the author behind the words, "It is, I believe, no sentimental illusion that mechanism is everywhere the enemy of joy : no less than the mechanical centralism of bureaucratic Utopians is the enemy of true citizenship" (EL, 81).

The awakening of the new consciousness in Chester is further accentuated by the tremendous hypnotic effect of the play, "Maria Marten" upon him. Chester has till now remained a man of cultivated conscience,by training if not by conviction,due to his father's influence, despite his occasional protests against oppression and poverty. The impracticability and the material uselessness of his father's faith in his cult has very often raised doubts in the minds of his children. But never have they allowed such feelings to come to the surface. Nevertheless the irresistible appeal of the evil

Cran, the gang leader with his exciting but unlawful schemes, has been lying dormant in Chester. "Cran was my hero, my joy. Why, you ask? Why did I, a child so carefully brought up, fall under the influence of this trickster, this petty thief? Because, in one word, to defy the law was brave and free. And how I worshipped that master of arts" (EL, 22). Ironically it is the same Cran who helps him to come into contact with this power of evil, once again in the form of the actor, enacting the role of Corder in the play "Maria Marten." Chester has felt the power of the oratory of a spellbinder on his father's congregation, but the atmosphere of the theatre with its illusory nature throwing the crowd in a state of mad enthusiasm and the actors radiating their powerful spell, is new to him. He feels as though "the blood had run out of my heart" (EL, 82). Cary artfully generalizes this experience, hoping to conceal his own passion for such spellbinders, and his belief that they become the indispensable force in the working of a democracy. "Is it that impersonation by itself has some secret and immemorial power over the growing spirit — some primitive urge older perhaps than humanity itself?" (EL, 84). This single movement in Chester's life seems to nullify the whole effect of the values built up by his father and there emerges a new Chester out of the old ashes, though the evangelist in him is still alive. "Our whole education as children turned on respect for the truth — falseness was a sin and falseness had a very wide meaning. Any kind of pretence, any kind of conduct having the least tincture of hypocrisy was not only a sin but a deadly trap. How often had I been told that the lie corrupts and poisons the very soul?" (EL, 86-87). But the very next moment, he indulges in self-deception when he convinces himself that seeing the play is not wrong : "' But this story is true. There is no sin in a true story truly represented'" (EL, 87).

The arrival of his sister, instead of surprising him, "made the occasion even more portentous, more exciting than before" (EL, 90). Naturally the "story of the cruellest kind of wrong inflicted by the rich upon the poor" (EL, 92), besides evoking sympathy for the girl, fills him with "fascinated admiration" (EL, 93) for the hero. He wonders, how "could any human being commit such villainies and stand there before a crowd of his fellows and own it — act it?" (EL, 93). This is the decisive moment in his life. He admits that "it seemed that something flashed from the very centre of evil into my deepest soul" (EL, 94). Chester's stirred feelings recall Cary's readiness to acknowledge and grant credibility to the Devil's grand defiance of God in pursuit of freedom.

It may be borne in mind that Cary has never failed to remind us that freedom can damn people. Chester who has realized the charm of the devil Satan finds the way open to him to become a free man notwithstanding the losing of his soul. The author in a sombre voice remarks : "... — power itself has a fascination for the young soul in its weakness and dependence. And when to power is added the guilt of blood, some horror of cruelty, its force can be hypnotic" (EL, 94). Chester acknowledges that he falls a prey to it. In Chapter II we looked into the influence of Blake on Cary's thinking in some detail. Blake's treatment of Milton's Satan is too well known to need elaboration here. Blake's vision of Evil, as noted in Chapter II, is dialectical. Cary could enhance his understanding of the thrust and cosmic function of Evil by a reading of Blake. It is this dialectical awareness on the part of Cary which frees him from the guilt of being a writer without a moral sense, as accused by critics like Robert Bloom and Dennis Hall.

When Chester leaves the Lilmouth Fair, he is a completely changed man. He begins to feel burdened with the heaviness of the sense of inequality and cruelty of social injustice for which he cannot merely blame the rich but "the forces beyond my understanding, the decree of a God whose ways were not my ways" (EL, 100). "Something moved in me that was not yet even an ambition — the mere ghost of aspiration." He adds with self-irony : "I was a king, a hero of the revolution. But without wrath — without even revolutionary principles" (*Ibid.*). The seeds have been sown at this stage but the direction of the growth is not yet determined and if it later tends to turn crooked it is largely the fault of the environment. The injustice meted out to his father by the mob's trampling upon him when he goes to save their life and later his arrest as one of the miners' leaders when he is least interested in labour politics, vitiates Chester's personality. The loss of his father's extra income leads to Chester's withdrawal from his school and that is the starting point of his becoming sullied both at physical and emotional levels : "I can say from experience that to be dirty and to accept dirtiness is to be half-way to the brute. He who resigns himself to filth in his person will come to delight in the bad thought, the filthy word" (EL, 109). However, he is aware that "There was planted in this rough dirty boy who spoke now habitually, as in spite against his lot, the broadest and crudest dialect, a vision of glory, of power, by means of the spoken word" (EL, 111).

Chester feels disconcerted when his father's calculation of Christ's Second Coming ends in a fiasco, for inordinate significance was attached in the congregation to the confident declaration of the elder Nimmo about Christ's Second Coming, "a doctrine appealing strongly to many lost and bewildered souls" (EL, 5). The fatal gig accident which kills the highly respected wife of G. happens only then. The people are "tormented deeply and anxiously by a terrible question — if a good woman could so die when a bad man was saved, where was the justice of God, where was any justice in earth or heaven?" (EL, 113). They look up to the elder Nimmo as their saviour who "offered an answer, an answer which, so he said, and we believed, was to be proved within a few weeks" (EL, 113). When his father's expectations fail, the bitter truth that both earthly justice and providential justice are beyond their reach, strikes Chester at his face. He confesses in a touching manner :

> In fact, this family disaster which had made my father a laughing-stock in the village, had a precisely opposite effect on Georgina and on me — it brought her closer to her father ... while it removed from me my complete trust in my father's wisdom and so opened the way to political agitation.
>
> ....my faith — the unquestioning faith of the child in what he has been told by his parents — had received a mortal wound. It was already bleeding to death (EL, 125).

Barbara Fisher asserts that "Like Bridget, and then Manus, in [*Castle Corner*] Chester turns from religion on discovering that his Father, and God, are not omnipotent, and instead seeks omnipotence in political power."[50]

The fire in Chester is fanned by the pamphlet 'The Great

Design' distributed in the Tarbiton market, highlighting the cruelty of poverty with the following arguments : religion is "the instrument of the rich to oppress the poor" (EL, 127) and "Either the omnipotent God was a tyrant and devil or there was no god at all — omnipotence being assumed as an all-embracing power over time and space, to subvert nature itself, to intervene at any moment in human fate" (EL, 128). His accidental meeting in Exeter with Dr. Lanza, a disciple of Proudhon, the French Liberal thinker, provides him with an antidote to his thwarted hopes and beliefs. Chester who is in no mood anymore to lend his ears to any kind of spiritual messages, is immediately won over by "one of the most brilliant orators" (EL, 135) who speaks of "no churches, no creeds, but only mankind and the soul" (EL, 134). This nihilist "believed government and property to be the source of all evil and despised organised religion as a branch of the police" (EL, 135). Lanza could make an immediate appeal to Chester mainly because he projects the familiar family love as "a holy thing, the foundation of all happiness and peace" (EL, 136). To Chester who has been in search of a new faith after his rejection of his father's God, Dr. Lanza provides a cult which restores his rejected God "under another name, that of humanity" (EL, 141). It also enables him to unite "under one majestic dome both my religious intuition and those vague political notions derived from so many sources — yes, and from all the ambition, the resentments, of a poverty — stricken childhood" (EL, 141). The thought of Proudhon makes his heart throb with delight and Dr. Dolling being the representative of his society quickly earns his admiration. He begins to worship the ground trodden by Dolling and he can hear him quoting from Mazzine : "'Humanity is a man who never does and never ceases to learn — he is the living thought of God upon Earth as the prophet of a divine law'" (EL, 149).

Chester becomes obsessed with the idea of revolution and "to defy the established authority of the land" (EL, 149) becomes his mission. However, Dolling's hold over Chester is soon lost mainly for the reason that the former is too much of an abstractionist whose Europeanized ways will not suit the British mentality which is rather pragmatic and soaked in religion. Chester's next idol, Pring, a powerful Marxist with his plan to call for a general strike, confounds the already confused mind though he is "revolted by the suggestion of violence" (EL, 189).

Chester starts the farm labourers' union at Shagbrook, and dreams of introducing a new millennium as suggested by Brodribb, the dockers' union chairman at Tarbiton. But he is compelled to countenance the reality of being a politician for the first time. Wilson poses a danger to him, with subtle threats of betrayal of the members of the union. Chester confesses that "... a fundamental question in politics, now for the first time presented to me, when and where is one justified in telling a flat lie?" (EL, 186). Cary prepares here the ground for the building up of a typical career of a politician by subjecting him to the bind of the intricate knot which every politician tries to untie but in vain, as in the case of Jim in *Prisoner of Grace*. Chester seems indeed to be opting for the *practical truth*, something that worked (PG, 219) in his political career as Nina puts it. Chester decides not to disclose the secret to Wilson and thinks of a suitable alternative stratagem. He starts playing tricks with Fred's feeling of suspicion about the relationship between Georgina and Wilson. Finally he manages to get rid of his enemy. But the sacking of the two boys of Doan by their landlord Mann and that of Bonnet by G. add to his trouble. Only a few writers like Cary can consciously describe the anguish of Chester trapped in the net of politics :

> I was like a man in some quiet town carrying a secret treasure in his pocket who is suddenly lost among the dark, unlit streets, and now he hears himself followed, a voice calls from the distance, a dark lantern flashes. He stops abruptly and the footfalls behind also stop, he tells himself they were only the echo of his own, that he is imagining these terrors — suddenly a whistle sounds and is answered from far ahead, he rushes on in rage and confusion saying that at least he will die game (EL, 204).

Chester feels baffled not only by the behaviour of outsiders who look down upon him as a trouble-maker but also by that of his own sister. In spite of her strong declaration of her hatred of the upper class, she sends the unwilling Ruth to the house of Lady Slapton as a sewing maid. Chester Nimmo cannot understand such class enemies like Wilson and Georgina. But the worst betrayal comes in the form of the assault of Chester by the three union men, Kimber, Dodman and Franc Don who suspect him to be the betrayer who has sold them for the money with which he has bought his new suit. "I realized now how much suspicion has gathered about me since I had put on a whole suit of cloth and gone to work in an office instead of the fields and ditches of the moor" (EL, 225). Chester is rescued by the dockers, but he has witnessed politics in its crudest form during this incident. The bitter truth about the complexity involved in politics and the ordeal of surviving in the chaotic world of politics with its innumerable waves of mistrust, suspicion, betrayal and opportunism, become graphically real to him. "It was the first time I had been made to understand the fearful condition of political life, the fundamental want of all security, the appalling risks of those who accept any large responsibility for their fellows" (EL, 226). Cary discusses this problem authoritatively in one of his articles :

> Power does not so much corrupt the ruler as the whole world in which he is compelled to work. It becomes for him, the moment he reaches power, a kind of Castle of Otranto, full of uncertain noises and vague threats, in which the very servants edge away from him as if he had the evil eye. And his friends become favourites and his closest friends can become his most dangerous enemies. For they, above all, have power; the power to deceive (CAF, 209).

Chester's initiation into the hard realities of life is further reinforced by his entry into London life. Witness Cary's description of London city as seen through the eyes of Chester :

> Nothing in my experience has prepared me for this world of atomies, mere corpuscles or droplets of life, whose difference from one another has no importance, whose dignity as individual human souls was, even to themselves, lost in the moving tide which alone had purpose and meaning (EL, 231-32).

First, he is repelled by the absolute obliteration of one's individuality in the sprawling crowded metropolis. However, the author constructs the scene in such a way that it adds to the challenging nature of the atmosphere, intoxicating Chester Nimmo more and more with a sense of glory. Pring, the "convinced and consistent Marxist" (EL, 241), gives some meaning to Chester's life by enabling him to live for a cause and Chester gets directly involved in the dreadful Lilmouth Dock strike. When Chester is questioned by Georgina whether he is responsible for the ambushing, he denies it, though with a feeling of pride which is not unmixed with a pang in his heart. "But in the same instant there arose in me a sense of glory and triumph, something quite unexpected in its force and puzzling even to myself — I had lied to Georgina for the cause" (EL, 254). He puts up with the horrible nature of the scheme "so coolly arranged in the office" (EL, 261) which leads to the death of many a dear man. Later he even criticizes Brodribb for his "weakness and treachery" (EL, 269) when he resigns from the committee protesting against Pring's rejection of the Allsend owners' negotiation for the good of everyone. But he cannot be long under the spell of Pring as he still remains a Christian at heart.

The reason for his separation from Pring may be attributed to a fight for power. But a thorough reading of the novel makes it clear that what enrages Chester Nimmo is Pring's tendency to sacrifice people in general for the 'cause' which is an abstraction. He realizes at one stage "that no one on earth counted with him beside the cause" (EL, 271) and "Pring loved power too much and men not at all" (EL, 272). The bitter truth that "there was too much loss in this strike and too little democracy" (El, 272) is too much for Chester to digest. This "is the discovery which wrenches Chester's sympathies from the militants. It prepares the way for his rediscovery of religion — the belief that all human emotions and endeavors are manifestations of God — and his subsequent espousal of the policies of Liberalism."[51]

We noted earlier that Nina's criticism of Chester Nimmo at the zenith of his political career is at once tempered with sympathy and laced with cynicism for the same reason. "She had never realized how little her 'devotion' meant to a man who was himself 'devoted' — not even to a human being but to something that seemed to his imagination (which had done so much to invent it) infinitely more beautiful and worthy — the Cause" (PG, 395). In such passages Cary consummately focuses on the ambivalence of the politcal predicament of Chester Nimmo as well as that of Nina. Cary's belief that power corrupts a person however much he is on guard against its insidious charm, finds its most complex expression in *Except the Lord*. It is indeed the record of Chester Nimmo's conscious but futile attempts to save himself from this kind of contamination. Chester, with his religious fervour, starts his career only with the good intention of promoting the poor. But the failure of the leaders to convince him of the logic behind their acts and the betrayal of the people who begin to politicize even his ordinary behaviour disillusion him. His inner conscience, already crushed by the oppression of poverty, easily yields to the magnetic words of the anarchists and socialists and he begins to seize avariciously every opportunity which brings him 'power.'

Cary, as is typical of him in his fashion, does not treat politics as the prerogative of a politician. *Except the Lord* too is full of people who perform their duties, as well as the politicians in their own field. As already mentioned, when there is a crisis in the family, even Georgina behaves like a politician. Her decision to marry Fred Coyte is politically motivated. She confides to Chester that "'It would be a good thing for you,.'... 'and father too — and Dick and all of us. We should have the farm. The only thing is I hate Fred so'" (EL, 160). Her management of her father is another sign of her instinctive political expertise. But what differentiates her from the other characters including Nina, is her unwavering faith in love as something prior to politics. She knows well that "'...politics isn't everything'" (EL, 213) and so she does take the risk of turning herself into a class enemy. Her every political move, if seen closely, has been motivated solely by her affection for her family members. When both Richard and Chester are daunted by the family disaster caused by their father, "it brought her closer to her father and nearly abolished from her mind all those strong political feelings which she had so suddenly revealed . . . after the fair" (EL, 125). Her decision to stick to her father, or her giving up William, serves her in two ways — to be a true daughter to her father till the end and to relieve herself of the only one sin in her soul, *i.e.*, deserting William Fred.

We may be justified in saying that Cary does not believe in treating man as a mere political animal. "Man is not a political or economic animal. He is moved by sympathies, tastes, faiths which have nothing to do with politics or cash, and he is always ready to fight for them" (PM, 35). The novel, *Except the Lord* shows with exceptional clarity how a set of people fight their battles each in his/her own way, moved by a whole host of motives, but ironically unable to refrain from a political handling of situation as a means to achieve them.

The last novel in the Second Trilogy, *Not Honour More* is dull and monotonous, as compared to the other two novels, for it hardly comprises anything save a few incidents in British History which are dealt with in detail by Jim. He shows how rotten the country has become and emphasizes the need for lynching such wanglers like Chester Nimmo who are responsible for the state of affairs. It is perhaps Cary's apparent affinity for this crusader for honesty which has led some critics like Barbara Fisher who are otherwise so very perceptive, to go astray in interpreting Cary's two main characters Chester Nimmo and Jim. Though, a major part of Barbara Fisher's criticism of *Except the Lord* seems to collide with the views of the author as explicitly stated in his treatises, letters, articles and essays, her analysis of the opening passage of the novel *Except the Lord* demands one's attention :

> The crisis is, surely, that people with Chester's aims have gained such power, since they want our civilization to collapse. That this is Cary's meaning seems proved by *Art and Reality*, where he writes of the 'power of the word, of rhetoric, of the demagogue,' which makes 'a great many people despair of civilization as it is. They expect the world to tumble once more into a thousand years of barbarism. That Cary himself felt this fear and despair seems certain.[52]

Barbara Fisher has chosen a passage where Cary has made a general comment, not relating it either to Jim or Chester Nimmo, and she has tried to prove her point, whereas there are plenty of instances where Cary has openly expressed his preference for Chester Nimmo.

The clarification of Joyce Cary's view of Chester Nimmo goes thus :

> Nimmo is meant to be like a real man with real thoughts. He often deceives himself about his own motives and that is pretty common among men of his type, that is to say men of action — spellbinders. They don't go in very much for self-criticism; they're too active; they are too interested in the world.[53]

On the other hand, in Cary's view Jim :

> ... doesn't call himself a fascist and he hates fascism but he has a fascist mind; he has been a soldier and he asks why a country can't be run like a good regiment, by men who believe in duty and discipline.... He is just like those people who hate drink, which is a real evil, and who say why don't we stop it by law. That is to say people — they're people who want to make the world good by law.[54]

Cary's own conviction, however, lies elsewhere : "The only way is by education and by trusting them and giving them a sense of responsibility as free men to behave like good citizens and they won't have a sense of responsibility if you push them around by law."[55]

Chester Nimmo himself expresses the need for a strong government. Considering the declining morality of the people he laments that it has led to distressing consequences :

> ...the very framework of Christian Society was tottering. Nothing could save us but an evangelical revival — a new Wesley.... 'It's not only the young — the masses are out of hand. It's the case of the Gaderene Swine over again. What we will need after this war is ten years of the strongest kind of government (PG, 310).

He even confesses that Lloyd George has failed to inspire the people. Chester Nimmo's anguish is the natural consequence of certain historical events and many of the Liberals of the day, shared his opinion. But they still believed in state action only as a means to increase the efficiency of the people, thereby boosting their morale. The same uneasiness made some turn to Fascism as the only way out and yet others to Communism. Cary's main intention seems to be to disclose the craze of such people who look at government as the ultimate source of salvation, not realizing the strength of human resourcefulness to sustain a nation's spirit. Cary belongs to the group of people whose trust in people remained unabated till the end. This even led to some patronizing comments. Witness, for *e.g.*, an anonymous writer in *Time* : "the world may be a grim place, but the British novelist Cary is not the man to learn from."[56] However such criticism loses its edge once the liberal mentality as represented by complex minds like Cary is understood. In Ian Bradley's assessment :

> The liberal spirit is incurably and eternally optimistic. This is not to say that it is smug and complacent. Liberals do not believe that all is well with the world — far from it; they are restless and impatient for change. But they have faith in the capacity of human beings, for all their weaknesses and frailty, to effect that change and make the world a better place.[57]

The novel *Not Honour More* is the record of the famous British political scenario of the General Strike of 1926 and the reaction to it is presented from various angles. It recaptures the time spirit as reflected in the mentality of two men, Chester Nimmo and Jim, of opposite poles to each other in their attitude. The whole novel seems to be resounding with the tall claims of Jim that he is out only for truth and justice. The very beginning of the novel indicates what a vain boast Jim's is, for, Jim's defense starts not with a discussion of any national problem, which finds Chester Nimmo standing opposite to him in the open court, but a purely domestic problem, maybe involving his honour as a husband. The book, in fact, opens with the repeated hints derived from various sources informing Jim about the recent, clandestine relationship between Nina and her former husband Chester who is staying as a guest in the Palm Cottage. Because of this basically personal grudge, all of Jim's talk about Chester Nimmo and his gang as the fountainhead of the corruption that defames the nation, looks like a child's prattle. Moreover, he gives himself away in admitting that it is Chester's interference with his wife which was the chief reason for his first attempt of murder on Chester. His main accusation against Chester is that : "I say he corrupted everything and everybody that came near him and stole this woman, my wife, from me when she was little more than a child and set to work to destroy her body and soul" (NHM, 8).

Jim's argument loses its ground at the very outset. For Chester's marriage with Nina is the master plan of Nina'sAunt and both Nina and Chester are the beneficiaries, as already mentioned. If anything, Jim is the scapegoat. Besides, it is Chester Nimmo who gives Nina the marital status and Jim is the culprit who continues to interfere with Chester Nimmo's wife.

Nina's insistent and continual defence of Chester Nimmo as "a good man — in his heart he was a true, good man, ..." (NHM, 14) may have surprised Jim. But the truth is, even Nina who loves Jim to the core can neither respect his spurious grandeur of thought nor believe his feelings for her. It is here that one notices the difference in the outlook of Nina and Jim. Both of them have been, at times, victimized by the cunning and deceit of Chester. "But Nina indulges in a long excited speech about Chester Nimmo's being the only hope of the country" (NHM, 14) Her tendency to tolerate his weaknesses as a man, is an indication of her liberal outlook whereas Jim's narrow-mindedness reduces him to a fanatic and too short-sighted to be a Liberal though he claims to be one.

Jim's hysterical rage is not directed against Chester Nimmo alone. His dealings with different cross-sections of society, starting from the press to law, give him no comfort. He finds the competition among various selfish people to distort truth raging very high everywhere. His desire to give a hand-out to the press after the murder of Nina confessing "the truth, the whole truth and nothing but the truth" (NHM, 27) is thwarted by the news reporter Drew's decision to delete that sentence which is of primary importance to Jim. Drew feels that "'Truth can be the worst kind of libel because doing more damages'" (NHM, 28) and so Chester Nimmo's offence of interfering with Jim's wife should not find a place in the hand-out. Jim does not take much time to conclude that "The writty chaps are only a tick better than the talky chaps, if ticks can win on bugs — both of them are out to suck the country's blood"

(NHM, 31). When Jim seems to be completely taken aback by the lack of appreciation and understanding of his action, Chester Nimmo brings the situation under his control by dismissing the whole thing as a mere accident. Cock-Nose's farewell words, "'But you have to take off your hat to the old bastard. Goodnight, captain, and good luck with it,'...." (NHM, 33) reflect upon the rather unenviable predicament of Jim.

As A.M. Brightman suggests in his letter to Jim, the latter by his hasty action gives an opportunity to Chester to use the occasion politically. Pretending before his supporters that Jim and he are good friends, Chester emerges with a clean image making Jim feel like an idiot. Chester takes him into his confidence, impressing upon him the necessity of handling the situation with skill : "'...you saw what you supposed to be something improper — you acted hastily, on the spur of the moment, and produced a certain situation — the situation we now have to deal with....'" (NHM, 48). He also drives home the point that Jim has been ready to sacrifice even Nina for the sake of what he considers as the truth : "'And in order to give them what you call a little bit of truth, you're prepared to sacrifice Nina — to throw her to the wolves. Yes, I understand. You wish to ruin me, to destroy me and, in doing so, you don't care if you destroy her'" (NHM, 48). The tremendous effect of Chester Nimmo's words upon Jim cannot be summed up better : "When Nimmo said it was because Nina followed her heart that she'd come back to me, he was very much on the point and I'm not pretending it didn't have a big effect. More than anything else he'd thrown at me" (NHM, 53). Later, when Jim seems to be thoroughly baffled about what is going on in his house, Chester Nimmo is quick enough to remind him of how both of them have really loved her but at the same time treated her brutally, making his argument very appealing by repeatedly employing Jim's favourite word 'truth' : "The truth — the whole truth ... let us face it, as guilty men. Let us have the courage to face it. You were a brute, you say, to that young girl, and I have loved her, let us say, too much ..." (NHM, 63). He further adds that the only way to repay her for all her tenderness and affection for them is by becoming friends and start it over all again. "'...with hearts renewed in sympathy, in our old tried friendship. Let us start again in truth — the truth of mutual sympathy, the reality of affection, the fact of today and its lesson ...'" (NHM, 65-66).

It is very difficult to discern Chester Nimmo's motive. Yet one cannot fail to notice the consistency in his admission of Nina's power over him and his need of her.

Cary indeed elicits the strength of his hero through his enemy himself. The rather simple, straightforward Jim cannot withstand any trick played upon his feelings by the resourceful Chester. He admits, "That was always Nimmo's game, to confuse things. Bunko. Whenever you went near Nimmo, you got in a blind spin, a mass of dirty fog full of wreckage like London in a November bomb raid. You could only bash yourself against the walls and break your nose if it wasn't your neck" (NHM, 70-71). Chester Nimmo compli(e)ments this furious abuse by paying a high tribute to Jim's sense of honour every now and then. But the truth which Chester Nimmo and Nina understand but Jim fails to grasp is that truth and honour as absolute ideals are rather elusive. As pointed out by Michael Echeruo, "Cary does not dispute [Jim] Latter's claim that 'nothing can save but the truth and the guts to take it.' But he does show in the novel that truth alone and the guts to take it may not always save either."[58] It is worth remembering here that Cary himself had been after the ideals of truth, honour and duty, in his own life and during the General Strike, had volunteered to work to keep the vital services to go on. However, Cary makes it clear that nothing can be achieved merely by talking about truth and honour without making them practical and humanly possible to realize. Jim, despite his fanatic commitment to truth and honour, can remain neither truthful to Nina nor maintain his honour as a family man as well as a public man, for he is a votary of abstraction. The irony lies in this discrepancy, as aptly pointed out by R.W. Noble :

> Captain James Latter sees himself as standing in descent from Colonel Lovelace, Sir John Suckling and those other gallants who tried to defend the order of the realm. But *Not Honour More* is an inversion of Lovelace's light witty poem. Latter's bitter defence of honour is ironically a sordid

> confession of hatred and murder, rather than a blithe assertion of the traditional gentlemanly verities.[59]

Cary's last novel in the Second Trilogy fails to sustain the reader's interest for a few reasons despite its serious tone. *Not Honour More* is more descriptive in its tone; it reads rather like a commentary on the General Strike of 1926 which started with a mighty ambition of bringing England to a standstill but turned out to be a wet squib. As a novel it seems to be an assortment of episodes which are not connected together properly into a coherent whole. The incongruities in the arrangement of events and their dates have been pointed out by critics. Moreover Jim has a tendency to get distracted and give more weightage to certain people and incidents which does not help him to strengthen his argument against Chester Nimmo. His lengthy description of Varney and his family as the epitome of goodness tracing the whole background, looks rather redundant in a serious novel like *Not Honour More*. Yet the very style of the book dramatizes the waywardness and the restlessness of Jim. "At times he writes almost inchoately, babbling like a paranoiac; his righteousness is very like that of some American reactionaries who damned President Roosevelt to the skies."[60]

Cary, in the least dramatic manner, brings out how the general strike was proposed as the panacea for curing all the social inequalities, by the different sections of people, all pushing each other for the sake of power but under the pretext of justice. The novel is filled with rhetorical speeches showing how the "talkie boys" like Chester and Binko, and the Communist leaders with their fiery speeches, entice the helpless mass who lose their control once they are seized of the idea. Jim sneers at the impact of Chester Nimmo's speech in the beginning of the novel : "He's promising the earth and they begin to lap it up. Fellows in middle distance straining their ears .... The ones at the back who can't hear a word are popping their eyes at celebrated saviour" (NHM, 17). Later he scoffs at the power of Pincomb's speech over the people who start roaring with anger. All this is no exaggeration, given a democratic set up. Ironically Jim with his frequent "speechifying" about honour equally attempts to win the hearts of the people as any other talky boy does but in vain. Cary thereby proves that "words" are part and parcel of political life and the evil lies not in them but in the way they are used.

Our initial response to Jim and Cary's artistic talent as his creator, is one of disappointment. Because we expect Cary to extol him as the hapless victim of the class disintegration. We expect the novelist to project him as a hero whose ideals are of no avail. But on a closer reading of the novel, we find the text subverting our wishful thinking. For Jim's predicament paradoxically throws the ideals which Cary cherished, in better light precisely because Jim turns out to be such a babble if not an 'ineffectual angel.' The text and its texture reveal the contradictions between the abstract and the real as boldly faced by the writer. Jim's fury is, no doubt infantile but on that score we cannot refrain from recognizing Chester Nimmo's self-centredness and self-aggrandizement. It also reflects upon the changes which had brought the British society at the crossroads. The apparent innocuousness of men like Jim is as deleterious as the consummate self-mastery and drive of men like Chester Nimmo.

Jim accuses Chester Nimmo on many grounds. He disapproves of Chester Nimmo's playing with the life of Varney by making him believe that if he acts according to reason, it will be applauded. Chester Nimmo's tact in using Varney as "a policeman without a policeman's powers" (NHM, 85) reminds him of his old days : "It is the old game they played on us in Africa — the everlasting Nimmo game. The everlasting game they always have played — nothing in writing. Nothing definite — nothing you can pin on them afterwards" (NHM, 85). Even Chester Nimmo's attempt to make him the chief of the specials has its own reason, Jim says : "It was plain enough why Nimmo wanted me to serve. I couldn't go shooting him while I was under his command. And I couldn't put out statements to the Press while I was a policeman" (NHM, 90). Chester Nimmo's Shagbrook address, almost similar to any Communist manifesto, rousing the people against the capitalists and the "new racket — stirring up feeling against the specials, saying that they were worse than the regular police, calling them the White Guard" (NHM, 114), complicates the situation further. Above all, Jim is taken aback by the knowledge of the secret agreement carried out between Chester Nimmo and the Communist leader

Pincomb ironically through the agency of his wife Nina because "this bargain was to sacrifice Potter's and the livelihood of three hundred families to the Bolshies in exchange for Bolshy support to Nimmo" (NHM, 119). "Nimmo's "policy of double-cross" (NHM, 110) in the case of the East Tarbiton bus incident proves to be rather repulsive to Jim, but he is strongly convinced that he "saved serious trouble" (NHM, 112) by his order. Jim also accuses Pincomb of inciting the people, goading them to revolution and imminent violence. The following speech of Pincomb in fact, captures the essence of the speeches made by the labour leaders who aspired to sow the seeds of Communism in England after the First World War which witnessed the decline of Liberalism :

> 'I should think any sensible man who saw the present state of Europe would want one. It's about the foulest mess in history. And it's dying of its own filth. But so are a few millions of people who can't help themselves. Don't you think it would be a good idea to help some of the filth down the drain and clear the air a bit?' (NHM, 118).

The unethical inclination of the relation between such determined agitators like Pincomb and the chairman of the Emergency committee responsible for law and order may look rather odd. But the tone of the novel and the way most of the people function without the least surprise, make it clear that such aberrations are taken for granted. Moreover, the political necessity of such compromises have to be considered from a pragmatic point of view. Robert B. Eckles and Richard W. Hale Jr., while discussing the 'collectivist Britain' between the two wars, explain :

> A symbol of a new age coming on the political world was the decline of the Liberal Party and the rise of the Labor Party. The Liberals had been pre-eminently the party of business, *laissez-faire*, and progress. Its platform had only recently turned toward socialization as the way to get progress and reform.[61]

The decision of Asquith during the critical year 1923 to keep Labour in office instead of supporting the Conservatives was on the ground of its unwavering faith in its own principles.

If Jim's inflexible approach to the situation is closely judged bearing in mind the context discussed above, it will become clear that Jim is somewhat of a silly sentimentalist. The very fact that Cary makes Varney, the favourite of Jim, doubt the sensibility and sanity of Jim is a ploy to reveal his own view that such unimaginative men like Jim may stand for the best ideals in life but they are not going to be of any use either to themselves or others. Varney's praise of Chester Nimmo as "the champion of the poor, the voice of a merciful god" (NHM, 93) is worth mention here. Despite Jim's claim that "as a Liberal I had always been against starvation wages anywhere" (NHM, 30), the General Strike terrifies him because "It will finish old England ..." (*Ibid.* 30).

Cary does not fail to bring out the irony of the situation where different leaders pretend to fight for the cause of justice for the poor. Jim's plan of revolution actually worsens the plight of the poor. Cary's view indeed concurs with that of George Orwell in this regard. For Orwell strongly feels that revolution cannot be the answer to the problems. "A revolution starts off with wide diffusion of the ideas of liberty, equality, etc. Then comes the growth of an oligarchy which is as much interested in holding onto its privileges as any other governing class."[62] Through his projection of one small firm called the Potter's, Cary shows the tragic consequences of a revolution. Potter's concern for its workers is genuine but how such firms and their dependents are sacrificed during the strike has been touchingly portrayed in *Not Honour More*. The argument between young Williams and Polly reflects the irony of the situation. Young Williams' view that "the only way to fight capitalism was the strike" (NHM, 122) is strongly refuted by Polly who shows the other side of the situation :

> 'I'm not talking about Frant's. Frant's can stand a strike. But this will finish Potter's off, and finish off the lot of us too. Except you at Frant's. Father's got no complaint against Potter's. He got good pay, and if Potter's shuts down, he'll be done for. He's sixty-four. How can he get another job at sixty-four with all them young chaps wanting work?' (NHM, 122).

Even the old Daddy Cooke becomes a butt of criticism when he tells the young rebels, "All you young chaps looking for trouble.

You say you want a fair deal for the workers but what you really want is war" (NHM, 123). Anyhow, the big leaders are not going to pay any heed to their voice for "It's a small firm and doesn't count much, either for political influence or votes" (NHM, 121) and they also know how to tackle the elements which may come up on their way. Jim is pushed into a position where his vocation prevents him from helping his friend Potter. Jim also gets caught unawares by the Communists who libel Chester and Jim together as "crypto-Fascist" (NHM, 150) and assert that Jim has already been "bought by Nimmo" (*Ibid.*, 150). Brightman addressing the students including Sally, further complicates the situation for Jim who is almost completely cornered. Jim also explains how he is tied down by certain liabilities which do not allow him to prove his honesty.

In the final analysis this novel though not as striking as the other novels in the trilogy, succeeds in providing a valid political commentary on the age. The admiration Sally and her group consisting volunteers have for Brightman as a source of hope and their search of a new leader and a new plan reflect one of the changing trends of the age. Williams and the young chaps with him represent another group. How well Cary has fictionally absorbed and recreated the zeitgeist may be understood in the light of the following observation :

> Liberals rejected the propaganda of the extreme left for colonial liberation by revolution, for intensification of the British class struggle by means of a general strike and for an outright socialist economy as a means of abolishing unemployment : and mass poverty. .... Liberals also rejected the propaganda of the extreme right, still demanding imperial consolidation, a tough line with nationalists in India and Egypt and with trade unionists at home....
>
> Yet both extremes seemed to be making headway between 1921 and 1931.[63]

Jim is astonished at Sally's conviction that "the old muddled England was finished and that a new plan was necessary" (NHM, 144). She also adds that "some of them are for the Fabian plan and some for the Communists. What they all want is a real plan of some kind'" (NHM, 144). The emergence of a new generation with a completely new set of ideas startles Jim, but greater and greater shocks are in store for him when he sees the change in most of the people belonging to the different cross-sections of the society.

> A lot like my niece were going Fascist. Raby, a chap who had been against everything for years, even the war, now came out everywhere about guild socialism which was simply Mussolini with a coat of paint. Some of my specials thought nationalization was the answer. Lots more officials to push more people about.
>
> Old Penrose, chairman of the bench, suddenly told me if it wasn't for the King, he'd go over to the strikers (NHM, 147).

Vicar Shermer's enthusiasm reminds him of the fact that "'... Indeed, the early Christians practised community of goods. Christ even laid it down for the apostles'" (NHM, 148). The confidence that the people have in Communism turns them blind to the seamy side of it though they are aware of it, as exemplified by Digweed, the grocer. He believes that "the Communist atrocities in Russia had been greatly exaggerated" (NHM, 149) and firmly hopes that "Communism in a civilized country like England would be quite a different thing" (NHM, 149). Palto with his dream of a world where "scientists were the aristocracy of the Soviet union" (NHM, 149) completes the circle.

However, in the novel, England proves to be strong enough to resist the temptation offered by the enchanting concepts of Communism and Fascism, may be owing to the maturity and political wisdom of a few people like Chester who rise to the occasion :

> '... the country is slipping into revolution, a revolution it doesn't even want. That nothing can save it now but a national government of all parties. A new government. For this is war. War for the soul of England — the very heart of liberal Europe.... if we threw in our weight with the workers, we could tell

> the Tories to get out,... And make such a revolution the world has never seen — it would transform history....' (NHM, 166).

The development of the conflicts and confrontations between Jim and Chester Nimmo, both at domestic and political levels taking place simultaneously, is rather striking, though it is better reflected in *Prisoner of Grace*. Jim's jealousy of Chester Nimmo as the corrupter of his wife assumes a different shape through his consequent attack of him as the corrupter of humanity as a whole. His struggle apparently becomes more or less a crusade, making him a martyr, though actually it is a little more than an outburst of a frustrated soul. In spite of Jim's contention that politics should not enter family life, it cannot be avoided in his own case. When Bootham comes with the letter from Chester Nimmo to Jim conveying his decision not to have anything more to do with Nina on condition that "Captain Latter undertakes not to proceed against Lord Nimmo in any manner likely to cause prejudice to his good name" (NHM, 133), Jim retorts "I didn't think husbands and wives ought to need political bumf, even if signed in duplicate, to keep their marriage straight" (NHM, 133). Jim is rather disgusted at the very idea of it, for it "simply drags down marriage into politics or business" (NHM, 134).

However, it is the odd relationship between Chester Nimmo and Nina which acts adversely on Jim when he strives to clear himself of the slur thrown upon him when being called a capitalist. Chester Nimmo's deposit of money and jewels in Nina's name after their separation is what precipitates the crisis. Nina has been tossed between the two men, sometimes allowing herself to be tossed and at other times forced by circumstance. Though her constancy can be questioned, she has been consistent in her attitude towards these two men. Her passionate love for Jim remains unabated till the end but her adoration of Chester Nimmo as a man with a cause very often overwhelms her. If her love for Jim enables her to forgive all his weaknesses, her conviction that Chester Nimmo is a saviour, turns her immune to his wangling and 'ratting' on promises. It is here that Nina emerges as an epitome of liberal morality whereas Jim who is obsessed with his hatred for the man Chester Nimmo, becomes blind to the reality around him.

Both Jim and Chester have experienced the power of Nina over them. But Chester has the courage to accept the fact that they cannot really love each other due to their difference in outlook, background and taste. He is prepared to accept her with all her fluctuations, whereas Jim is rather curt and possessive of her. The latter wants to believe that "she was still the gentlest, the kindest, the cleverest woman I'd ever known" (NHM, 137) though his heart knows that "she was as tricky as a set of Japanese boxes" (NHM, 57), as Chester puts it to him. His ego is rather pleased when she tries to kill herself. He remarks that "'She had the truth in her soul — she was ready to die for it'" (NHM, 173). Chester Nimmo though sharing Jim's view, reacts in a different manner : "'Have we killed her between us? Don't tell me its my fault. I know that too well. I am guilty before her and before you and before God ...'" (NHM, 172). Chester Nimmo's feeling for Nina exceeds the limit of politics, though he has undoubtedly used her for his own political gains.

Though the green-eyed monster in Jim is already awakened by his wife's idol-worship of Chester Nimmo, what precipitates the situation, simmering since sometime, is the persecution of Maufe. Jim feels that Maufe is a hero of the finest kind, for his "magnificent action" (NHM, 158) of arresting Pincomb who deliberately incites the crowd, thereby averting a "situation of the highest danger" (NHM, 158) in the dock area. The way in which this case is distorted as a "complaint of unprovoked criminal assault" (NHM, 160) and the shocking realization of the role played by Nina in weakening the evidence of the witness Bell who could have helped Maufe out, strike despair in Jims' heart. The pretence on the part of Chester Nimmo as though it were a mere accident that he was brought inside the Palm Cottage and his "yarn about the phone call to Nina from the Town Hall" (NHM, 171) aggravate the situation and strengthen Jim's suspicion of Chester and Nina. Though the storm outside has subsided, in Jim's heart the battle is still going on, in pursuit of the "*real true everlasting cross-my-heart rock-bottom truth*" (NHM, 191), both in his private and public life. Jim declares that he is living "the lowest form of animal life — an honest freeman" (NHM, 206). In his view Chester Nimmo has to pay for his corruption of the good soul and she has to die for making marriage a political game.

> I say I never loved this sweet woman so much as now when I knew she had to die. Because of the rottenness. Because of the corruption. Because all loyalty was a laugh and there was no more trust. Because marriage was turned into a skin game out of a nice time by safety first. Because of the word made dirt by hypocrites and cowards. Because there was no truth or justice anywhere any more. Because of the grabbers and tapeworms who were sucking the soul out of England (NHM, 220).

It was not a murder but "an execution" (NHM, 223) according to him and he "killed her for an example because it was necessary" (NHM, 222). It is such bombastic statements which betray Jim's conceitedness. He murders Nina when he realizes that everything about his family life has gone beyond his control and there is no way of extricating Nina off Chester Nimmo's spell. If Jim had confessed that he murdered his wife as a deceived husband, his act may be considered as a case of a self-respecting man who esteemed his honour more than his love for Nina. But since he claims that he does it in order to save the honour of the country, the gravity of the action invites serious speculation which will undoubtedly swallow him as its fragile victim. His act of murder raises a serious question, whether shooting or persuading, which way is a better solution to a problem and how far practical it is in each case. Charles Hoffman argues that "The injustice suffered by John Maufe is not erased by the injustice done to Nina and Nimmo; Latter's crusade for honour and truth merely multiplies the fundamental injustice of the world."[64]

Jim's tendency from the beginning to see anything with a jaundiced eye, makes him an inefficient judge of the overall perspective. It may be recalled that Nina, even by mistake, does not seem to remember any mention of Pincomb's fall in Bell's report and her frank statement that she thinks Maufe was guilty and Chester Nimmo was justified in criticizing him, gives an impression that Maufe might not have been an innocent victim.

Cary's failure to give a clear picture of what really has happened may be ascribed to his lack of concentration, as a result of his illness while writing this novel. However, never does he suggest that Jim is a level-headed man who is capable of rational thinking and wise judgement. Jim's instability is evident in the very style of his narration. To use the words of Elizabeth R. Bettman, "Cary catches Latter's incoherent indignation admirably in a staccato telegraphic style perfectly suited to Latter's desperate shut in-feeling."[65] Jim needs a cause in life because he is groggy by nature and the ideal of 'honour' catches his fancy after his failure with the Luga mission in Africa. Unfortunately he can never grasp the essence of it and there lies his weakness. He is only fit to run like a bridled horse to whom a wider world with its vicissitudes does not exist at all, and so he can have only one solution, *i.e.*, to shoot the enemy. "Latter's way leads to madness and murder (the attempted murder of Nimmo and the actual murder of Nina) and to anarchy or dictatorship. Nimmo's way, for all its compromises, expediency and opportunism, is less evil, more free."[66]

Cary is charged by many critics as having no single point of view or any moral focus. But Anthony West holds a different view : "There is nothing wrong with a writer who handles experience from an idiosyncratic point of view, but what Cary has is not a point of view but an enclosure with a high wall of certainty round it."[67] Yet there are some critics like Alan Kennedy and John Teeling, S.J., who hold that there are a few clues built in his novels for his readers. John Teeling, S.J. focuses, for instance, on how Chester Nimmo's life ends in disaster as a childless man.

Cary perceives, like Yeats, the antinomies of politics. He does believe in love and tolerance as the basis of life. But he also regards the people and their welfare as the goal of party politics. Our conclusion therefore may be formulated thus : Cary's prerequisite for happiness is freedom. But he knows, to be sure, that politics is a game in which both the public and private men indulge in, though their arena may differ in scope and range. But the touchstone by which the worth of such acts may be measured is the capacity to exercise one's free will. When the free will is motivated by love and tolerance, it adds grace to one's action though it has a touch of immorality sometimes. Cary's characters, especially his women protagonists, Sara and Nina, are more accommodative in the liberal sense than his men; they are life givers of more than one man in their lives. However they seem to win the admiration of Cary chiefly perhaps on the strength of their steadfast intention to face moments of crisis imaginatively, not yielding to abnegation. Besides making themselves happy, they make others happy. And this calls for flexibility. Cary has countenanced a lot of attack on the ground that his characters are immoral or worse still, amoral. This problem may be set in the context of the tussle between the paradigm of essentialism and a paradigm centred in temporal and historical concerns. Cary is an essentialist in the sense that he is one of the few writers who deals with a much neglected field, "the whole bread-winning aspect of life, the routine, the problems, the clash of personalities, the daily crises of men at work," according to Orville Prescott.[68] However, in infusing his characters with the typical liberal sense of morality, he is also a typical product of his age. Ernest Jones points out that :

> It has been very easy since Fielding and Sterne for English novelists to exalt sound feelings and the good heart over all other virtues. Neither Mr. Cary nor his characters are fooled for a minute by this sort of nonsense. They are protestants in the original sense of the word. Their Protestantism, their rebellion, is of the will which is free.[69]

It is this latent power in men to exercise their free will which can enhance the power of any government, for the government on its own is powerless. In Cary's view, "The best that can be hoped from any government is that it will navigate among unknown rocks and unexpected hurricanes without sinking the ship and drowning the crew."[70] But the tragedy of Cary's time is that people after the crisis of the two World Wars have been desperately searching for some sort of government which can save them from disaster, rejecting freedom as unwanted and useless. As R.W. Noble points out, "Of course, this political trilogy is neither a defence of nor a programme for egalitarian democracy."[71] Jennifer Ramage, examining the political trilogy makes an incisive observation when she points out how long before it was fashionable, Cary was interested in the rise of 'pressure-group democracy' *i.e.*, "one man is not wholly represented by any one pressure group, but can belong to many...." She shows that Cary upholds the system of democracy as an alternative to anarchy or oligarchy because it employs all the 'arts of persuasion' (lobbying, public relations, advertising, media), and the pressure groups use these arts as "alternatives to violence."[72]

Cary, nevertheless, strongly believes in democracy as the most open sort of government which gives the maximum opportunity for the people to exercise their free will. But he is not a millenarian. Not willing to accept the inevitable reality of life, some look for a millennium on earth through one or the other kind of government, but none of them has withstood the test of time whereas the freedom of the will alone has remained undestroyed. Cary notes :

> ... autocracy with a sword is followed by democracy with a cheka; the capitalist with his wage slaves gives way to a minister of production and the concentration camp; but thug, student, minister, each has somewhere a home, and in every home, throughout the centuries in all the world, women ask themselves the question : How shall we ensure peace? How shall love be served?
>
> Their politics are the everlasting politics of love and truth, beauty and cleanness (EL, 216).

It is this power to love which is born of understanding and demands freedom of will to achieve it, which can save the world. Cary's solution, to conclude, is not given in the form of his faith in the efficacy of any single political system but in his rendering of the creed of liberalism as an attitude of the mind. Cary's unshakable belief in the freedom of the will may have led him occasionally to cross the limits of credibility and even decency sometimes, but it is the age in which he lived which is largely responsible for it. The anguish of another famous writer of his age substantiates this view.

> The twentieth century knows more history ... and more psychology, and has suffered more; its disillusion over peace in 1914 has been swiftly followed by its disillusion over democracy today.....And consequently many people do not believe in freedom any more, and the few who do regard it as something that must be discovered, not

> recovered. They think that it is a blessing which we have never possessed upto now.[73]

It does not mean that Cary is not aware of the evils peculiar to a democracy. In his *Republic*, Plato denounces democracy for "never giving a thought to the pursuits which make a statesman, and promoting to honour any one who professes to be the people's friend."[74]

> ...; but that the true pilot must pay attention to the year and seasons and sky and stars and winds, and whatever else belongs to his art, if he intends to be really qualified for the command of a ship, and that he must and will be the steerer, whether other people like or not — the possibility of this union of authority with the steerer's art has never seriously entered into their thoughts or been made part of their calling. How in vessels which are in a state of mutiny and by sailors who are mutineers, how will the true pilot be regarded? Will he not be called a prater, a star-gazer, a good-for-nothing?[75]

Cary answers this question in his novels which are discussed in this chapter. His contention seems to be that people like Chester Nimmo alone can persuade people into action as the situation demands, instead of shooting them if they do not act. The price a people have to pay for this may be both tolerance of the lies and falsities the rulers indulge in, but this forgiving spirit is the starting point of their freedom, as shown earlier. Cary never claims democracy to be the purest form of government but as the best among the lot and his mixed feelings are very well reflected in the following couplets :

> Tyrants hate Truth, death takes them by surprise,
> Hail Democrats, who love the larger lies (TP, 395).
>
> God loves democracy; the proof is plain
> It cannot die; tho' hopelessly insane (TP, 358).

However, it is not the mere study of Cary's political ideology which constitutes the main charm of his works but his realization of the tradition of British thought which is explained by Harold J. Laski as follows :

> Its value is its denial of politics as a science distinct from other human relations; and that is why Adam Smith can write of moral sentiments no less than wealth of nations. The 18th century saw clearly that each aspect of social life must find its place in the political equation.[76]

To conclude, Cary emerges as a successful as well as a significant political novelist mainly by infusing his novels with this spirit of politics, which has always been typical of the British consciousness.

6

'Polyphony' and the Caryan Political Novel

Having considered the wide range and scope of the political novel and in particular, Cary's ambivalent treatment of this volatile subject in the foregoing chapters, it is imperative to discern his calibre as a political writer and to ascertain his position in the arena of the English literary scene.

Joyce Cary's novels, no doubt, fulfil many of the requirements of the orthodox political novel. As Joseph Blotner remarks :

> A political novel invariably reveals the attitude of its author toward the national groups from which its characters come. Often the author may seek to draw a national portrait by describing political behaviour which he believes is particularly characteristic of Spaniards or Greeks or English men.[1]

Cary's novels do not fail to capture the national character of the English, the protestant and nonconformist spirit, though sometimes, in a very subtle manner : "She [England] is the wandering Dutchman, the pilgrim and the scapegoat of the world which flings its sins upon her as the old world heaped its sins upon the friars..." (TP, 498). This may be read as a sentimental exaltation of the Englishman or as an instance of self-irony by a shrewd English author.

The Englishman's and naturally the English writer's unemotional approach to politics, when compared to that of American writers, has been widely discussed by many critics of the genre of the political novel. The extreme radicals rarely appear and revolutionaries are hardly present in English novels, save a few like

Conrad's *The Secret Agent*. Cary is no exception and his novels are scattered with 'conservatives' and 'liberals,' and 'radicals' who differ from them more in degree than in kind. We earlier noted their predicament in the political milieu in which in they lived.

Like any other orthodox political novel, Cary's political fiction is also centered in contemporary events and ethos. The important question of the role of the churches in the British life of the nineteen twenties and the declining religious hold over the people has been one of the pre-occupations of the writers of this age. The emergence of the new thought with its new prophets, Marx, Darwin and Freud, smashing the very base of the Victorian system of values namely religion, in the next generation, gave rise to a set of satirists, like Evelyn Waugh and the Bloomsbury group of writers. The novelists who wrote with a political direction, on the other hand, fell into two main groups. While discussing the line of political thinkers from Plato down to John Dewey, Will Durant explains in a poetic manner the conflict between the individual and the state and the solutions offered by the divided camps in Europe :

> Here is the old vicious cycle; men from institutions and institutions from men; where could change break into the ring? Voltaire and the liberals thought that intellect could break the ring by educating and changing men, slowly and peacefully; Rousseau and the radicals felt that the ring could be broken only by instinctive and passionate action that could break down the old institutions and build, at the dictates of the heart, new ones under which liberty, equality and fraternity would reign. Perhaps the truth lay above the divided camps.[2]

Using this comment to the scene of the English Novel, we find for instance, C.P. Snow, a trained scientist, focusing more on the 'head' whereas D.H. Lawerence laments the slow disappearance of 'fully developed hearts.' Lawrence, in fact, declares that "My great religion is a belief in the blood, the flesh, as being wiser than the intellect."[3] E.M. Forster wistfully murmurs, 'Only Connect' in his Epigraph to *Howards End*. And Cary makes an earnest attempt to seize the 'truth' suggested by Will Durant, 'which lay above the divided camps,' for he acknowledges the mutually enhancing capacity of reason and emotion on the one hand and the individual and the state on the other.

Cary is never fascinated by abstract values which are rather flat and lifeless. And so he upholds pragmatism with its creed of flexibility, adaptability, tolerance and ingenuity, and above all, creative imagination as the basis of both public and private life. When Galsworthy, H.G. Wells and Bernard Shaw had offered Fabian Socialism as the only way of curing the evils of society, Forster and Joyce Cary unhesitatingly affirmed the central tenet of Liberalism, namely the significance of the 'individual' and the sacredness of personal relationship and the private world. Cary emphatically says that "Freedom is the power to gratify frustrated desires, curiosity, ambition, love, family hopes; and in its instinctive, incessant drive for gratification, its everlasting battle with all authority, it has transformed the political world" (SE, 217). And only that type of Government which can satisfy this basic urge in man for freedom, can in the long run survive. As a true disciple of John Stuart Mill, Cary rates the democratic form of government as the best kind of all, mainly on account of the importance it attaches to human personality. As a realistic thinker, Cary, like Forster, does not regard democracy as the ideal form of government, for he knows its inadequacies as well. At the same time, in his view democracy with all its defects, postulates personal freedom. Moreover it contains within it the seeds of dissolution and decay, as well as life and progress, and as such better suited to the human temperament and the nature of our life than any other system. Cary's perception of the dialectics of democratic ideology and machinery is again dialogic because it admits warring claims both by characters and by their critics, discussed earlier in this book.

It may be remembered here that Cary continued to emphasize democracy even during and after the period which saw a stout reaction against democracy (1918-39) and when dictatorships became the order of the day. The toppling of the Liberal government in Italy and the setting up of the Fascist dictatorship in 1922 and Germany's replacement of the Republican government by the Nazi dictatorship in 1933 along with the rise of dictators in Spain, Portugal and Yugoslavia, appeared totally to undermine the Western intellectuals' faith in democratic principles. Some who had been under the wrong impression that democracy and peace were synonymous, sought other forms of government as their refuge, but not Cary. He boldly declared that autocracy and dictatorships have to yield to democracy at one stage or the other, for "The people of the world are bent on liberty, and that in their minds democracy is the only kind of government that can secure their liberty" (SE, 270). The experimentation with democracy which is at its initial stage in the post-Communist Russia in the 1990's has been witnessing the kind of disintegration which Cary visualized as the fate of any autocracy.

Cary had also the burning conviction to declare the value of international organizations for peace when there was a strong sense of resentment towards international law, especially in America, and there was a growing disappointment even among those who relied on such Leagues before the World Wars. E.M. Forster, spells out his loss of hope in world organizations in the essay, "What I believe." But Cary explains how "the United Nations has replaced the League of Nations when the latter failed to achieve its purpose and all this organization, driven by increasing pressures of urgency, grows steadily in comprehensiveness and power."[4] He declares :

> World affairs have a direction and it is towards a general world law, and world peace. It can be checked but it is not to be reversed. And the effect of any check, like that of Hitler war, is to dam and build up the force behind, until it breaks through and rushes forward with still greater speed and weight.[5]

Cary's exploration of the religious appeal of politics and the political appeal of religion, makes him stand out distinctly in the galaxy of modern British political writers. Joseph Blotner makes an assessment when he observes that "when the Englishman does allow emotion to surge into his politics, it may be mixed with religion."[6] The poignancy of Cary's novels lies in the religious zeal with which he speaks about the political behaviour of man. Kinley Robey, has gone to the extent of placing Cary in the tradition of Langland and John Bunyan saying that "William Blake, Bunyan, Langland, and others of their kind wrote out of conviction that they had encountered the truth and were God-bound to reveal it."[7]

The attempt made in the foregoing chapters to estimate Cary as a political novelist has shown that his merit lies mainly in his skill in preventing his novels from becoming a mere monological record of history or a literary thesis on Imperialism or Liberalism. His refusal to treat his subjects neither exclusively in a centrifugal nor in a centripetal manner compels our attention. Cary's works, in fact, stand to gain much, if they are read in the 'dialogic' perspective, as advocated especially by the currently popular fiction theorist Mikhail Bakhtin.

In Bakhtin's view, the novel is the only genre which allows enough latitude for the writer to juxtapose several world-views about one particular idea, message or event, thereby shaping cultural history. Some writers, whether consciously or unconsciously, have introduced certain techniques in their novels which pose complex questions, in other words, challenges to the readers and critics. These writers do not intend to utter the final word because "...nothing conclusive has yet taken place in the world, the ultimate word of the world and about the world has not yet been spoken, the world is open and free, everything is still in the future, and will always be in the future."[8] They believe that they would rather not offer any solution to a given issue but just participate in the process of speech communication which carries the ideology within it. Cary belongs to the above group of writers. In being so, he has indeed incurred the displeasure of the readers and critics alike, especially those who have been moulded by the unitary notion of literature, language, society as well as 'power.' Cary's world view is 'dialogic' and hence he is unwilling to be confined to one strand of ideas. Cary has, indeed, skilfully exploited the genre of the political novel to express his dialogic perspective of life, both private and public, by rendering it as, "another speech in another language ('heteroglossia' *i.e.*, variety of social languages) serving to express authorial intentions but in a refracted way," to use the words of Bakhtin. Bakhtin goes on to say, significantly, "Such speech constitutes a special type of *double-voiced discourse*.....In such discourse there are two voices, two meanings and two expressions....Double voiced discourse is always internally dialogic."[9] When viewed in this light we can understand how Cary arrived at his complex perception of politics as embedded in history as determined by power relation. Cary resists, if not overcomes, his temptation to discover a single political vision, unlike writers like Benjamin Disraeli, C.P. Snow, Aldous Huxley and George Orwell.

Cary has no intention of writing novels to vindicate the claims of any political party as is the case with Disraeli, the pioneer of the political novel form in England. Disraeli himself has made his position clear in the preface to the fifth edition of *Coningsby* :

> The main purpose of its writer was to vindicate the just claims of the Tory party to be the popular political confederation of the country....It was not originally the intention of the writer to adopt the form of fiction as the instrument to scatter his suggestions, but, after reflection, he resolved to avail himself of a method which, in the temper of the times, offered the best chance of influencing opinion.

Disraeli, a true believer in conservatism, with his natural flair for writing, successfully arrives at a unitary notion of a revitalised Tory Party in his Young England Trilogy, comprising *Coningsby, Sybil* and *Tancred*.

Aldous Huxley and George Orwell, on the other hand, use fiction more as a platform for making their passionate appeal for human liberty by painting a gory picture of the Totalitarian State in their distopias. Orwell's pungent political satires *Animal Farm* and *Nineteen Eighty-Four* and Huxley's *Brave New World* undoubtedly exhibit the authors' brilliant journalistic acumen marked by an extraordinary power of clarity and vigour. At the same time, they also confirm their relative lack of 'historical perspective.' According to Tom Hopkinson, "He [Orwell] saw the world of his day with peculiar intensity because he saw extremely little of its past, and he regarded the future as simply a continuation and extension of the particular present which he knew."[10] Huxley, when compared to Orwell, turns out to be more optimistic and less biased. However, he too cannot resist the temptation to totalize the present, ignoring the temporality of history. The single aim of Huxley and Orwell, as in the case of Disraeli, is to use their novels as political instruments, displaying their unitary notion of power.

C.P. Snow, with whom Cary is generally compared, excels in focusing on a particular aspect of a political act of a particular kind. His famous novel, *The Affair*, captures the misfiring of justice in a Cambridge college. The whims and fancies of men and their arbitrary decisions which topple a man who seemed to have every chance of survival a short time ago, form the core of the novel. In *Corridors of Power*, Snow introduces an excellent Whitehall diplomat and the intricate process of the working of human psyche behind the scene, precipitating major political events. Cary is, no doubt, more akin to C.P. Snow in the adoption of a comparatively traditional narrative form, but the similarity stops there. For, "He [Cary] does not pursue one thesis like Snow, but showers us with hot fragments."[11] Moreover, Cary's novels are not concerned with the *Polis* in its simplistic sense.

What one finds in common among the above mentioned writers brought in for a comparison with Cary, is their preference for a monological discourse, confining themselves to the logic of a restrictive sort where there is only one opinion. But Cary has allowed the coexistence of several discourses within a single discourse of the novel, in spite of being himself a liberal by conviction and an ardent supporter of Democracy as a political system. Cary has been widely regarded as an exponent of Liberalism both as a popular creed and as a political ideology. But what distinguishes him from scores of political writers of Liberal persuasion is his tacit acknowledgment of the text as 'a competing centre of cultural powers.' Cary is bold enough to allow in his works the unpleasant aspects and the inadequacies of Liberalism to come into play. The novels also reflect, how well he has captured the changing contours of its reception since the Victorian times. It is here that Cary's choice of a controversial character like Chester Nimmo, ironically enough, to embody the spirit of Liberalism, demands our attention. A reading of Cary's political trilogy in the light of some of the insights provided by Bakhtin on the dialogic novel confirms the analysis offered in the earlier chapters. Special mention must be made of Bakhtin's concepts of the 'carnivalesque' and 'subversion' for a fruitful application of his model of reading to Cary.

The two opposing ideologies of Liberalism and Fascism as

represented by Chester and Jim with their credos 'freedom' and 'honesty' respectively, are always shown in tension in the Second Trilogy. Both Chester and Jim claim to have led exemplary political as well as personal lives. Bakhtin says,

> The activity of a character is always ideologically demarcated, he lives and acts in an ideological world of his own (and not in the unitary world of the epic), he has his own perception of the world that is incarnated in his action and in his discourse.[12]

However, in the process of depicting the greatness of Chester, Liberal ideology stands subverted at various instances by the 'honest' Jim and his passionate plea for a corruption-free political life. It may be recalled here that several subversions of this kind, discernible at all levels, have been highlighted in the earlier chapters. Cary's novels, especially the African novels and the political trilogy, are resplendent with 'carnivals' *i.e.*, the playful toppling of hierarchy where characters are seen flouting the stability of order. While Bakhtin discusses the concept of carnival, he explains how 'carnival' allows, "a special type of communication [which is] impossible in everyday life" :

> All the symbols of the carnival idiom are filled with this pathos of change and renewal, with the sense of the gay relativity of prevailing truths and authorities. We find here a characteristic logic, the peculiar logic of the 'in side out' ..., of the 'turnabout,' of a continual shifting from top to bottom, from front to rear, of numerous parodies and travesties, humiliations, profanations, comic crownings and uncrownings.[13]

For instance, in *An American Visitor*, the defender of Birri is finished off by Birri men and the exploiter Cottee restores normalcy. In *The African Witch*, the rational Aladai is vanquished by the witch Elizabeth. In *Mister Johnson* the title itself has an aspect of 'carnival,' for after all Johnson is a simple man who serves an English Officer as a clerk. But he triumphs in the end by making his master shoot him, thereby conferring glory on him. In *Prisoner of Grace* on the other hand, Chester undergoes a different kind of treatment in the hands of his wife Nina. Chester who appears to be God-like in one instance evokes pity like a baby and terror like a devil in Nina, who finally ends up with a complex portrayal of her husband who is the Liberal War-Minister.

Cary is dealing with a grim political world where various contradictory forces are to be reckoned with. Hence, there is a collision of several ideas at various levels, but rarely accompanied by explicit authorial commentaries. He assumes 'silence' and it has been misinterpreted by many critics. In the poetics of Bakhtin, silence becomes a 'part of carnival.'[14] and it can assume many forms of expression like 'reduced laughter' as in the case of Cary.

When the author allows the characters to have free will, the question of 'power' arises. In Cary's world, power is not only institutional but is also in the individual and it becomes political in its inclusive sense. It is significant to note how the shifting power structures present an interesting site in Cary's novels. In order to achieve his purpose, Cary has gone quite far, adopting the best modes of fiction wherever he found them, starting from the picaresque tradition of Defoe to the social novels of the nineteenth century and that of the Georgian symbolists. However, his deviation from the 'structure of a cobweb,' characteristic of the modernist novelists, has led some critics to classify him as a traditionalist along with C.P. Snow and treat him slightly if not slightingly as an old fashioned realist. The reason behind this misconception of the author lies in his reluctance to cast his views into a monological discourse, despite his affinities for traditional fictional techniques. In other words, his modernity lies in his approach rather than in the narrative forms he adopts in his novels. For instance, his use of the trilogy form is better understood within the framework of a dialogic mode of representation. This form gives him scope for using the method of layering-that is, the recurrence of characters, a few kernel situations viewed from varying perspective leading to versions, layered one upon the other, sometimes in all the three novels, sometimes not. (*e.g.*, Nina's murder by Jim, Nina's adultery as viewed by Chester Nimmo and Jim and Chester's machinations). The deft handling of the trilogy form enables Cary to analyze in a dialogic manner the worthiness of a given system which operates in politics. It helps him to avoid some of the limitations of the multiple-point-of-view narration. In the modernist kaleidoscopic or multiple-point-of-view narration, a central object is metaphysically scrutinized, giving importance to the epistemological process. This method is effective in writing 'introverted' or 'lyrical' novels. But Cary's conception of history as the history of a people's consciousness adds a new dimension to the trilogy form. A political trilogy on 'pressure group democracy,' as noted by Jennifer Ramage (Vide Chapter V), is a rare achievement in the history of English fiction.

Again Cary's guilt-free, objective approach to the subject of colonialism is better understood in the light of all that we have said above. He does not belong to the group of Imperialists headed by Kipling who finds the natives the 'white man's burden' and idealises the entire "rank and file of those who...maintained an empire through dust and heat, bringing...beneficent rule to 'new caught, sullen peoples, Half devil and half child.'[15] At the same time, his plight is not that of the Liberal humanists like E.M. Forster and George Orwell who suffer from 'white man's guilt.' Cary has no doubts about the liberating power of Britain. His conviction that Englishmen have enlarged the potential for freedom among the colonized by exposing them to civilization, checks him from nourishing any kind of feeling of guilt like Forster or Orwell has towards India (which included Burma where Orwell served). At the same time, Cary does not revel in his novels in the portrayal of 'Poor Africa' turned to paradise by white man's entrance into the Dark Continent. On the contrary he unflinchingly presents the muddle 'civilization' and Western culture have created in the life of an antithetical people. In Molly Mahood's view, Cary "found relief from guilt, not in kicking against the pricks with Orweil and Woolf, but in developing a historical perspective that allowed him to see the colonial intrusion as an inevitable disturbance in a world of continual change."[16] However, Cary's bold declaration in *The Case for African Freedom* (1941) that "the worst exploitation of native labour, all over the world, in Africa, India, China has been by native employers the worst oppressors of the African people have been their own native rulers"(12) seems to offset Molly Mahood's view that "Guilt is also a recognizable element in Joyce Cary's *Mister Johnson*."[17]

It may be pointed out here that Cary has by-passed the atrocities and the repressive measures of at least some white administrators and traders which led to the victimization of the innocent, ignorant natives. If at all the British officers in his African novels have been guilty of anything, it is only their apathy and indifference towards the natives. This inability in Cary to see the horrors caused by the white men along with the blessedness they brought to the native land, robs his liberal humanism of its humanity when compared to E.M. Forster or George Orwell. However, he remains a 'typical Briton' who "feels in fact, even when he hardly recognizes his own convictions or their source, that man is essentially an individual, and that as an individual he has a unique claim to individual consideration" (SE, 219). There is no gainsaying the fact that Cary has always been considerate towards the worth of an 'individual' whether he is an African or English. Whereas writers like Forster treat places like Italy and India for instance, not merely as places but as congeries of mysterious notions and values rendering them as menacing symbolic suggestions, Cary has treated the natives more as real living people, though the temptation to indulge in metaphorical connotation is reflected to some extent in *Aissa Saved* and *The African Witch*.

It is this unwavering interest in the individual which impels Cary to go deep into the political conditions which can be more conducive to the enlargement of human potential. Wilfred Stone points out that E.M.Forster and D.H.Lawrence were "prophetic vitalists opposed to the machine age; both were pagans haunted by Christianity, trying to discover in the forms of the creative imagination a new vision of the whole."[18] Joyce Cary is also a prophetic vitalist like them and his staff too is creative imagination. But the source of his philosophy is Protestant Nonconformism. Moreover, Cary does not share the sentiment of D.H. Lawrence towards civilization that it is the source of all evil. It is the contact with the Englishmen, the harbingers of civilization to Fada which inspires Johnson's artistic imagination. Cary's closeness to the real living tribal men during his career as a political officer in Nigeria and his first-hand knowledge of the unfelt sorrows and unheard agonies of the natives, unlike in the case of E.M. Forster who had only a slender chance of getting to know the Indians, impels him to resist the temptation to be overwhelmed by the apparent charm of the vitalistic tribal people. Cary's African novels, save *Mister Johnson*, do not abound in scenes, exhibiting vitality in Lawrentian sense, but on the other hand, visualize, how the Africans crave for civilization. Johnson is no doubt presented as an embodiment of the intensity of life, but Cary's main concern is to show how this original creative artist should have led a more constructive, vital life, had he been better educated and more civilized. Unlike D.H.Lawrence who believes that modern civilization threatens to repress the 'consciousness,' other than mental, Cary emphasizes that while the 'power' in man to create imaginatively cannot be suppressed by external forces, it can be enhanced if placed in a more congenial atmosphere. Sara, Lucy, Bridget, and above all Johnson and Gully Jimson who live more intensely than others, bear this truth out. The way the individual autonomy of these characters has been preserved against the violent, external forces, may confer on Cary the title of the celebrant of individual autonomy but not that of Life Force as claimed by some critics.

The main reason behind the above criticism may be traced to Cary's obsession with people with a peculiar temperament, described by William James thus : "the healthy-minded temperament, the temperament which has a constitutional incapacity for prolonged suffering, and in which the tendency to see things optimistically is like a water of crystallization in which the individual's character, is set."[19] William James further explains how this temperament becomes the basis for a particular type of religion and says that, though it was common in the Romish Church, "even in Protestantism they have been abundant enough; and in its recent 'liberal' development of Unitarianism and latitudinarianism generally, minds of this order have played and still are playing leading and constructive parts."[20] It is worth mentioning here that the above-mentioned book has been one of the chief sources of inspiration for Cary and his most popular characters belong to the type described here by James. In his novel, *To be a Pilgrim*, such characters have been effectively pitted against characters like Edward and Tom Wilcher, men with adequate political and social consciousness. But what is striking about Cary's characterization is that, till the end, the author rarely gives an indication of his partiality for any particular character. Here we find dialogism operating at the level of characterization.

Bakhtin in his discussion of Dostoevsky emphasizes the significance of the "plurality of independent and unmerged voices and consciousnesses" in a polyphonic novel. In his view "a genuine polyphony... unfolds not a multitude of characters and fates in a single objective world, illuminated by single authorial consciousness; rather a plurality of consciousness, with equal rights and with its own world, combined but not merged in the unity of the event."[21] We cannot say for certain that a conservative remains in Cary's fiction conservative all through or for that matter a radical maintains his subversive spirit till the end. The same ambivalence is reflected in the case of his treatment of women characters especially. The female characters, who are basically 'nest-builders,' ironically turn out to be the creators of policies and policy makers. Nina and others are obviously averse to politics. But willy nilly they are drawn into the vortex of it. Of course even Nina plays the perfectly conservative role of the woman behind a successful man. But Cary does not shrink from presenting the innate shrewdness and self-interest with which she subverts an accepted situation to gain mastery. Cary has excelled in powers of androgyny in unravelling the mystery of the female psyche.

The close examination of the Second Trilogy makes it clear that there is no defining male voice and the struggle between Nina and Chester is a clash of equals. Being a strategist by herself, she refuses to be treated as the constructed 'other.' Cary's treatment of women beginning with his powerful depiction of the African Witch Elizabeth Aladai followed by Sarah, Lucy and Nina hint at Cary's ambivalence towards the changing image and status of women. If the women characters of the First Trilogy typify maternal feminism and commodity feminism in various forms, Elizabeth stands out in her triumphant displacement of male power. On the other hand, in the Second Trilogy, we find Cary very effectively maintaining an equilibrium between male space and female space.

One may hear several voices speaking simultaneously in Cary's novels. It is this simultaneity of several dialogues which leads to a larger polyphony of social and discursive forces which Bakhtin calls "heteroglossia" that makes Cary's novels polyphonous. The heteroglossia is present not only in the art of characterization but more centrally in Cary's pitching the very ideology of Liberalism at the centre of his novels discussed here. In one sense the inherent dialectics of Liberalism itself generates heteroglossic possibilities.

The liberals of the twenties were repelled by the approach of the extreme Leftists with their idea of colonial liberation and achievement of equality through revolution. And equally abhorrent to them was the attitude of the extreme Rightists who continued to cling to the concept of Imperial consolidation by ruthlessly dealing with the nationalists, whether in India or in Ireland. The predicament of the mature, wise liberal of the day was itself potentially protean. For he was required to be at one moment a nationalist, at another an imperialist, at yet another a colonist, and still further a humanist. The shifting demands made on the ideology by the times reflected on the man who held on to the creed.

The anguish of Harry Jarvis in *Castle Corner* is that of the author too. But it is tempered by the realization that nationalism and racialism are insurmountable natural feelings in every man. Indians and Africans as well as the other colonized people will not acknowledge the beneficent nature of the British rule, for men are primarily nationalists. With a tinge of pain, Cary seems to accept the fact that the constructions of otherness, (in post-colonial terminology) stand in the way of a proper unbiased appraisal of the colonizer by the colonized. Cary explains that nationalism is an 'idea' because

> it has no basis in any real difference. All North Europe, from Shannon to Danzig, is the same racial mixture. Africa has much more variety of race and colour, so has India. But North Europe is a dozen national units; Africans and Indians talk and think of their continent as one. It is the name that matters, the symbols, the embodied idea. Men live by such symbols, such ideas, whether political or religious, and die joyfully for a word or a flag (SE, 245-46).

Cary is sensitive to the emotive power "of personal pride, ambition, and distrust of the stranger-feelings very easily worked up by a demagogue into arrogance and hatred, fear and revenge" (SE, 245). Cary lived long enough to see Europe torn to pieces by the human tendency to feel in terms of symbols, as he anticipated. Unlike Voltaire who hated war as the greatest of all crimes (since very often the crime is coloured with a seeming concern for justice), and was rather apathetic towards nationalists, Cary is fully aware of the magic of both war and nationalism. It is his sense of nationalism which makes him feel elated to see the triumph of Britain, but surprisingly, he extends the same prerogative to the Africans as well as to the other colonized people. This is the source of the conflicts and contradictions in his African novels. And this can be accounted for only by an appeal to the Bakhtinian notion of heteroglossia.

We discussed in Chapter II at some length why Cary held Blake in veneration because for him the individual soul's freedom was precious and a pre-condition for creation. One of the best modern exponents of Blake, Northrope Frye observes : "What Blake demonstrates is the sanity of genius and the madness of the commonplace mind, and it is here that he has something very apposite to say to the twentieth century with its interest in the arts of neurosis and the politics of paranoia."[22] Cary's appeal to the twentieth century readers is of the same order. Cary, in one sense, brought the dialectics of Blakean vision to bear upon his understanding of the dialogic nature of politics. Hence, he was able to give a new intellectual framework for the genre of the political novel.

NOTES

CHAPTER 1 : THE CASE FOR CARY

1. Morris Edmund Speare, p. IX.
2. *Ibid.*, p. 23.
3. Joseph L. Blotner, p. 1.
4. Irving Howe, p. 17.
5. Vide SE.
6. Morroe Berger, p. 82.
7. Michael Wilding, p. 5.
8. Harish Trivedi, p. V.
9. Joyce Cary, Prefatory Essay in *Prisoner of Grace*, p. 5.
10. Joyce Cary, Prefatory Essay in *The African Witch*, p. 309.
11. In this book, Foster had laid special emphasis on men and matters influencing Cary's writing.
12. The works of Barbara Fisher (1980, 1986) are the outcome of the great pains she had taken over a long period to equip the readers with the relevant material collected from various sources not easily accessible to scholars, especially those working in places outside England.
13. Frederick Karl, p. 195.
14. A.C. Ward, p. 84.
15. G.S. Fraser, p. 167.
16. Vide Chapter III.
17. Andrew Wright, "A Note on Joyce Cary's Reputation," p. 207.
18. *Ibid.*, p. 209.
19. Anon. *Time*, p. 46.
20. Michael Wilding, p. 16.
21. Max Cosman, p. 598.
22. M. Foster, *Joyce Cary : A Biography*, p. 453.
23. G.D.H. Cole, p. 17.
24. J.A. Morris, pp. 17-18.
25. Interview with John Burrow and Alex Hamilton, p. 50.

26. Robert Boyers, p. 28.

CHAPTER 2 : THE PHILOSOPHICAL AND POLITICAL BASIS OF CARY'S IDEOLOGY

1. David Daiches, p. 207.
2. Basil Willey, p. 16.
3. Thomas R. Edward, p. 38.
4. "My Religious History," Preliminary draft, Cary Collection. Cited from M. Foster, *Joyce Cary : A Biography*, p. 34.
5. Immanuel Kant, p. 58.
6. Interview with John Burrow and Alex Hamilton, p. 56.
7. *Ibid.*, p. 11.
8. OC Box 233. Cited from Hazard Adams, *Joyce Cary's Trilogies*, p. 9.
9. William Blake, "The Marriage of Heaven and Hell," p. 152.
10. William Blake, "A Vision of the Last Judgement," p. 615.
11. Northrop Frye, p. 24.
12. William Blake, "Jerusalem" III, p. 709.
13. K.D. Sethna, p. 149.
14. William Blake, "Jerusalem" II, p. 663.
15. William Blake, "A Vision of the Last Judgement," p. 605.
16. Michael Echeruo, *Joyce Cary and the Dimensions of Order,* p. 72.
17. *Ibid.*, p. 74.
18. Spinoza, pp. 167-68.
19. *Ibid.*, p. 157.
20. Spinoza, p. 125.
21. "The Split Mind of the West." Cited from M. Foster, *Joyce Cary : A Biography*, pp. 285-86.
22. Hazard Adams, "Reappraisals : Joyce Cary's Swimming Swan," p. 237.
23. Interview with John Burrow and Alex Hamilton, pp. 52-53.
24. M. Foster, *Joyce Cary : A Biography*, pp. 277-78.
25. Cited from D.J. Manning, p. 18.
26. Cited from E.K. Bramsted and K.J. Melhuish, eds., p. 4.
27. John Stuart Mill, p. 51.
28. *Ibid.*, p. 53.
29. M. Foster, *Joyce Cary : A Biography*, p. 308.
30. Foreword, E.K. Bramsted and K.J. Melhuish, eds.
31. Cited from D.J. Manning, p. 17.

32. Private letter (16 November 1948). Cited from M. Foster *Joyce Cary : A Biography*, p. 292.
33. Cited from E.K. Bramsted and K.J. Melhuish, eds., p. 128.
34. Cited from Will Durant, p. 260.
35. M. Foster, *Joyce Cary : A Biography*, p. 106.
36. Pierre — Joseph Proudhon, p. 57.
37. M. Foster, "Fell of the Lion : Fleece of the Sheep," p. 260.
38. "Interview with John Burrow and Alex Hamilton," pp. 50-51.
39. Henry Bergson, p. 107.
40. *Ibid.*, p. 109.
41. Cited from Will Durant, p. 21.
42. Joyce Cary, "The Sources of Tension in America," p. 35.
43. *Ibid.*
44. Ian Bradley, pp. 65-66.
45. Cited from M. Foster, *Joyce Cary : A Biography*, pp. 309-10.
46. Cited from Barbara Fisher, Joyce Cary, *The Writer and His Theme*, pp. 2-3.
47. 'M.S. Cary 250/N.16, fol.2' from Barbara Fisher, *Joyce Cary : The Writer and His Theme*, p. 6.

CHAPTER 3 : WHITE IMPERIALISM AND THE 'NOBLE SAVAGE'

1. Emmanuel Obiechina, p. 20.
2. 'M.S. Cary 268/S.5. E a. JC.' Cited from Barbara Fisher, *Joyce Cary : The Writer and His Theme*, p. 139.
3. E.K. Bramsted and K.J. Melhuish, eds.,p. 284.
4. John Stuart Mill, p. 127.
5. Robert Bloom, p. 39.
6. S.H. Kanu, p. 43.
7. Molly Mahood, *Joyce Cary's Africa*, pp. 125-26.
8. *Ibid.*, p. 129.
9. William Van O' Cannor, p. 19.
10. Malcolm Foster, *Joyce Cary : A Biography*, p. 318.
11. Molly Mahood, *Joyce Cary's Africa*, p. 191.
12. S.H. Kanu, p. 44.
13. Kinley E. Robey, p. 20.
14. Barbara Fisher, *Joyce Cary : The Writer and His Theme*, pp. 162-63.
15. R.W. Noble, p. 14.

16. S.H. Kanu, p. 54.
17. R.W. Noble, p. 15.
18. Dennis Hall, p. 32.
19. Malcolm Foster, *Joyce Cary : A Biography*, p. 293.
20. Dennis Hall, p. 27.
21. Charles Hoffman, *Joyce Cary : the Comedy of Freedom*, p. 22.
22. S.H. Kanu, p. 48.
23. *Ibid.*, p. 51.
24. Joyce Cary, Prefatory Essay in *An American Visitor*, p. 10.
25. William Van O'Connor, p. 18.
26. Michael Echeuro, *Joyce Cary and the Novels of Africa*, p. 44.
27. Charles Hoffman, "Joyce Cary' African Novel : There is a War on", p. 237.
28. George Steinbrecher, p. 390.
29. Molly Mahood, *Joyce Cary's Africa*, p. 148.
30. Andrew Wright, *Joyce Cary : A Preface to His Novels*, p. 60.
31. Virginia U. Ola, p. 95.
32. Molly Mahood, *Joyce Cary's Africa*, p. 162.
33. Cited from S.H. Kanu, p. 39.
34. Emmanuel Obiechina, p. 22.
35. Virginia U. Olo, p. 97.
36. George Steinbrecher Jr., p. 390.
37. Joyce Cary, Prefatory Essay in *Castle Corner*, p. 8.
38. B.R. Smith, p. 10.
39. William Van O'Connor, p. 22.
40. R.W. Noble, p. 32.
41. Molly Mahood, *Joyce Cary's Africa*, p. 170.
42. Ngugi Wa Thiong'o, p. 92.
43. Frederick Karl, p. 189.
44. Arnold Kettle, p. 165.
45. J.Z. Kronenfeld, pp. 70-71.
46. Robert Bloom, pp. 58-59.
47. K.K. Sharma, p. 35.
48. Anon, "Cheerful Protestant," p. 48.
49. Kinley Robey, p. 29.
50. Joyce Cary, "The Idea of Progress," pp. 334-35.
51. Chinua Achebe, "Named for Victoria, Queen of England," p. 70.
52. Molly Mahood, *Joyce Cary's Africa*, p. 79.

53. Robert M. Wren, p. 50.
54. Frantz Fanon, *Black Skin White Masks*, p. 47.
55. *Ibid*., p. 60.
56. Chineua Achebe, "Named for Victoria, Queen of England," p. 70.
57. *Ibid*., pp. 67-68.
58. D.R.C.R. Goonetilleke, p. 102.

CHAPTER 4 : WHITE IMPERIALISM AND THE CELTIC PEASANT

1. W.B. Yeats, p. 118.
2. Dennis Hall, p. 44.
3. Joyce Cary, Prefatory Essay in Castle Corner, p. 5.
4. Robert B. Eckles and Richard W. Hale, Jr., p. 109.
5. R.W. Noble, p. 25.
6. William Van O'Connor, p. 31.
7. Barbara Fisher, *Joyce Cary : The Writer and His Theme*, p. 182.
8. James Simmons, p. 147.
9. Enid Starkie, pp. 126-27.
10. Barbara Fisher, *Joyce Cary : The Writer and His Theme*, p. 175.
11. Matthew Arnold, "The Nadir of Liberalism," *Essays, Letters and Reviews*, p. 272.
12. William Blake, "Jerusalem III, p. 689.
13. Paul Arthur, p. 10.
14. *Ibid*.
15. Charles Hoffman, "They want to be happy, Joyce Cary's Unfinished Castle Corner Series," p. 218.
16. Alan Bullock and Maurice Shock, eds., pp. 106-7.
17. *Ibid*., p. 231.
18. Ian Watt, p. 156.
19. *Ibid*., p. 158.
20. Burbara Fisher, *The House as a Symbol : Joyce Cary and 'The Turkish House*,' p. 53.

CHAPTER 5 : THE LIBERAL DILEMMA

1. Ian Bradley, p. 29.
2. Joyce Cary, "Three New Prefaces," p. 12.
3. Michael Bell, ed., pp. 95-96.
4. Anon, "Cheerful Protestant," p. 51.

5. Fred Stockholder, p. 237.
6. Charles Hoffman, *Joyce Cary : The Comedy of Freedom*, p. 84.
7. Andrew Wright "A Note on Joyce Cary's Reputation," p. 208.
8. Andrew Wright, *Joyce Cary : A Preface to His Novels*, p. 121.
9. Charles Hoffman, *Joyce Cary : The Comedy of Freedom*, p. 81.
10. The historical truth of how Edwardian young men and women in general viewed their Victorian inheritance with suspicion and disgust is highlighted in *The Twentieth Century* Mind, Vol. I.
11. Enid Starkie, p. 112.
12. George Steinbrecher, p. 392.
13. Edward Galligan, p. 585.
14. Cornelia Cook, pp. 115-16.
15. John Ruskin, *Sesame and Lilies,* p. 29.
16. Eckles and Hale, pp. 699-700.
17. Sidney Monas, p. 469.
18. Randall Stevenson, p. 103
19. Interview with John Burrow and Alex Hamilton, p. 55.
20. Ian Bradley, p. 68.
21. Sidney Monas, pp. 468-69.
22. Aldous Huxley, *Brave New World Revisited*, p. 50.
23. Quoted in Malcolm Foster, *Joyce Cary : A Biography*, p. 450.
24. Ernest Barker, p. 10.
25. Elizabeth R. Bettman, p. 266.
26. Cecil David, "The Novelist at Work," p. 18.
27. Elizabeth Janeway, p. 5.
28. Joyce Cary's radio talk, 1957 qtd. by Cornelia Cook, p. 186.
29. Giles Mitchell, p. 267.
30. Charles Hoffman, "Joyce Cary : Art and Reality," p. 278.
31. Michael Echeruo, *Joyce Cary and the Dimensions of Order*, p. 99.
32. Barbara Fisher, *Joyce Cary : The Writer and His Theme*, p. 270.
33. Cornelia Cook, p. 188.
34. Dennis Hall, p. 111.
35. Hazard Adams, *Joyce Cary's Trilogies*, p. 160.
36. George Watson, pp. 161-62.
37. Cornelia Cook, p. 189.
38. Malcolm Foster, *Joyce Cary : A Biography*, p. 479.
39. Cited from Michael Rosenthal, p. 338.

40. Robert Bloom, p. 198.
41. Cited from Andrew Wright, *Joyce Cary : A Preface to His Novel*, p. 154.
42. Joyce Cary, Prefatory Essay in *Prisoner of Grace*, p. 5.
43. E.K. Bramsted and K.J. Melhuish, eds., p. 677.
44. Michael Echeruo, *Joyce Cary and the Dimension of Order*, p. 109.
45. Alan Kennedy, p. 180.
46. Aldous Huxley, *Brave New World Revisited*, p. 65.
47. Malcolm Foster, *Joyce Cary : A Biography*, p. 487.
48. Golden Larsen, p. 190.
49. S.H. Kanu, pp. 233-34.
50. Barbara Fisher, *Joyce Cary : The Writer and His Theme*, p. 292.
51. Cornelia Cook, p. 211.
52. Barbara Fisher, *Joyce Cary : The Writer and His Theme*, p. 281.
53. Broadcast on "Political Novel" quoted by Malcolm Foster, *Joyce Cary : A Biography*, p. 492.
54. *Ibid.*, p. 489.
55. *Ibid.*
56. Cited from Andrew Wright, "A Note Joyce Cary's Reputation," p. 208.
57. Ian Bradley, p. 71.
58. Michael Echeruo, *Joyce Cary and the Dimensions of Order*, pp. 128-29.
59. R.W. Noble, p. 93.
60. George Steinbrecher Jr., p. 395.
61. Robert B. Eckles and Richard W. Hale, p. 663.
62. 'War-time Diary,' 24 June 1940. *The Collected Essays, Journalism and Letters of George Orwell*, Vol.II, p. 355.
63. Fred Reid, p. 121.
64. Charles Hoffman, *Joyce Cary : The Comedy of Freedom*, p. 154.
65. Elizabeth R. Bettman, p. 271.
66. Charles Hoffman, "Joyce Cary : Art and Reality," pp. 280-81.
67. Anthony West, p. 176.
68. Orville Prescott, p. 182.
69. Ernest Jones, p. 186.
70. Joyce Cary, "Three New Prefaces," p. 12.
71. R.W. Noble, p. 99.
72. Jennifer Ramage, p. 58.
73. E.M. Forster, "The Menace to Freedom," *Two Cheers for Democracy*, p. 10.
74. R.W. Livingston, ed., p. 487.

75. *Ibid.*, pp. 119-20.
76. Harold J. Laski, pp. 12-13.

CHAPTER 6 : 'POLYPHONY' AND THE CARYAN POLITICAL NOVEL

1. Joseph Blotner, p. 48.
2. Will Durant, p. 248.
3. Cited from Walter Allen, *Tradition and Dream*, p. 14.
4. Joyce Cary, "The Idea of Progress," p. 335.
5. *Ibid.*, p. 337.
6. Joseph Blotner, pp. 49-50.
7. Kinley Robey, p. 119
8. Mikhail M. Bakhtin, *Problems of Dostoevsky's Poetics*, p. 166.
9. Mikhail M. Bakhtin, *Dialogic Imagination*, p. 324.
10. Tom Hopkinson, p. 7.
11. Paul West, p. 112.
12. Mikhail M. Bakhtin, *Dialogic Imagination*, p. 335.
13. Mikhail M. Bakhtin, *Rabelais and His World*, pp. 10-11.
14. Mikhail M. Bakhtin, *Speech Genres and other Late Essays*, p. 149.
15. Rudyard Kipling, "The White Man's Burden," *Rudyard Kipling : Selected Poems*, p. 82.
16. Molly Mahood, *The Colonial Encounter*, p. 168.
17. *Ibid.*
18. Quoted in John Colmer, p. 18.
19. William James, p. 125.
20. *Ibid.*, p. 80.
21. Mikhail M. Bakhtin, *Problems of Dostoevsky's Poetics*, p. 6.
22. Northrope Frye, p. 13.

WORKS CONSULTED

PRIMARY SOURCES

Works of Joyce Cary

Fiction

Aissa Saved. 1932. Carfax Edition. London : Michael Joseph,1952.

An American Visitor. 1933. Carfax Edition. London : Michael Joseph, 1976.

The African Witch. 1936. Carfax Edition. New York : Harper & Brothers, 1962.

Castle Corner.1938. Carfax Edition. London : Michael Joseph,1952.

Mister Johnson. 1939. Harmondsworth, Middlesex : Penguin, 1980.

Charley is My Darling. 1940. Carfax Edition. London : Michael Joseph, 1974.

A House of Children. 1941. Carfax Edition. London : Michael Joseph, 1951.

Joyce Cary Triptych : Herself Surprised, To Be a Pilgrim, The Horse's Mouth. Harmondsworth, Middlesex : Penguin, 1985.

The Moonlight. 1946. Carfax Edition. London : Michael Joseph, 1959.

A Fearful Joy. 1949. Carfax Edition. London : Michael Joseph, 1952.

Prisoner of Grace. 1952. London : Michael Joseph, 1954.

Except the Lord. 1953. Carfax Edition. London : Michael Joseph, 1953.

Not Honour More. 1955. Carfax Edition. London : Michael Joseph, 1975.

The Captive and the Free. 1959. Harmondsworth, Middlesex : Penguin, 1985.

Spring Song and Other Stories. London : Michael Joseph, 1960.

Political Treatises

Power in Men. 1939. Seattle : U of Washington P, 1963.

The Case for African Freedom and Other Writings on Africa. Austin : U of Texas P, 1962. Includes *The Case for African Freedom* 1941, revised and enlarged, 1944; *Britain and West Africa* 1946, republished in 1947; "Africa Yesterday : One Ruler's Burden," *Reporter* 15 (May 1951); "Christmas in Africa," *Esquire* (Dec. 1953); "Catching Up With History : A Review of *Black Power* by Richard Wright," *Nation* 16 (Oct. 1954).

Other Works

Art and Reality. Clark Lectures. Cambridge : Cambridge UP, 1958.

Joyce Cary : Selected Essays, ed. A.G. Bishop. London : Michael Joseph, 1976.

"A Novel is a Novel is a Novel." *Adam International Review* 18.212-13 (Nov.-Dec. 1950) : 1-3.

"The Way a Novel Gets Written." *Adam International Review* 18.212-13 (Nov.-Dec. 1950) : 3-11.

"Three New Prefaces." *Adam International Review* 18. 212-13 (Nov.-Dec. 1950) : 11-14.

"The Sources of Tension in America." *The Saturday Review* 23 (August 1952) : 6-7 and 35.

"The Idea of Progress." *Cornhill Magazine* 167 (Summer 1954) : 331-37.

"A Prefatory Essay." *Prisoner of Grace*. By Joyce Cary. Carfax Edition. London : Michael Joseph, 1954.

SECONDARY SOURCES

Achebe, Chinua. *Things Fall Apart*. London : William Heinemann Ltd., 1989.

—— "Named for Victoria, Queen of England." *Morning Yet on Creation Day Essays*. London : Butler Tanner, 1975. 65-70.

Adams, Hazard. "Joyce Cary's Three Speakers." *Modern Fiction Studies* 5 (Summer 1959) : 108-20.

—— "Blake and Gulley Jimson : English Symbolists." *Critique* 3 (Spring - Fall 1959) : 3-14.

—— "Reappraisals : Joyce Cary's Swimming Swan." *American Scholar* 29.2 (Spring 1960) : 235-39.

—— Introduction. *Power in Men*. By Joyce Cary. Seattle, Washington : U of Washington P, 1963.

—— *Joyce Cary's Trilogies : Pursuit of the Particular Real.* Gainsville, Florida : UP of Florida, 1983.

Adams, Robert H. "Freedom in *The Horse's Mouth*." *College English* 26 (Feb.-May 1965) :451-60.

Allen, Walter. "Joyce Cary." *British Writers* Vol.VII ed. Ian Scott-Kilvert. Under the Auspices of the British Council. New York : Charles Scribner's Sons, 1984.185-96.

—— *Tradition and Dream : The English and American Novel from Twenties to our Time*. London : Chatto & Windus, Hogarth, 1986.

Appadorai, A. *The Substance of Politics*. 7th ed. Madras : Oxford UP, 1954.

Arnold, Matthew. *Essays, Letters and Reviews*. Collected and Edited by Fraser Neiman. Cambridge, Massachusetts : Harvard UP, 1960.

—— *Culture and Anarchy*. 1869. Edited with an Introduction by J.Dover Wilson. Cambridge : Cambridge UP, 1969.

Arthur, Paul. *Political Realities : Government and Politics of North Ireland*. 2nd ed. London : Longman Group, 1984.

Ashcroft, Bill, Gareth Griffiths and Helen Tiffin. *The Empire Writes Back : Theory and Practice in Post-Colonial Literature*. London : Routledge, 1989.

Bakhtin, Mikhail, M. *Dialogic Imagination : Four Essays*. Ed. Michael Holquist. Trans. Caryl Emerson and Michael Holquist. Austin, Texas : U of Texas, 1981.

—— *Rabelais and His world*. Trans. Héléne Iswolsky. Bloomington, Indiana : Indiana UP, 1984.

—— *Problems of Dostoevsky's Poetics*. Ed. and Trans. Cary Emerson. Manchester : Manchester UP, 1984.

—— *Speech Genres and Other Late Essays*. 1st ed. Trans. Vern W. McGee. Eds. Caryl Emerson and Michael Holquist. Austin, Texas : U of Texas, 1986.

Barker, Ernest. *The Values of Life*. Bombay : Blackie & Son,1951.

—— *Principles of Social and Political Theory*. Oxford : Oxford UP, 1956.

Barr, Donald. "A Careful and Profound Thinker." *Adam International Review* 18. 212-13 (Nov.-Dec. 1950) : 30-31.

Barry, Peter. *Beginning Theory*. Manchester : Manchester University Press, 1995.

Battaglia, Francis Joseph. "Spurious Armageddon : Joyce Cary's *Not Honour More*." *Modern Fiction Studies* 13 (Winter 1967-68) : 479-91.

Bellow, Saul. "A Personal Record." A Review of *Except the Lord*.

By Joyce Cary. *New Republic* 130 (Feb. 24 1954) : 20-21.

Berger, Morroe. *Real and Imagined Worlds : The Novel and Social Science*. Cambridge, Mass : Harvard UP, 1977.

Bergson, Henri. *Creative Evolution*. Authorized Translation. Arthur Mitchell. London : Macmillan, 1912.

Bettman, Elizabeth R. "Joyce Cary and the Problem of Political Morality." *The Antioch Review* 17.3 (Summer 1957) : 266-72.

Blake, William. *The Complete Writings of William Blake. With Variant Readings*. Ed. Geoffrey Keynes. London : Oxford UP, 1966.

Blamires, Harry. *Twentieth Century English Literature*. Macmillan History of Literature. 2nd ed. London : Macmillan, 1986.

Bloom, Robert. *The Indeterminate World : A Study of the Novels of Joyce Cary*. Philadelphia, Penn. : U of Pennsylvania P, 1962.

Blotner, Joseph. L. *The Political Novel*. New York : Doubleday, 1955.

Booth, Wayne C. *The Rhetoric of Fiction*. Chicago : Chicago UP, 1963.

Boyers, Robert. *Political Fiction : Atrocity and Amnesia : The Political Novel since 1945*. New York : Oxford UP, 1985.

Bradley, Ian. *The Strange Rebirth of Liberal Britain*. London : Chatto Windus, Hogarth P, 1985.

Bramstead, E.K., and K.J. Melhuish, eds. *Western Liberalism : A History of Documents from Locke to Croce*. London : Longman Group, 1978.

Brawyer, Judith. "The Triumph of Defeat. A Study of Joyce Cary's First Trilogy." *Texas Studies in English Literature and Language* 10.4 (Winter 1969) : 629-34.

Bullock, Alan, and Maurice Shock, eds. *The Liberal Tradition : From Fox to Keynes*. London : Adam & Charles Black, 1956.

Burgess, Anthony. *English Literature : A Survey for Students*. London : Longman, 1974.

Burrows, John, and Alex Hamilton. "Joyce Cary." *Writers at Work : The Paris Review Interviews*. Ed. Malcolm Cowley. London : Secker & Warburg, 1958. 49-61.

Cecil, David. "The Novelist at Work; A Conversation Between Joyce Cary and Lord David Cecil." *Adam International Review* 18. 212-13 (Nov.-Dec. 1950) : 15-25.

"Cheerful Protestant." *Time* 60 (20 Oct. 1952) : 46-52.

Chinweizu, Onwuchekwa Jemie and Ihechukwu Madubuike, eds. *Toward the Decolonization of African Literature*.London : Cambridge UP, 1980.

Christian, Edwin Ernest. "Joyce Cary's Major Poems." *Ariel* 17.2 (April 1986) : 33-46.

Cole, G.D.H. *Politics and Literature*. London : Hazell, Watson & Vinay, 1929.

Colmer, John. *E.M. Forster : the Personal Voice*. London : Routledge & Kegan Paul, 1975.

Cook, Cornelia. *Joyce Cary : Liberal Principles*. London : Vision, 1981.

Cosmon, Max. "The Protean Joyce Cary." *Commonweal* 69. 6 (March 1959) : 596-78.

Cox, C.B., and A.E. Dyson. eds. *The Twentieth-Century Mind :*

History, Ideas and Literature in Britain 1900-1918. Vol.I. 1972. London : Oxford UP, 1974.

—— eds. *The Twentieth-Century Mind : History, Ideas and Literature in Britain 1918-1945*. Vol.II. London : Oxford UP, 1972.

Creelman, Melbakuddy. "Beyond Modernism : Critical Attitudes in Some Unpublished Joyce Cary Materials." *Contemporary Literature* 24.1 (1983) : 15-25.

Cuddy, Keane Melba. "Conflicting Feminisms and the Problem of Male Space : Joyce and the Fifties." *Cultural Critique* (Fall 1994) : 103-128.

Daiches, David. "Religion, Poetry and the Dilemma of the Modern Writer." *Literary Essays*. London : Oliver Boyd, 1956. 206-225.

David, Dan. "Five Windows Darken : Recollections of Joyce Cary." *Encounter* 44.6 (June 1975) : 24-33.

Davis, Robert Con, and Ronald Schleifer. "Mikhail Bakhtin, V.N. Volosin 1895-1975." *Contemporary Literary Criticism*. New York : Longman, 1989. 391-410.

Disraeli, Benjamin. *Sybil*. Ed. Thom Braun. Intro. R.A.Butler. New York : Viking Penguin, 1980.

—— *Coningsby*. New York : Revisionist, 1979.

Durant, Will. *The Story of Philosophy : The Lives and Opinions of the World's Greatest Philosophers from Plato to John Dewey*. Pocket Library Edn. New York : Pocket Books, 1954. 4th printing 1957.

Eastman, Richard M. "Historical Grace in Cary's *A Fearful Joy*." *Novel* (Winter 1968) : 150-57.

Echeruo, Michael J.C. *Joyce Cary and the Novels of Africa*. London : Longman Group, 1973.

—— *Joyce Cary and the Dimensions of Order*. London : Macmillan, 1979.

Eckles, Robert B. and Richard W. Hale Jr. *Britain, Her Peoples and the Commonwealth*. Indian edn. Bombay : Allied Publishers, 1962.

Edwards, Thomas R. *Imagination and Power : A Study of Poetry and Public Themes*. London : Chatto & Windus, 1971.

Fanon, Frantz. *Black Skin White Masks*. 1952; 1967. Trans. Charles Lam Markmann. London : Pluto Press, 1986.

—— *The Wretched of the Earth*. 1961;1967. Trans. Constance Farrington. Preface Jean-Paul Sartre. Harmondsworth, Middlesex : Penguin, 1978.

Fisher, Barbara. *Joyce Cary : The Writer and His Theme*. London : Colin Smythe, 1980.

—— *The House as a Symbol : Joyce Cary and 'The Turkish House'*. Amsterdam : Rodopi, 1986.

Forster, E.M. *Two Cheers for Democracy*. Vol. II Ed. Oliver Stallybrass. London : Edward Arnold, 1972.

—— *A Passage to India*. London : Charnwood, 1981.

—— *Howards End*. Ed. Oliver Stallybrass. Harmondsworth, Middlesex : Penguin, 1983.

Foster, Malcolm. "Fell of the Lion, Fleece of the Sheep." *Modern Fiction Studies* 9 (Aug. 1963) : 257-61.

—— *Joyce Cary : A Biography*. London : Michael Joseph, 1969.

Fraser, G.S. *The Modern Writer and His World*. London : Verschoyle, 1953.

Freeden, Michael. *The New Liberalism : An Ideology of Social Reform*. London : Clarendon Press, 1986.

Friedman, Alan Warren. "Joyce Cary's Cubistic Morality." *Multivalence : The Moral Quality of Form in the Modern Novel*. Baton Rouge : Louisiana State UP, 1978. 54-76.

Frye, Northrop. *Fearful Symmetry : A Study of William Blake*. 4th edn. Princeton : Princeton UP, 1969.

Fyfe, Christopher. "Colonial Situation in *Mister Johnson*." *Modern Fiction Studies* 9 (Aut. 1963) : 226-30.

—— Introduction. *The Case for African Freedom and Other Writings on Africa*. By Joyce Cary. Austin, Texas : U of Texas P, 1962, xiv-xix.

Galligan, Edward L. "Intuition and Concept : Joyce Cary and the

Critics." *Texas Studies in English Literature and Language.* 8.4 (1967) : 581-87.

Gardner, Helen. "The Novels of Joyce Cary." *Essays and Studies.* Collected by Ellodt for the British Council Library. London : John Murray, 1975. 76-93.

—— Foreword. *Joyce Cary : Selected Essays.* By Joyce Cary. Ed.A.G. Bishop. London : Michael Joseph, 1976. vii-xii.

Giddings, Robert. Ed. *Literature and Imperialism.* London : Macmillan, 1990.

Gooch, G.P. *Political Thought in England From Bacon to Halifax.* Home University Library. 6th imp. London : Thornton Butterworth, 1933.

Goonetilleke, D.R.C.R. "Ironies of Progress : Conrad and Imperialism." See Robert Giddings.

Graham, Gorden. "Political Liberalism." *Politics in its Place : A Study of Six Ideologies.* Oxford : Clarendon Press, 1986. 79-102.

Hall, Dennis. *Joyce Cary : A Reappraisal.* London : Macmillan, 1983.

Hardy, Barbara. "Form in Joyce Cary's Novels." *Essays in Criticism* 4 (April 1954) : 180-90.

Hoffman, Charles G. "Joyce Cary : Art and Reality : The Interaction of Form and Narrator." *University of Kansas City Review* 26.4 (1960) : 273-82.

—— "Joyce Cary's African Novels : 'There's a War On'" *South Atlantic Quarterly* 62.2 (1963) : 229-43.

—— "They want to be Happy : Joyce Cary's Unfinished Castle Corner Series." *Modern Fiction Studies* 9 (Aut. 1963) : 217-25.

—— "The Captive and the Free Joyce Cary's Unfinished Trilogy." *Texas Studies in English Literature and Language* 5.1 (Spring 1963) : 17-24.

—— "The Genesis and Development of Joyce Cary's First Trilogy." *PMLA* 78 (Sept. 1963) : 431-39.

—— *Joyce Cary : The Comedy of Freedom.* Pittsburg : U of Pittsburg P, 1964.

Holloway, John. "Joyce Cary and the 'Sustaining Power'." *The Colours of Clarity*. London : Routledge Kegan & Paul, 1974. 52-59.

Holquist, Michael. *Dialogism : Bakhtin and His World*. London : Routledge, 1990.

Hopkinson, Tom. "George Orwell." *British Writers* Vol. VII. Gen. Ed. Ian Scott, Kilvert. Under the Auspices of the British Council. New York : Charles Scribner's Sons, 1984, 273-87.

Howe, Irving. *Politics and the Novel*. New York : Horizon Press, 1957.

Huxley, Aldous. *Brave New World Revisited* : *The Collected Works of Aldous Huxley*. 1959. London : Chatto & Windus, 1974.

—— *Brave New World*. London : Chatto & Windus, 1966.

Hynes, Samuel. *The Auden Generation* : *Literature and Politics in England in the 1930's*. London : Bodley Head, 1976.

James, William. *The Varieties of Religious Experience*.Toronto : Random House of Canada, 1929.

Janeway, Elizabeth. "A Great Man Who Was My Husband." *The New York Book Times Review* 12 Oct. 1952 : 5, 28.

Jeffares, A Norman. "Ireland." *Literatures of the World in English*. Ed. Bruce King. London : Kegan Paul, 1974, 98-116.

Jones, Ernest. "The Double View." *The Nation* 170 (25 Feb. 1950) : 184-86.

Johnson, Pamela Hansford. "Three Novelists and the Drawing of Character : C.P. Snow, Joyce Cary and Ivy Compton-Burnett." *Essays and Studies* 1950. Vol. III : 82-99.

Kant, Immanuel. *Critique of Pure Reason*. Introduction by A.D. Lindsay. Trans. J.M.D. Meikle John. London : J.M. Dent & Sons, 1974.

Kanu, S.H. *A World of Everlasting Conflict : Joyce Cary's View of Man and Society*. Ibadan : Ibadan UP, 1974.

Karl, Frederick R. "Joyce Cary : The Moralist as Novelist." *Twentieth Century Literature* 5.4 (Jan. 1960) : 183-196.

Kennedy, Alan. "Language, Mimesis and the Numinous in Joyce

Cary's Second Trilogy." *The Protean Self* : *Dramatic Action in Contemporary Fiction*. London : Macmillan, 1974. 99-149.

Kettle, Arnold. "Joyce Cary : *Mister Johnson*." *An Introduction to the English Novel*. Vol. II. London : Hutchinson, 1972. 159-165.

Kipling, Rudyard. *Rudyard Kipling : Selected Poems*. Ed. Peter Keating. London : Penguin Books, 1993.

Kronenfeld, J. Z. "In Search of Mister Johnson : Creation, Politics and Culture in Cary's Africa." *Ariel* 7.4. (Oct. 1976) : 69-97.

Larsen, Golden L. *The Dark Descent : Social Change and Moral Responsibility in the Novels of Joyce Cary*. New York : Ray Publishers, 1966.

Laski, Harold J. *Political Thought in England : From Locke to Bentham*. Home University Library. London : Thornton Butterworth, 1937.

Livingston, R.W. ed. *Plato : Selected Passages*. London : Oxford UP, 1951.

Lone W. Lancaster. ed. "Peter Alexeyevich Kropotkin (1842-1921)." *Masters of Political Thought : Hegal to Dewey*. London : George G. Harrap, 1959. 244-266.

Lucas, C.P. *A Historical Geography of the British Colonies : West Africa*. Vol. III. London : Oxford UP, 1913.

Mahood, M.M. *Joyce Cary's Africa*. London : Camelot Press, 1964.

—— *The Colonial Encounter : A Reading of Six Novels*. London : Rex Collings, 1977.

McEwar, Neil. *Africa and the Novel*. London : Macmillan, 1983.

McLeod John. *Beginning Postcolonialism*. Manchester : Manchester University Press, 2000.

Majumdar, Bimalendu. *Joyce Cary : An Existentialist Approach*. New Delhi : Associated Publishing House, 1982.

Maini, Darshan Singh. "The Politics of Henry James." Lecture at The British Council, Madras. 150th Birth Anniversary of Henry James, 16 April 1993.

Manning, D.J. *Liberalism*. Modern Ideologies. London : J.M. Dent & Sons, 1976.

Mill, J.S. *On Liberty and Considerations on Representative Government*. Ed. with an Introduction by R.B. McCallum. Oxford : Basil Blackwell, 1948.

Mitchell, Giles. "Joyce Cary's *Prisoner of Grace*." *Modern Fiction Studies* 9 (Aut. 1963) : 63-75.

Monas, Sidney. "What to do with a Drunken Sailor." *Hudson Review*. 3.3 (Aut. 1950) : 466-474.

Morris, J.A. *Writers and Politics in Modern Britain* 1880-1950. London : Hodder & Stouton, 1977.

Naipaul V.S. "New Novels." *New Statesman* 14 (March 1959) : 376.

Noble, R.W. *Joyce Cary*. Edinburg : Oliver and Boyd, 1973.

Obiechina, Emmanuel. *Culture, Tradition and Society in the West African Novels*. African Study 14. London : Cambridge UP, 1975. 1-30.

O'Brien, Colin Joseph. *Art and Reality in the Novels of Joyce Cary*. New Delhi; Commonwealth Publishers, 1990.

O'Connor, William Van. "*Joyce Cary*." Columbia Essays on Modern Writers 15. Ed. William York Tindall. New York : Columbia UP, 1966. 3-43.

Ola, Virginia U. "The Vision of Power : Joyce Cary and African Women." *Ariel* 9.1 (Jan. 1978) : 85-97.

Orwell, George. Foreword to the 1941 Edn. of *The Case for African Freedom and other Writings on Africa*. By Joyce Cary. Austin, Texas : U of Texas P, 1966.

—— *The Collected Essays, Journalism and Letters. My Country Right or Left* : 1940-1943. Vol.II. Ed. Sonia Orwell and Ian Angus. London : Secker and Warburg, 1969.

—— *Selected Essays of Orwell*. Introduction by M.G. Nayar. Madras : Macmillan India, 1986.

—— *Nineteen Eighty Four* (&) *Animal Farm*. London : Chancellor Press, 1984.

Owen, B. Evan. "The Supremacy of the Individual in the Novels of

Joyce Cary." *Adam International Review* 18. 212-13 (Nov.-Dec. 1950) : 25-29.

Prescott, Orville. "Two Modern Masters : Cozzens and Cary." *In My Opinion; An Inquiry into the Contemporary Novel.* Indianapolis : Bobbs-Merrill, 1952. 180-199.

Pritchett, V.S. "Books in General." *New Statesman and Nation* 27 (Oct. 1951) : 464-65.

Proudhan, Pierre-Joseph. *Selected Writings of Pierre-Joseph Proudhan.* Ed. Steward Edwards.Trans. Elizabeth Fraser. London : Macmillan, 1969.

Ramage, Jennifer. "Poet of the Pressure Group : Joyce Cary's Myth." *Encounter* 73.1. (June 1989) : 55-60.

Randall, Stevenson. *The British Novel Since the Thirties*. London : Batsford, 1986.

Reed, Peter J. "Holding Back : Joyce Cary's *To be a Pilgrim.*" *Contemporary Literature* 10.1 (1969) : 103-16.

Reid, B.L. "Joyce Cary's First Trilogy." *Sewanee Review* 98 (Wint., 1990) : 50-74.

Reid, Fred. "The Disintegration of Liberalism, 1895-1931." *The Context of English Literature* 1900-1930. Ed. Michael Bell. London : Methuen, 1980. 94-123.

Robey, Kinley E. *Joyce Cary.* Twayne's English Authors 377. Boston : Twayne Publishers, 1984.

Robson, W.W. "From Auden to Orwell." *Modern English Literature.* London : Oxford UP, 1970. 125-151.

Rosenthal, Michael. "Joyce Cary's Ambiguous Chester Nimmo." *South Atlantic Quarterly* 10.3 (May 1971) : 332-40.

Ruskin, John. *Sesame and Lilies.* Madras : Macmillan India, 1991.

Salz, Paulina. "The Philosophical Principles in Joyce Cary's Work." *Western Humanities Review* 20.1 (Winter 1966) : 159-65.

Schorer, Mark. "The Socially Extensive Novel." *Adam International Review* 18. 212-13 (Nov.-Dec. 1950) : 31-32.

Seltzer, Alvin J. "Speaking out of Both Sides of *The Horse's Mouth* : Joyce Cary *Vs.* Gulley Jimson." *Contemporary Literature* 15.4 (Aut. 1974) : 488-502.

Sethna, K.D. *Blake's Tyger : A Christological Interpretation.* Pondicherry : Sri Aurobindo Ashram, 1989.

Seymour-Smith, Martin. "Joyce Cary." *Who's Who* in *Twentieth Century Literature*. New York : Mcgraw-Hill, 1977, 72-73.

—— "Zero and the Impossible : Ray Campbell; Wyndham Lewis; Joyce Cary; John Middleton Murry." *Encounter* (Nov. 1957) : 38-51.

Shapiro, Stephen. "Leopold Bloom and Gulley Jimson : The Economics of Survival." *Twentieth Century Literature*. 10.1 (April 1964) : 3-11.

—— "Joyce Cary's *To Be a Pilgrim* : Mr.Facing-Both Ways." *Texas Studies in Literature and Language* 8.1 (1967) : 81-91.

Sharma, K.K. *Joyce Cary : His Theme and Technique. A Modern Variation on the Major Tradition of the English Novel.* Ghaziabad, U.P : Vimal Prakashan, 1976.

Simmons, James. "Joyce Cary in Ireland." *On the Novel : A Present for Walter Allen on his 60th birthday from his Friends and Colleagues*. Ed. B.S. Benedikz. London : Dent, 1971. 140-60.

Smith, B.R. "Moral Evaluation in *Mister Johnson*." *Critique* 2 (1969) : 101-10.

Snow, C.P. *The Masters*. London : Macmillan, 1951.

—— *Corridors of Power*. Harmondsworth, Middlesex : Penguin, 1964.

—— *The Affair*. Harmondsworth, Middlesex : Penguin, 1973.

Speare, Morris Edmund. *The Political Novel : Its Development in England and in America*. New York : Russel and Russel, 1966.

Spinoza. *The Philosophy of Spinoza : Selected from His Chief Works*. Ed. Joseph Ratner. New York : Charlton House, no year.

Starkie, Enid. "Joyce Cary : A Personal Portrait." *Virginia Quarterly Review* 37.1 (Winter 1961) : 110-34.

Steinbrecher, George Jr. "Joyce Cary : Master Novelist." *College English* 18 (May 1967) : 387-95.

Stevenson, Lionel. "Joyce Cary and the Anglo-Irish Tradition." *Modern Fiction Studies* 9 (Aut. 1963) : 210-216.

Stevenson, Randall. *The British Novel Since the Thirties*. London : B.T. Batsford, 1987.

Stewart, J.I.M. *Eight Modern Writers*. Oxford History of English Literature. Eds. F.P. Wilson and Bonamy Dobree. Oxford : Oxford UP, 1963.

Stockholder, Fred. "The Triple Vision in Joyce Cary's First Trilogy." *Modern Fiction Studies* 9 (Aut. 1963) : 231-44.

Teeling S.J., John. "Joyce Cary's Moral World." *Modern Fiction Studies* (Aut. 1963) : 276-83.

Thiong O, Ngugi Wa. *Decolonising the Mind : The Politics of African Literature*. London : James Currey, 1987.

Thomson, David. *England in the Twentieth Century,* 1914-63. Harmondsworth, Middlesex : Penguin, 1966.

Trilling, Diana. "Fiction in Review." *Nation*. 28 (May 1949) : 618-20.

Trivedi, Harish. ed. *The American Political Novel : Critical Essays*. New Delhi : Allied Publishers, 1984.

Van Horn, Ruth G. "Rx for Joyce Cary." *Nation* 189.19 (11 May 1957) : 42.

Ward A.C. *Twentieth-Century English Literature* 1901-60 Bombay : B.I. Publications, 1974.

Watson, George. *Politics and Literature in Modern Britain*. London : Macmillan, 1977.

Watt, Ian. *Conrad in the Nineteenth Century*. London : Chatto & Windus, 1980.

Weintramp, Stanley. "*Castle Corner* : Joyce Cary's Buddenbrooks." *Contemporary Literature* 5.1. (1964-65) : 54-63.

West, Anthony. "Footloose and Fancy Free — Charley is my Darling." *New Yorker* 36. (30 April 1960) : 170-76.

West, Paul. *The Modern Novel*. Vol. I. London : Hutchinson & Co. Ltd., 1967.

Wilding, Michael. *Political Fictions*. London : Routledge and Kegan Paul, 1980.

Willey, Basil. *The Eighteenth-Century Background : Studies on the Idea of Nature in the Thought of the Period*. London : Chatto & Windus, 1974.

Wren, Robert M. "'Mister Johnson' and the Complexity of 'Arrow of God'" *Studies in Commonwealth Literature*. Ed. C.D. Narasimhaiyah. New Delhi : Sterling Publishers, 1978. 50-61.

Wright, Andrew. *Joyce Cary : A Preface to His Novels*. London : Chatto and Windus, 1959.

—— "A Note on Joyce Cary's Reputation." *Modern Fiction Studies* 9 (Aut. 1963) : 207-09.

Yeats, W.B. *Selected Prose*. Ed. with an Introduction and Notes by A. Norman Jeffares. London : Macmillan, 1964.

INDEX

D

E

F

G

H

I

J

K

L

M

N

O

P

R

S